From Good King Wenceslas to the Good Soldier Švejk

A Dictionary of Czech Popular Culture

From Good King Wenceslas to the Good Soldier Švejk

A Dictionary of Czech Popular Culture

ANDREW ROBERTS

Central European University Press
Budapest New York

Published in 2005 by
Central European University Press

An imprint of the
Central European University Share Company
Nádor utca 11, H-1051 Budapest, Hungary
Tel: +36-1-327-3138 or 327-3000
Fax: +36-1-327-3183
E-mail: ceupress@ceu.hu
Website: www.ceupress.com

400 West 59th Street, New York NY 10019, USA
Tel: +1-212-547-6932
Fax: +1-646-557-2416
E-mail: mgreenwald@sorosny.org

ISBN 963 7326 26 X cloth

Library of Congress Cataloging-in-Publication Data

Roberts, Andrew Lawrence, 1970-
    From Good King Wenceslas to the Good Soldier Svejk : a dictionary
    of Czech popular culture / by Andrew Roberts.
        p. cm.
    Includes bibliographical references.
    ISBN 963732626X
    1. Popular culture--Czech Republic--Dictionaries.   I. Title.
    DB2244.R63 2005
    306'.094371'03--dc22
                                2005023289

Printed in Hungary by Akadémiai Nyomda, Martonvásár

To Lenka and Radko for showing me
what it means to be a Czech

Table of Contents

Preface

The intent of this dictionary is not to provide a complete account of Czech history and culture. I am neither a historian nor cultural critic, merely an observer of everyday life. My aim is simply to introduce the reader to a number of concepts—people, places, songs, games, slogans—common in Czech popular culture. These concepts generally do not appear in dictionaries, textbooks, or histories, or at least not in the form they do here. Where they do occur—mainly in daily newspapers or ordinary conversation—they are usually not explained.

Yet all of them are well known to Czechs living in the latter half of the twentieth century. They are the furniture of his or her mental universe. Czechs allude to them when talking to friends, situate new phenomena in relation to them, and assume them to be a natural part of the world. This dictionary thus tries to explain both their literal meaning and the set of associations that has grown around them.

In choosing the entries for the dictionary, I have followed one simple rule. All of the concepts are known to ordinary Czechs. Every Czech with a standard secondary school education should recognize virtually all of the entries even if they may be hazy on some of the details. In fact, most of the research for this dictionary involved simply quizzing Czechs about their lives and opinions. Another title for this dictionary might be: *Things That Every Czech Knows, But No Foreigner Does.*

My model in this task—though I am less comprehensive and knowledgeable than he—is István Bart. His *Hungary and the Hungarians: The Keywords* is a minor treasure. It is the only book I know of that acquaints the reader with the range of images that citizens of a culture take for granted. Here is how Bart explains his approach:

> Language is not just words and grammar, it works by metaphors and allusions that make up (and also hide away) meanings which are indecipherable without knowledge of the cultural code. Every student of a foreign language is painfully aware how this meta-language lurking behind even the simplest of turns of phrase can make reception of even everyday speech such a precarious affair. For there may be worlds in a word, not unlike the boxes within boxes within boxes of a Chinese puzzle. And bilingual dictionaries, constructed on the principle of equivalence, do not help here, because they do not try to invoke the thoughts, concepts and images that are invoked for the native speaker

upon hearing the name of a town or a region, a festival, a form of address, a dish peculiar to his country or the lines of a song. For languages are made up of popular memories, myths and beliefs, customs and ever changing usage, words ring bells—and if our ears don't hear their toll, life is merely a silent movie.

This book was born out of innumerable futile efforts to explain to visitors what is behind a gesture or a melody, a name, an attitude. It is both a guide to the "secrets" of the Hungarians' code-language and a concise cultural encyclopaedia of Hungarianness.

My aim is similar to Bart's, but with a few limitations. I have largely avoided high culture because it has been described better elsewhere. In any case, high culture is not well known by ordinary people—they are aware of it, but do not feel it in their bones. I have also focused more on communism than other eras because it is a particular interest of mine. It is also the era with which contemporary Czechs are most familiar.

Most importantly, I am limited as a foreigner. I have tried to capture some aspects of the Czech cultural language, but everything came to me second-hand. I had to learn these terms and their associations; I did not grow up with them. In fact, I did not come to know Czech culture until I was in my early twenties. I publish this dictionary only in the hope that these concepts are not lost before someone better qualified takes up the task of documenting them.

The dictionary is meant to serve a number of purposes. First, it is a handbook for those exploring Czech popular culture. One often comes across allusions to individuals or subjects that are difficult to track down in conventional reference sources. Consider Michal Viewegh's *Bringing Up Girls in Bohemia*, probably the most translated Czech novel of the nineties. Its numerous references to Czech popular culture, usually unexplained, include the following entries to this dictionary: *Lidové noviny*, Mácha, semtex, *omáčka*, *pohádka*, *Major Zeman*, *Becherovka*, Masaryk, Vinnetou, *Pyšná princezna*, *pantofle*, *Pionýr*, *odboj*, *lidovka*, *ruština*, *Prodaná nevěsta*, *Sametová revoluce*, *Sparta*, Fučík, ÚV KSČ, *Lidové milice*, *Švanda dudák*, *kádrový spis*, Čapek, *jmeniny*, *Dušičky*, *cikán*, and Baťa.

The dictionary will also help students of history and popular culture who are interested in how Czechs are similar to and different from citizens of other countries. One will find numerous entries common to all modern societies, like television serials and popular musicians, though often with a unique Czech twist. Others are distinctively Czech, like "the meaning of Czech history" (→ *smysl českých dějin*). A quick comparison with Bart's dictionary of Hungarianness shows many commonalities. The entries from his dictionary on pig roasts, coffeehouses, and fairytale introductions could almost be reproduced intact here (see *zabíjačka*, *kavárna*, and *Kdysi dávno*).

The entries may also be of use to a certain type of tourist. Even a quick tour of Prague will bring encounters with many of the concepts and symbols described here. They can be found on street signs, billboards, and magazine covers. Of course, this dictionary is no substitute for a tourist guide. I have intentionally excluded much of the content of guidebooks because they include things more of interest to tourists than to

Czechs. The industries that have grown up around Magical Prague or Franz Kafka are dealt with only tangentially here, as befits their role in the Czech imagination.

The dictionary is not meant to be read from start to finish. Readers may start anywhere they wish and are advised to skip around. The entries are organized alphabetically with distinctive Czech letters grouped with their closest English counterparts (for example, words starting with *č* are listed under c). Arrows (→) in the text refer readers to related entries. Abbreviations are used where they are common in Czech. The text is interspersed with poll results, top ten lists, and restaurant menus that are meant to supplement the main entries and let the reader draw his or her own conclusions.

Finally, I would like to thank those who helped make this dictionary possible. First of all are the students at the Universum Language School in Brno, whose innocent conversational references to many of these concepts sparked my interest. Next come Kerr Houston who taught me how to live in a foreign country and sample its culture, and Jonathan Bolton who showed me that it was possible to be a scholar of Czech.

As the dictionary began to take shape, among those who patiently answered my questions were Martin Lux, Petr Matějů, Kateřina Skutilová, Petr Sunega, and Jiří Večerník. Very useful unsolicited advice came from Jeronym Klimeš. A large thank you goes to those who read and commented on versions of the entire manuscript: Jonathan Bolton, Ben Frommer, Michael Henry Heim, Martina Horáková, and Blanka Navrátilová. Most of all I want to thank my wife Lenka and my good friend Radko Bohatec. I can't count the hours I spent with both of them discussing the Czech culture. This book is really a compilation of their lives.

Naturally, these helpers should not be held responsible for any mistakes that remain. In fact, the scope of this project means that many areas fall outside of my competences, and I fear that some mistakes may have been overlooked. I apologize for these in advance and only hope that a second edition, and more time spent among Czechs, will give me an opportunity to correct them.

A Short Guide to Czech Pronunciation

For readers who wish to pronounce the words in the dictionary, a brief pronunciation guide follows. Czech is almost entirely phonetic (one letter equals one sound), so knowing the spelling means knowing the pronunciation. All Czech words have stress on the first syllable. Vowels are continental: *a* = ah, *e* = eh, *i* and *y* = ee, *o* = oh, and *u* = ew. Long marks over the vowels simply lengthen them: thus, *á* = aaahhh, *ů/ú* = ewwww; they do not indicate stress. Consonants that do not correspond to English pronunciation are the following:

c = ts as in bits

č = ch as in church

ch = a single letter pronounced as in Bach

j = like the consonant y (the English j sound is spelled *dž*)

ř = rzh as in Dvořák

š = sh as in shower

ž = zh as the s in pleasure

One final note on language is that formation of the plural in Czech often leads to consonant changes at the end of the word. This explains the discrepancy in spelling when I use both the singular and plural in some entries.

A Brief Chronology of Czech History

5–6th c.	Arrival of the Slavs
830–907	Great Moravian Empire (→ *Velkomoravská říše*)
863	Arrival of → Cyril and Methodius
885	The first Premyslid (→ *Přemyslovci*), Bořivoj, founds the Prague Castle
929	Death of St. Wenceslas (→ Svatý Václav)
13th c.	Germans settle in Czech lands
1278	Přemysl Otakar II defeated at Moravian Field (→ *Moravské pole*)
1308	Extinction of the Premyslid Dynasty
1346–1378	Rule of Charles IV (→ Karel IV)
1415	Jan → Hus burned at the stake
1419	Start of the Hussite Wars (→ *Husité*)
1434	Battle of → Lipany
1526	Ferdinand Habsburg elected King of Bohemia, beginning of Habsburg rule
1618	Defenestration and beginning of Thirty Years' War (→ *Třicetiletá válka*)
1620	Battle of White Mountain (→ *Bílá hora*)
1740–80	Rule of → Maria Theresa
Late 18th c.	Start of Czech National Revival (→ *Národní obrození*)
1848–1916	Rule of → Franz Joseph
1849–59	Bach's Absolutism (→ *bachův absolutismus*)
1868	Founding stone of National Theater (→ *Národní divadlo*) laid
1874	Young Czech Party (→ *Mladočeši*) founded
1918	Independent Czechoslovakia founded (→ *28. říjen*)
1938	Sudetenland given to Germans at Munich (→ *Mnichov*)
1939	German invasion
1945	Liberation by Soviet Army (→ *Den osvobození*)
1948	Communists take power in coup (→ *Vítězný únor*)
1968	Prague Spring (→ *Pražské jaro*) and Soviet invasion (→ *srpnová invaze*)
1970s and 80s	Normalization (→ *normalizace*)
1989	Fall of communist regime (→ *Sametová revoluce*)
1992	Separation of the Czech Republic and Slovakia (→ *Sametový rozvod*)
1999	Czech Republic enters NATO
2004	Czech Republic enters European Union

A

Akce Z (Campaign Z). "Voluntary" program of maintaining public spaces introduced under communism. Proclamation of an *Akce Z* by the local national committee (→ *národní výbor*) meant that groups of designated workers or students were required to clean up or repair sidewalks, soccer fields, and highway shoulders in their local community. These campaigns were one of several forms of forced, unpaid labor (the Z is said to stand for *zadarmo* or free), in which the communists specialized. See also → *pracovní sobota*.

Alpa (brand of liniment). A universal cure-all found in all Czech medicine cabinets. Known by its brand name, Alpa is an alcoholic solution containing essential oils, fragrant herbs, and menthol. Its uses are myriad. Rubbed on to the skin, it is said to relieve rheumatism and soothe aches and pains. Applied to the temples, it makes headaches go away. Gargled, or, for children, dripped on to a sugar cube, it is a cure for the common cold. It even serves as a disinfectant and antiseptic.

Američan z Vysočan (American from Vysočany). Rhyming phrase used under communism to refer to those who sported Western styles, whether sunglasses or brand-name clothes. Vysočany is a quarter of Prague.

Amerika (America). Communist propaganda described America as the home of abject poverty, divisive racism, and war-mongering politicians who wanted nothing more than to destroy the Czech socialist paradise and enslave its citizens. Only fellow-traveling Americans,

like the well-known Angela Davis, were given positive play in the media. Though most adults saw through the propaganda, for many children these tales produced nightmares. Even children, however, borrowed from American culture, playing at cowboys and indians (→ Vinnetou) and listening to rock music. A new set of illusions about America emerged after the revolution (→ *Sametová revoluce*), when the tidal wave of American entertainment made Czechs think of the U.S. as the land of beautiful blonde women and incredible riches. Frequently decried, however, is the purported American obsession with political correctness and feminism. The allegedly overzealous enforcement of sexual harassment laws in the U.S. is a popular topic of conversation. Another warhorse is the comparison of Czech gypsies (→ *cikán*) with American blacks. Interestingly, Czech-Americans were among the few Eastern European immigrants not to return to their homeland in mass numbers after the fall of communism as they had assimilated too well into American life. Among famous Czech-Americans are the film director Miloš Forman, the tennis player Ivan Lendl, and the mayor of Chicago Anton Cermak.

"Andělíčku, můj strážníčku" (Little angel, my little guardian). The beginning of the most common children's bedtime prayer. It continues, "Protect my soul/Protect her all day and all night/From the devil and from evil."

apolitická politika (apolitical politics). Before he became president, → Masaryk coined this term to suggest that the Czech struggle for political autonomy should be conducted not at the level of parliamentary politics, but in the lives of ordinary individuals working to build a better nation. Such a principled commitment to avoid politics and even an aversion to political activity has been a running theme in Czech history. It was picked up most strongly by the dissident (→ *disident*) movement, but it can be seen in other guises throughout Czech history, particularly in the belief that great powers would recognize the ethical goodness of the Czech people and thus refrain from harming them. Distrust of politics and politicians remains high even under the new democracy.

Aš. A small town that is known both for its short name and its position as the westernmost town in the country.

B

Baarová, Lída (1914–2001). Baarová was one of the most beautiful film actresses of the thirties and a frequent star of the drawing room comedies that were popular at the time. Memories of her, however, are tarnished by her romantic affair with Joseph Goebbels, which infuriated Czechs and Nazis alike. After the war, she was handed over to the Czechs and served a prison term, though upon her release she was able to resume her career in Germany and Italy. In her best-selling autobiography, *Útěky* (Flights), she attributes her mistakes to youthful naiveté and a trusting nature. Still mixed feelings about her were raised after her death in 2001, when few former friends and colleagues dared to attend her funeral. A similar fate befell Adina Mandlová, another star of interwar film. False rumors had her romantically involved with Karl H. Frank, one of the brutal rulers of the Protectorate (→ *Protektorát*). Though she was never tried after the war, she immigrated to Britain and never acted again. The allure of both is the universal story of an ingénue in distress who knows she has to take advantage of her beauty while she still has it.

Babička (Granny). The classic Czech novel of the nineteenth century. Written in 1855 by Božena → Němcová, *Babička* begins with the title character coming to live with her daughter and take care of her four grandchildren, including Barunka, her favorite. She teaches the children thrift, religiosity, and love of the Czech nation and language, while at the same time dispensing folk wisdom to the local baroness. The novel itself, as its subtitle suggests, consists of "Pictures of Country Life." It is centered on the four seasons through which it describes age-old Czech customs, holidays, and superstitions. The best remembered story in the novel is that of crazy Viktorka, who, having been seduced by a foreign soldier, now haunts the town. Indeed, in a trope widely repeated by Czechs, virtually all of the troubles described in the novel are the result of foreigners disrupting harmonious Czech life. The grandmother dies in the end, though she retains such a place in Czech hearts that three films have been made of the book, and the village, in which she reputedly lived, Staré Bělidlo in northeast Bohemia (→ *Čechy*), has become a tourist attraction. The novel leaves all Czechs weepy and sends them rushing to their own grandmothers who continue to enjoy the fortune of Sunday afternoon visits from their children and grandchildren.

Babinský, Václav (1796–1879). According to legend, one of the country's greatest criminals and murderers. In reality, the tales about his dastardly deeds were largely of his own invention, and he was actually just a small-time thief. This in fact might be taken as typical of a general Czech habit of talking big but avoiding violence (→ *holubičí povaha*). Babinský's name was immortalized in a popular children's song in which he is improbably imprisoned in Africa. The real murder king of the old days was Grasel whose name gave Czech the word *grázl* meaning "scoundrel" or "crook."

Bachův absolutismus (Bach's Absolutism). Period of political repression in the 1850s.

Even before communism, there were names that the Czechs associated with brutal repression, and Baron Alexander Bach (1813–1893) was at the top of the list. Named Interior Minister of the Austrian Empire after the unrest of 1848, Bach's job was to quell nationalist revolts and restore order. His ruthless methods earned him the nickname Minister of the Barricades, and the period of his rule is referred to as Bach's Absolutism. Among his victims was the political journalist Karel → Havlíček Borovský, who was one of the very few with the courage to defy Bach's persistent secret police. Even today Bach's legend lives on in the expressions *bachař* (prison guard) and *dej si bacha* (watch out).

Barrandov. Film studios that occupy the same place in Czech consciousness that Hollywood does for Americans. The studios, along with luxury residences, were built on the Barrandov hills to the south of Prague in 1931 by Miloš Havel—the uncle of Václav → Havel. They started production in 1933 and soon came to dominate the Czech film industry, producing nearly thirty films annually, most of them drawing room comedies. The studios were nationalized at the end of the war and immediately put to use by the communists in creating images of a better tomorrow. They reached their artistic height in the sixties when they were home to the Czech New Wave (→ *Nová vlna*). By the seventies and eighties, Barrandov was again producing as many films as in the thirties and had rebuilt a stable of superstars (→ Bohdalová, → Brzobohatý). In accord with Czech tastes, its most popular products at the time were light comedies (→ *S tebou mě baví svět*) and filmed fairy tales (→ *pohádka*). Though Barrandov was privatized in 1993 and has largely ceased to produce domestic films—its facilities are now mainly in the service of foreign productions—for Czechs, the name still symbolizes the magic of film.

Baťa. The first family of Czech industry. In 1894, Tomáš Baťa (1876–1932) founded a shoe factory in the town of Zlín that became one of the country's largest and most success-

ful companies and a symbol of the growing might of the Czech economy. Among Baťa's innovations were assembly-line production, a system of bonuses for workers, modern advertising, and profit sharing with employees. He also turned Zlín into a model company town, providing workers with apartments and homes as well as pleasant surroundings. The company's habit of pricing goods in numbers ending in 9—the infamous 19.90—meant that these numbers are known in Czech as Batavian. The company was nationalized after the war by the communists, and the Baťa family emigrated and continued production in the West. The new regime set about erasing memories of Baťa who had become a symbol of bourgeois values and prosperity. The shoe factory was renamed Svit, the town itself was rechristened → Gottwaldov after the first communist leader of Czechoslovakia (→ Gottwald), and a propaganda film entitled *Botostroj* (The Shoe Machine) became required viewing. The communists also unintentionally managed to destroy Baťa's business credo—Our Customer, Our Master—and instituted a tradition of poor service that lasts to this day. Since 1989, the Baťas have returned to the country and reopened their shoe stores. Like Leningrad, Gottwaldov has resumed its former name.

bažant (recruit; literally "pheasant"). Slang term used for new army recruits. When army service lasted for two years, first-year soldiers or *bažanti* were subject to hazing and had to wait hand and foot on soldiers who were in their second year of service. These older soldiers, known as *mazáci*, were free to lounge around for the remainder of their mandatory term. See → *vojna*.

Becherovka. An herbal liqueur that along with beer (→ *pivo*) and → *slivovice* forms the triumvirate of favorite Czech alcoholic beverages. Sold in patented green bottles, it tastes something like cough medicine and can be consumed on just about any occasion, including and especially during sickness. Becherovka was invented by an English

Family Silver

These are the firms that Czechs call their family silver; that is, firms which they consider of great value to the nation whether symbolic or real. They were chosen by readers of the newspaper *Lidové noviny* in the year 2002. Other well-known brand names, some of which no longer exist, are: Dermacol cosmetics, Elite stockings, Esko and Favorit bicycles, Fruta, Hamé, and Vitana packaged foods, Jawa motorbikes, Jitex clothing, Kara furs, Karat jewelry, Karosa buses, Léčiva medicines, Liaz trucks, Meopta cameras, Nanuk ice cream, Rico hygienic needs, Supraphon records, Svit shoes, and Tatra cars.

Name	Products	Headquarters	Founding
Barum Continental	tires, car parts	Otrokovice	1932
Baťa	shoes	Zlín	1894
Budějovický Budvar	beer	České Budějovice	1895
Brisk Tábor (formerly Jiskra)	spark plugs	Tábor	1935
Crystalex	glass, crystal	Nový Bor	1948
ČKD Holding	heavy machinery, locomotives	Prague	1927
Český porcelán	porcelain	Dubí	1864
Egermann	crystal	Nový Bor	19th c.
ETA	household appliances	Hlinsko	1943
FAB	locks	Rychnov nad Kněžnou	1911
Granát	garnet jewelry	Turnov	1953
Hartmann-Rico	hygienic products	Veverská Bítýška	1820
Hellada	cosmetics	Prague	1920
Chlumčanské keramické závody	ceramics, building materials	Chlumčany	–
IPS Skanska	construction	Prague	1953
Jan Becher	liquor	Karlovy Vary	1810
Jemča	tea	Jemnice	1960s
Jitex Písek	clothing	Písek	1949
Karlovarský porcelán	porcelain	Karlovy Vary	1911
Kasalova Pila	sawmill, joinery	Jindřichův Hradec	1928
Keramost	ceramics	Most	1945
Koh-I-Noor	writing instruments	České Budějovice	–
Kovohutě Příbram	metalworking	Příbram	1786
Kostelecké uzeniny	sausage	Kostelec	1917
Lonka Příbor	socks, hosiery	Příbor	1872
Mattoni	mineral water	Kyselka	1867

Name	Products	Headquarters	Founding
Mora Moravia	ovens, stoves	Mariánské údolí	1825
Moser	crystal	Karlovy Vary	1857
Nábytek Exner	furniture	Kutná hora	1914
Národní hřebčín Kladruby	horse breeding	Kladruby	1562
Okula Nýrsko	spectacles	Nýrsko	1895
Olma	dairy products	Olomouc	1965
Opavia	snack foods	Opava	1840
Orion	chocolate	Prague	1896
Petrof	pianos	Hradec Králové	1864
Plzeňský Prazdroj	beer	Plzeň	1842
Praga Čáslav	motorcycles, buses	Čáslav	1907/1955
Pribina	dairy products	Přibyslav	1923
Prim	watches	Nové Město nad Metují	1949
Rako	tiles	Rakovník	1883
Sklárny Kavalier	glass	Sázava	1837
Solo Sirkárna	matches	Sušice	1839/1903
Škoda Auto	automobiles	Mladá Boleslav	1895
Tatra	automobiles	Kopřivnice	1897
Tesla	radios, tvs	Mladá Vožice	1921
Ton	furniture	Bystřice pod Hostýnem	1856
Tonak	hats	Nový Jičín	1799
Triola	women's lingerie	Prague	1920s
Veba	textiles	Broumov	1856
Viadrus	heating equipment	Bohumín	1885

Source: Lidové noviny, 16 September 2002.

chemist visiting the spa (→ *lázně*) → Karlovy Vary at the beginning of the nineteenth century and entrusted to the local German-speaking Becher family. Said to cure digestive problems, the secret blend of herbs was a hit with visitors to the spa and even became a favorite of the emperor → Franz Joseph. The recipe has always been a closely guarded secret—at one point the only two people to know it had to travel in separate cars lest they both perish at once. Under communism, court battles with the Becher family—who had been expelled to Germany (→ *odsun*)—led to two separate Becherovkas on the world market, a Czech and a German variety. Becherovka was frequently seen in the hand of the recent Prime Minister Miloš Zeman and is considered a national treasure despite its German or rather English origin.

Beneš, Edvard (1884–1948). Beneš stood at the founding of the state of Czechoslovakia. He promoted the state abroad during World War I, served as the new country's foreign minister, and succeeded → Masaryk as president. He is remembered, however, not for his patriotism and devotion to the Czech cause, but for two fateful decisions. In 1938, he allowed the Germans to take the Czech borderlands without a fight (→ *Mnichov*), judging that the blood lost would gain nothing. And, in 1948, again as president, he accepted the resignation of several democratic ministers, thus allowing the communists to take power (→ *Vítězný únor*). For these decisions, he enjoys a checkered reputation among Czechs. He is, however, despised among Sudeten Germans (→ *sudetští Němci*) for his decrees confiscating their property (→ *Benešovy dekrety*), an action that is lauded by Czechs.

Benešovy dekrety (Beneš Decrees). The common designation for a series of decrees issued by then president Edvard → Beneš, with the approval of the government, at the end of World War II. Though most were innocuous laws aimed at postwar reconstruction, the most infamous ones deprived the German population of their citizenship and confiscated their property (→ *odsun*). Popular at the time and ignored under communism, the decrees became a live political issue after 1989 when German and Austrian descendants of those expelled called for the revocation of the decrees as a condition of Czech membership in the European Union. Belief in their justness and fear of having to return immense tracts of property have led the vast majority of Czechs to defend the decrees with passion. The issue in fact is almost entirely symbolic.

betlém (nativity scene). A common Christmas (→ *Vánoce*) tradition is to build or visit a nativity scene. An invention of St. Francis of Assisi, who used a live donkey and ox to celebrate Christmas mass, nativity scenes arrived in the Czech lands in the sixteenth century, carried there by Jesuits (→ *jezuité*) spreading the Counter-Reformation (→ *katolická církev*). By the eighteenth century the tradition was adopted wholeheartedly by villages and towns across the country. In addition to the holy family and three wise men, the scenes often feature elaborate background sets and a host of characters as well as mov-

ing parts and music boxes. Ornate nativity scenes can now be found in churches and regional museums (the largest, measuring sixty square meters and containing 1,400 figures, is in the town of Jindřichův Hradec); many families construct their own more modest versions out of paper or cardboard.

Běž domů, Ivane! (Go home, Ivan!). This phrase was widely scrawled on walls after the Soviet invasion (→ *srpnová invaze*) and was even set to music, in a song entitled "Well-Intentioned Advice." It was often followed by references to Ivan's girlfriend Natasha, who was waiting for him at home in Russia or was having an affair with his best friend.

Bezruč, Petr (1867–1958). Poet of the proletariat (→ *dělník*). Bezruč first gained fame in the early 1900s as the author of a book of poems that detailed the grim lives of the miners (→ *Jsem horník a kdo je víc*) of Silesia (→ *Slezsko*) and created a literary sensation for its brutal imagery. His reputation today, however, rests on the cult that the communists later made of his progressive writing. His poems became required reading (→ *povinná četba*) in schools, and factories were named after him. In reality Bezruč produced little after his first book, entitled *Songs of Silesia*, and spent only a year among the miners he described. Other poets elevated to canonical status under communism for their proper political stance included Marie Majerová, S.K. Neumann, and Marie Pujmanová. What they all had in common was a real talent which they sold out in the name of ideology.

Bible kralická (Kralice Bible). The standard Czech translation of the Bible. It was produced by members of the Protestant sect, the Union of Brethren (→ *Jednota bratrská*), who under increasing pressure from the Counter-Reformation set up a secret printing press in the small Moravian town of Kralice. Working from 1579 to 1594, they created an accurate and historically-informed translation of the Old and New Testaments that rivaled any in Europe at the time. Though it was not the first appearance of the holy book in Czech, it far exceeded previous versions in the depth of its scholarship and the poetry of its language. Though the Brethren were suppressed soon after the Bible appeared, their handiwork had a profound effect on Czech language and literature, and its lines continue to be cited.

Bican, Josef "Pepi" (1913–2001). The best Czech soccer (→ *fotbal*) player of all-time and one of the greatest goal scorers the world has ever known. Born to a Czech family in Austria, he first gained fame as a striker with a nose for the net playing for the Vienna club Rapid. In the thirties, he transferred to Prague's Slavia (→ Sparta/Slavia) though he did not get his citizenship papers in time for the 1938 World Cup, when with the goalie František Plánička he might have delivered the title to the Czechs. His goal scoring, however, continued unabated even through the war years. He finished his career with an incredible five thousand goals (643 in league play), a total that became the title of his best-selling autobiography. The communists, however, banished him from his beloved Slavia to the backwater of Hradec Králové and after his career had ended put him to work as an ordinary laborer on the Holešovice docks. As if these humiliations were not enough, the bureaucrats in charge of world football records voted not to make him the top goal scorer of all time (they argued that his wartime goals should not count), and Czech sports fans did not choose him as the best player of all-time (possibly because he was not sufficiently Czech for their tastes).

bigbít (rock and roll). Instead of using the term rock and roll, Czechs are more likely to refer to the music as *bigbít* (pronounced big beat). *Bigbít* arrived in Czechoslovakia at the end of the fifties, but due to harassment from the regime, it did not make it beyond student clubs until the mid-sixties. The country's version of the Beatles, the supergroup → Olympic was founded in 1963 and became a launching pad for virtually all of the country's stars. Other icons of Czech rock include the blues-oriented Vladimír Mišík, the ubiquitous Slovak combo Elán, and Katapult—the first hard rock group to attain wide popularity. A number of more avant-garde rock bands like the → Plastic People and Pražský výběr meanwhile became important symbols of the underground and dissident movements. The dissident-turned-president Václav → Havel is a self-acknowledged fan of the music and received Frank Zappa and Lou Reed among his first official guests. Czech tastes in foreign *bigbít* run toward the Beatles and Rolling Stones, but not so much Led Zeppelin and Jimi Hendrix. Patti Smith, Nick Cave, and Freddie Mercury meanwhile are probably better known to Czechs than to Americans. To actually see these bands live under communism, Czechs had to make the trip to Hungary (→ *Maďarsko*), the only state in the Soviet bloc to regularly play host to Western acts. Rock, however, has never been the majority taste in music; rather top forty (→ Gott) rules the airwaves and plays constantly in shops and restaurants.

Bílá, Lucie (1966). The leading star of the postcommunist music scene. Bílá was the first singer to learn how to exploit the tabloidization of Czech journalism to rise to the top of her profession. With both provocative songs—her biggest hit sang of boys going with boys and girls with girls—and a very public love life, she became the most followed and written about celebrity of the nineties.

Bílá hora (White Mountain). Site of a decisive battle during the Thirty Years' War (→ *Třicetiletá válka*) that meant the end of Czech Protestantism and independence. Rather than celebrating military victories, of which there are few, Eastern European countries often prefer to remember their great defeats. Where Serbs have *Kosovo Polje* and Hungarians *Mohács*, Czechs summon up *Bílá hora*. In 1620, soldiers paid by Czech nobles met the army of the Habsburg monarchy at a field near White Mountain not far from Prague. The cause of the battle was the effort of the largely Protestant Czech estates to resist the growing centralism of the Catholic Habsburg monarchy. In the end, the Czech mercenary army, underpaid by its patrons, put up only feeble resistance and quickly fled the battlefield. More traumatic than the loss itself were the consequences, which included the destruction of the Czech aristocracy (most had their property confiscated or were exiled), the forced recatholicization of the country (at the time most Czechs were Protestants), and the end of Czech as a language of state. Most memorably, twenty-seven Czech noblemen were executed on Old Town Square in Prague. It was after the battle that → Komenský and other carriers of Czech culture and learning emigrated, leaving German speakers as the sole intellectual elite. Many have compared the trauma of *Bílá hora* to the imposition of communism in 1948, though the consequences of White Mountain stretched far longer, for almost three centuries. The battle also produced the Czech Benedict Arnold in the person of Albrecht of Valdštejn, who sold out his people before being murdered by his new masters. For many patriots, *Bílá hora* is the tragedy that haunts all of Czech history and prevented the development of an independent and democratic state in the heart of Europe (→ *smysl českých dějin*).

Bílá paní (White Lady). A mythical denizen of the country's castles and chateaux (→ *hrady a zámky*). It is said that while she lived, her husband treated her so cruelly that she cannot rest even in death and must remain in her old castle. Dressed in a white robe with a tall pointed hat and a veil across her face, the White Lady haunts these old estates and plays tricks on their human inhabitants. She is often associated with the real-life Lady Perchta of Rožmberk, who, according to family legend, appears wearing white gloves whenever an heir is about to be born and black gloves when a family member is about to die. The actress Jiřina → Bohdalová starred in a popular film comedy about the White Lady.

Blaník. An ancient folk myth that claims a secret army of the country's greatest heroes lies in wait under the mountain Blaník in central Bohemia (→ *Čechy*). Led somewhat incongruously by the pacifist Saint Wenceslas (→ Svatý Václav), the army will supposedly awaken and save the nation when the Czechs are in dire straits—leading many to remark that the worst is yet to come. Inhabitants of the surrounding areas claim to hear rumblings coming from beneath the mountain (→ Cimrman believes the army spends its spare time bowling) and when a stray mortal somehow ventures into their hiding place, one day spent with the Blaník knights is transformed into a year of normal time. The myth forms the basis for artistic works by musicians like → Smetana and Fibich, and writers like Tyl and Jára → Cimrman. It might be taken as typical of a Czech willingness to put their fate in the hands of others. The legend though is not the Czechs' alone: secret, hidden armies that will save the nation are widespread (and universally ineffective) in Eastern Europe.

bobříky (little beavers). *Bobříky* are tests of strength and ability for young boys and girls. They were set down in Jaroslav → Foglar's *Rychlé šípy* (Fast Arrows) books, and their name is derived from the Beaver River near which the book's young heroes had their adventures. Among the best known of the thirteen *bobříky* are silence (not saying a word for twenty-four hours), bravery (staying alone all night in the woods), and nobility (no lying or cursing). The remaining tasks are nimbleness (various running and jumping tests), precision (stone throwing), rescue, swimming, good deeds (one hundred must be performed), flowers (fifty species of plant must be identified), loneliness (ten hours without being seen or heard), handiness (manufacturing a useful object), strength (five pullups), and hunger (a day-long fast). To this day kids perform *bobříky* and sew a patch on their sleeve whenever they "hunt" one down. *Bobříky* have even penetrated the adult world: when a politician lets slip something better left unsaid, for example, he is said not to have held to the little beaver of silence.

bodování úklidu (cleanup rating). One of the rituals of summer camp. Every morning counselors rate all of the tents and cabins on how well their resident campers have cleaned them up. The tentmates with the best score are awarded a special prize. Another well-known exercise is the *stezka odvahy* (trail of bravery) where campers have to make their way through the woods alone at night.

Bohdalová, Jiřina (1931). The most popular actress in the last quarter of the twentieth century. A perky, wide-eyed redhead, Bohdalová burst onto the film scene in the late sixties as a star of musicals and wacky comedies. In one classic role, she played a streetcar ticket inspector who cleverly punishes her unfaithful husband. While her style and appearance remind one of Lucille Ball, she showed her acting range in the New Wave (→ *Nová vlna*) classic *Ucho* (The Ear) as the wife of a communist functionary who discovers that their house is bugged. She remains known and loved, however, mainly for her countless television roles where she excelled in short comedy sketches with a variety of male partners. Even today, with most of her career behind her, Bohdalová regularly wins popularity contests. She remains for Czechs the epitome of the fun-loving, sharp-tongued, occasionally ditzy, but down-to-earth and good-hearted mother and wife.

Bohouš. The title of a popular short film from the late sixties that is traditionally shown on television on New Year's Eve. The actor Vladimír → Menšík plays a customer in a pub who bets that he can eat more items off the pub's menu than the bartender's Saint Bernard, Bohouš. Menšík wins the bet when the dog turns its nose up at slices of bread.

bony (coupons). Coupons introduced in the fifties that allowed citizens to buy imported goods—like Levi's jeans, Swiss chocolate, or Adidas sneakers—at special → Tuzex shops. *Bony* were obtained from the state in exchange for foreign currency, which citizens were required by law to turn in to the gov-ernment who needed it to cover perpetual foreign exchange shortages. By the eighties, black-market sellers of *bony* (→ *vekslák*) had become a common sight on street corners, whispering to passersby, "Need some *bony*" or "Wanna buy *bony*." A popular eighties film called *Bony a klid* (Bony and Peace) provided a surprisingly honest look at the world of *bony* trading. Prices quoted in bony in fact were probably the only accurate prices in the country under communism (→ *koruna*).

boží muka (wayside cross; literally "divine suffering"). A short column with a shrine containing a small statue, picture of a saint, or inscription. These shrines are an indelible part of the Czech landscape, appearing on the side of roads as well as in forests and fields. They once pointed the way to pilgrimage sites (→ *pouť*) for journeying Christians or memorialized the site of accidents.

brambory (potatoes). Though they arrived in Europe only after the discovery of the New World, potatoes quickly became a staple of Czech cuisine. Several recipe books are devoted entirely to the potato and they include such favorites as boiled potatoes, mashed potatoes, potato salad, potato dumplings stuffed with sausage, and even so-called American potatoes (potato slices baked on oil and then topped with cheese and ketchup). Street stands sell large, spicy potato pancakes called *bramboráky*.

branná výchova (defense education). As a communist country on the frontline of any potential war with the imperialists, Czechoslovakia had to be kept in constant military readiness. For adults this meant service in the military (→ *vojna*) or → *Lidové milice*. Children meanwhile were trained through the → *Spartakiáda* and *branná výchova* in schools. The latter consisted not just of hiding in bomb shelters, but also of learning to fire air rifles, crawl on one's stomach, and use a compass. These exercises even became the object of interscholastic competitions. Most hated was the drill known as IPCHO (*Improvi-*

zovaná protichemická obrana/Improvized Anti-chemical Defense) where students had to don gas masks and plastic suits (rarely washed from their previous users) and run around outdoors to practice for a chemical attack. Jokes had it that the purpose was to make sure the corpses were well-wrapped for burial. These exercises were no relic of the fifties as in America, but continued until the very end of the regime. Recently there have been moves to reintroduce *branná výchova* to prepare for terrorist attacks.

Brejchová, Jana (1940). If the Czechs have a silver screen femme fatale in the postwar era, it is Jana Brejchová. Her blonde hair, doe-like eyes, and innocent expression made her a sex symbol under a regime that preferred to keep sexiness out of public life. Her best-known role was as the wife of Emperor → Karel IV in the musical adaptation of the comedy *Night in → Karlštejn*. In addition to her countless film roles both at home and in Germany, Brejchová was married to the director Miloš Forman and the popular actor Vlastimil Brodský. Her sister Hana played the ingénue in Forman's classic film *Lásky jedné plavovlásky* (Loves of a Blonde).

brigáda (work brigade). A term referring to part-time work. Under communism, school days in the fall months were regularly taken up by brigades as entire classes were shepherded into the fields to help with the potato harvest. While such brigades were mandatory, young people often made extra money in the summer months on brigades picking hops (→ *chmel*), an activity immortalized in the popular film → *Starci na chmelu* (The Hops Pickers). Today *brigáda* refers not only to these summer jobs (mandatory brigades have disappeared), but also to any sort of temporary work, whether in a factory or a restaurant.

Brno. The second-largest Czech city. An industrial center in south Moravia (→ *Morava*), Brno suffers from an inferiority complex in relation to Prague (→ *Praha*). Though it boasts a proud history—it was the site of

Gregor Mendel's pea experiments and was known as the Manchester of Moravia for its factories—it inevitably loses its most talented sons and daughters to the capital. As a result, it covets its own idiosyncrasies, especially its distinct way of speaking (→ *hantec*).

Broučci (Fireflies). One of the most popular Czech children's books of all time. Written by the part-time theologian Jan Karafiát in 1876, it allegorically describes a utopian world inhabited by fireflies and other bugs. Its main character is Young Firefly, who learns from his parents the value of Christian humility and obedience to the divine order as well as the importance of being helpful and useful. The book, however, does not lack for fantasy, kindness, and an understanding for human frailty. Each chapter memorably ends at sunrise with the lines: "And they slept and slept. Oh, how they slept." Though it went through fifty editions before the war, *Broučci* was suppressed by the communists and published only briefly in the thaw of 1968. Like the books of Jaroslav → Foglar, it circulated widely in the form of old editions lent among friends.

Brzobohatý, Radoslav (1932). Sex symbol of sixties and seventies film. His chiseled features, tough-guy persona, and classical training made Brzobohatý directors' first choice to play dramatic leading men during his prime. He starred most famously as an independent farmer who opposes collectivization (→ JZD) in Vojtěch Jasný's classic film *Všichni dobří rodáci* (All the Good Countrymen). As a result of that film, viewed as too anticommunist under the normalization (→ *normalizace*) regime, he had to humble himself in a number of lesser roles before returning to his accustomed position as star. He is the actor who would have won "The Sexiest Man Alive" contest if it had been held in communist Czechoslovakia.

budovatelský (constructive). Used most frequently in the fifties, the high point of enthusiasm for communism, this adjective described the efforts of committed communists to build a new and better society. The word could be applied to nouns like plans, work, thoughts, camps, songs, and novels. One could even act in a constructive manner. It is often used as a synonym for politically engaged communist art that in English is referred to as socialist realist (→ *sorela*). *Budovatelský* stories and films followed a set of standard plots. They typically had as their hero a hard-working communist who reformed his enterprise's workplace to achieve higher production by inspiring his co-workers and foiling the plans of imperialist or counterrevolutionary saboteurs. This art had mostly vanished by the mid-sixties, except in statues and mosaics, as enthusiasm for communism waned. Today the term is used almost exclusively in a negative or at best ironic sense.

bufet (cafeteria/snack bar). These restaurants were the Czech equivalent of fast food. Customers would stand in line with trays, order from a variety of pre-made hot and cold dishes, and then consume their food while standing at high counters. Among the typical offerings at these cafeterias were a wide selection of open-faced sandwiches (→ *chlebíčky*) and mayonnaise-based salads (→ *vlašský salát*) as well as soups (→ *polévka*), goulash (→ *guláš*), and fried cheese (→ *smažený sýr*). A close relative of these enterprises were the so-called *mléčné bary* (milk bars), which served mainly dairy dishes in a similar setting. These buffets have recently been dying out due to competition from Western-style fast food chains.

Bulharsko (Bulgaria). Czechs know Bulgaria for Black Sea resorts like Golden Sands, Varna, and Sunny Beach, all common summer destinations under communism when travel to the West was virtually prohibited. To reach these beaches, one had to suffer through a day and a half train or bus ride. Most can tell humorous stories about misunderstandings stemming from the fact that Bulgarians nod their heads to indicate "no" and shake them to mean "yes."

burčák (young wine). A popular milky brownish beverage that forms at an early stage in the process of wine fermentation. It has a sweet taste like apple juice, but packs an alcoholic punch. In the wine-growing region of South Moravia, *burčák* is cause for celebration. Vintners taste their wine frequently in the early fall and at the exact moment it turns into *burčák*, whether morning or night, they invite all their friends over to their wine cellar for a drinking bender. Though *burčák* contains only about five percent alcohol, it catches up on drinkers quickly because its taste is so sweet and because it reputedly continues to ferment in one's stomach. It is commonly served at grape harvest festivities, known as → *vinobraní*.

Burian, Vlasta (1891–1962). Known to Czechs as the king of comics, Burian was the most popular star of Czech film and theater in the thirties and forties. A scrawny, mustachioed figure, Burian began as a comic actor in a theater which he owned and whose plays he wrote. As the writer Josef Škvorecký describes him, "He was something of a Czech Groucho Marx. He had the same mercurial energy, was capable of similar verbal floods, and stupefied the audience with wisecracks, explosive gags, aggressive conquests of women, and fantastic mimicry." With the coming of sound films, he became the country's most marketable star. Many of his films were adapted from his own plays and most involved mistaken identities. Thus in *Přednosta stanice* (The Station Master), he plays a ticketless train passenger who is taken for the stationmaster. The same kind of mix-up inspired *U pokladny stál* (He Stood at the Till) where hospital staff believe he is a VIP and *C. a k. polní maršálek* (Imperial and Royal Field Marshal) where he is mistaken for an Austrian field marshal. Burian had the misfortune of being at the top of his career when the Nazis invaded. Though his collaboration with the invaders was of a lesser degree than that of many communist leaders—he once made fun of Czech politicians and Jews on a radio broadcast—he was hauled before a tribunal after the war. He was banned from performing and most of his great fortune was confiscated (his luxurious lifestyle was probably the real reason for his punishment). Though he eventually returned to the stage and film, he never recaptured his prior zaniness. His association with the bourgeois First Republic (→ *První republika*) also meant that his films were shown only intermittently under communism. Since the Velvet Revolution (→ *Sametová revoluce*), Burian's work has been enjoying a revival. Hardly a week goes by without a film of his appearing on television, and his remains were recently reburied in the national cemetery →*Slavín*.

buržoazní původ (bourgeois origin). Under communism, being of bourgeois origin was a fatal blotch on one's record. It meant that one could not advance at work and one's children would be disadvantaged at school. Bourgeois pastimes like dining out, wearing elegant clothes, and drinking cocktails were likewise frowned upon. Such discrimination against the middle class seemed natural to many Czechs who were brought up to see poor peasants or at least manual laborers as the soul of the nation (→ *rovnostářství*).

"Byl pozdní večer—první máj" (It was late evening, the first of May). The start of the most cited stanza in Czech poetry. It comes from the poem *Máj* (May) by the romantic Karel Hynek → Mácha, and, in Edith Pargeter's translation, sounds thus: "Late evening, on the first of May / The twilit May—the time of love. / Meltingly called the turtledove, / Where rich and sweet pinewoods lay." The poem itself, probably the most influential work in all of Czech literature, tells the story of Vilém, who is thrown out of his home as a child and becomes a bandit. When Jarmila, the woman he loves, is seduced by an older man, Vilém kills the man only to learn that it was his father, Hynek. Vilém is then sentenced to the gallows and Jarmila drowns herself. More than the story, Czechs remember the poem for its romantic imagery of nature, love, and loneliness, and

most know only the first stanzas that they are made to memorize in school. A recent billboard for cell phones featured the poem's last line: Hynek! Vilém! Jarmila!

"Byli jsme před Rakouskem, budeme i po něm" (We were here before Austria, we will be here even after it). The historian → Palacký's famous assessment of relations between the Czechs and the Habsburg state. In Palacký's influential formulation of Czech history, Czechs and Germans were in constant conflict over the Czech lands, and it was the Czechs whose claim was stronger. The quotation's emotional force comes from its appeal to an ancient, primeval nation that can survive any adversity including four centuries of Habsburg rule. Nevertheless, it represents not just Czech patriotic feeling, but also the sort of naïve hope in the ultimate triumph of their good cause that characterizes much Czech nationalism (→ *Pravda vítězí*). It seems to highlight simple survival and the miraculous disappearance of enemies rather than the militant struggle typical of other Eastern European nationalists. All students learn the line in schools and it is frequently cited in conversation. Jára → Cimrman tacked the words *"kdoví jestli"* (and who knows if that) to the end of the formulation, and a popular radio show—parodying a typical Czech family—is subtitled *"Byli jsme a budem"* (We Were and We Will Be).

Bylo nás pět (There Were Five of Us). A popular comic novel by the author Karel Poláček (1892–1944) that describes life in a small town between the wars. The story is told from the point of view of a young boy who, with his four friends—altogether the five of the title—finds various ways of getting in trouble. Indeed, the book feels much like *Tom Sawyer*, with a solid grounding in the details of Czech small-town life. Though a carefree, nostalgic feel pervades the work, it was actually written just before the author was deported to a concentration camp and was not published until after the war. Paradoxically, it was the Jewish Poláček who more than any other was able to understand and speak to the provinciality (→ *maloměšťáctví*) of the Czech mentality in books like *Dům na předměstí* (House on the Periphery)—about a landlord who tyrannizes his tenants—and *Muži v offsidu* (Men Offsides)—about fans of Prague's three main soccer clubs (→ Sparta/Slavia, → *fotbal*).

C

čaj (tea). Served at all times of the day, tea is the country's staple drink and even more popular than juice and soft drinks. The whole family usually drinks tea in the morning and again at dinner. Children are served heavily sweetened tea with their lunch at school. Most languages use a similar word to refer to tea as it is derived from the Chinese word *cha*.

Čapek, Karel (1890–1938). The symbol, for Czechs, of all that a writer should be. Čapek was not just a great and prolific author, he was also a public intellectual and ethical role model. His deep-felt humanism and skeptical rationalism set the moral tone of his age. In his most famous works, like the plays *R.U.R.* (the source of the word → robot) and *The White Sickness,* as well as the novel *War with the Newts,* he tells in Robert Pynsent's words of "humanity threatened by its own endeavours to master the world." As important was his writing style which evokes in Czechs a feeling that this is the way their language should be written. As a person, Čapek epitomized the bourgeois values of the First Republic (→ *První republika*). Indeed, he played a major role in forming that culture through the weekly meetings he held with his *pátečníci* (Friday Men), where leading artists and opinion-makers from across the political spectrum gathered to discuss culture, philosophy, and politics. Čapek's own politics were defiantly liberal—he was close to → Masaryk and published a famous interview with the president entitled *Conversations with T.G.M.*—and he was an ardent supporter of Czechoslovak democracy. His reputation was such that even the communists could not completely remove him from the canon of Czech literature. He is also remembered for his newspaper feuilletons (→*fejeton*) and a children's book about his fox terrier Dášeňka. Čapek's death on Christmas Day in 1938, not long after the capitulation at Munich (→ *Mnichov*), marked the death knell of the First Republic.

Čáslavská, Věra (1942). Olympic champion gymnast. The blonde-haired Čáslavská first won hearts at the 1964 Tokyo Olympics where she collected four medals, including three golds. More inspirational was her performance at the 1968 Olympics in Mexico City. After the Soviet invasion (→ *srpnová invaze*) in August of that year, it was unclear if Czechoslovakia would even send a team to the games. Though she arrived too late to acclimatize to the high altitude, Čáslavská provided some satisfaction for the humiliating invasion by overwhelming her Soviet rival and taking home four golds and two silvers. In a time of national depression, her victories, like those of the hockey team, were seen as a slap in the face of the occupiers. Čáslavská disappeared from public life after the victory, but returned to become an advisor to Václav → Havel after the fall of communism. Other female athletic heroes include the figure-skater Alena Vrzáňová, who emigrated rather than be sent to Russia to train skaters, and the muscular sprinter, Jarmila Kratochvílová.

Čech. The eponymous founder of the Czech nation, often called forefather Čech. Legend has it that he arrived on the territory of

100 Books Every Czech Should Read

According to the book *Fakta do kapsy* (A Pocket Book of Facts), "This thoroughly problematic selection includes books (without regard to the age of the reader) readable and less readable, read or today unread, celebrated or cursed; books which are part of popular consciousness; books which "established" norms or high points of literary genres or entire epochs. Others became bestsellers in their time (sometimes artificially), or were on the other hand banned; last but not least, they are works which essentially (though often falsely) established images about our past...The selection can be taken as 100 books which everyone should read or at least know about." Asterisks (*) indicate books that have been translated into English.

Czech Title	English Title	Author	Date	Notes
Anna Proletářka	Anna the Proletarian	Ivan Olbracht	1928	Epitome of socialist realism
→ Babička*	Grandmother	Božena → Němcová	1855	Classic sentimental realist novel
Báječná léta pod psa	The Wonderful Years That Sucked	Michal Viewegh	1992	Bestseller about growing up in 70s and 80s
→ Broučci*	Fireflies	Jan Karafiát	1876	Children's book with religious subtext
→ Bylo nás pět	There Were Five of Us	Karel Poláček	1946	Humorous novel about small-town friends
Cesta slepých ptáků	Journey of the Blind Birds	Ludvík Souček	1964	Popular science fiction
Cirkus Humberto	Circus Humberto	Eduard Bass	1941	Comic novel about circus life
→ Černí baroni	Black Barons	Miloslav Švandrlík	1969	Comic novel about army life
Česká kronika	Czech Chronicle	Václav Hájek	1541	Classic chronicle of Czech history
Dalimilova kronika	Dalimil Chronicle	-	1315	Verse chronicle of Czech history from the biblical flood to 1310
Dědeček automobil	Grandfather of the Automobile	Adolf Branald	1955	Novel about pioneers of the automobile, later filmed
Devět bran	Nine Gates	Jiří Langer	1957	Hasidic themed novel; among the most translated from Czech
→ Domácí kuchařka	Home Cookbook	Magdaléna Rettigová	1826	Key work in the National Revival
Don Pedro, Don Pablo a Věra Lukášová	Don Pedro, Don Pablo and Věra Lukášová	Božena Benešová	1936	Story of the inner life of a 13-year-old girl

Czech Title	English Title	Author	Date	Notes
Edison	Edison	Vítězslav Nezval	1928	Poems about human creative force
Einsteinův mozek	Einstein's Brain	Josef Nesvadba	1960	Science fiction
Elegie	Elegy	Jiří Orten	1947	Poetry by a rising talent who died at the age of 22
→ Ferda Mravenec	Ferda the Ant	Ondřej Sekora	1936	Among best known children's books; famous illustrations by → Lada
Fimfárum	Fimfárum	Jan → Werich	1960	Clever fairytales by a national icon
Hodina mezi psem a vlkem	An Hour Between the Dog and the Wolf	Jan Skácel	1962	Poetry
Hostinec u kamenného stolu	The Stone Table Inn	Karel Poláček	1941	Comic novel
Hovno hoří	Shit Burns	Petr Šabach	1994	Bestseller about growing up in the sixties
Hovory s T.G.M.*	Conversations with T.G.M.	Karel → Čapek	1928	Life and opinions of the first president
Hrad smrti	Castle of Death	Jakub Deml	1912	Novel by a Catholic author
Jak jsem potkal ryby*	How I Came to Know Fish	Ota Pavel	1974	Jewish and outdoor-themed stories by a famous sports journalist
Kája Mařík	Kája Mařík	Felix Háj/ Marie Černá-Wagnerová	1926	Children's bestseller in the First Republic
Kámen a bolest	Stone and Pain	Karel Schulz	1942	Historical novel
Klabzubova jedenáctka	Klabzub's Eleven	Eduard Bass	1922	Comic novel about a family soccer team
Klíč kacířské bludy	Key for Recognizing Heretical Errors	Antonín Koniáš	1729	Counter-Reformation propaganda
Klokočí	Klokočí	Jiří Suchý	1964	Poems, better known in musical form
Kniška Karla → Kryla	Karel Kryl's Little Book	Karel Kryl	1972	Protest songs
Kohout plaší smrt	The Cockerel Frightens Death	František Halas	1930	Classic modernist poetry
Kronika česká	Bohemian Chronicle	→ Kosmas	1125	First chronicle of Czech history
Krvavý román	Bloody Novel	Josef Váchal	1924	Parody of pulp fiction

Czech Title	English Title	Author	Date	Notes
Krysař	The Pied Piper/ The Ratcatcher	Viktor Dyk	1915	Poetic story of Pied Piper
Kytice z pověstí národních	Bouquet of National Legends	Karel Jaromír → Erben	1853	Collection of national fairytales
Liška Bystrouška	The Cunning Vixen	Rudolf Těsnohlídek	1920	Newspaper articles about forest life
Lovci mamutů	Mammoth Hunters	Eduard Štorch	1918	Adventure novel for children
→ Máj*	May	Karel Hynek → Mácha	1836	Romantic ballad
Maminka	Mother	Jaroslav Seifert	1954	Poems by a Nobel Prize winner
Manon Lescaut	Manon Lescaut	Vítězslav Nezval	1940	Drama in verse
Markéta Lazarová	Markéta Lazarová	Vladislav Vančura	1931	Novel of medieval life; known for its style
Měsíc s dýmkou	Moon with a Pipe	Hana Prošková	1964	Detective story
Město v slzách	City in Tears	Jaroslav Seifert	1921	Proletarian poetry by a future Nobel laureate
Mirákl*	The Miracle Game	Josef Škvorecký	1972	Chonicle of Prague Spring (→ Pražské jaro)
Miss Otis lituje…	Miss Otis Regrets…	Josef Kainar	1969	Blues lyrics
Modlitba pro Kateřinu Horowitzovou*	A Prayer for Kateřina Horowitzová	Arnošt Lustig	1964	Jews during WWII
Moje první lásky*	My First Loves	Ivan Klíma	1981	Stories by dissident author
Modrý a rudý	Blue and Red	Fráňa Šrámek	1906	Anarchistic poetry
Moskva-hranice	Moscow-Border	Jiří Weil	1937	Novel about life in the USSR; banned
Mstivá kantiléna	Vengeful Cantilena	Karel Hlaváček	1898	Classic Czech decadence
Muži v offsidu	Men Offsides	Karel Poláček	1931	Comic novel about Prague football fans (→ Bylo nás pět)
Němá barikáda	Silent Barricade	Jan Drda	1946	Socialist realism about WWII
Newtonův mozek	Newton's Brain	Jakub Arbes	1877	Early science fiction
Nikola → Šuhaj, loupežník*	Nikola Šuhaj the Outlaw	Ivan Olbracht	1933	Novel about legendary thief in Subcarpathia (→ Podkarpatská Rus)

Czech Title	English Title	Author	Date	Notes
Noc s Hamletem	A Night with Hamlet	Vladimír Holan	1964	Meditative poems
Nový epochální výlet pana Broučka, tentokrát do XV. století	The Excursion of Mr. Brouček to the Fifteenth Century	Svatopluk Čech	1889	Parody of Czech provincialism
Obsluhoval jsem anglického krále*	I Served the King of England	Bohumil → Hrabal	1964	Story of a waiter's peregrinations through the 20th century
O kocourovi Mikešovi	About Mikeš the Cat	Josef Lada	1934	Czech version of Puss in Boots with illustrations by the author
Ostře sledované vlaky*	Closely Watched Trains	Bohumil → Hrabal	1964	Coming of age story set during WWII
Osudy dobrého vojáka → Švejka*	The Good Soldier Švejk	Jaroslav → Hašek	1921–23	Classic comic novel of WWI
Petrolejové lampy	Petroleum Lamps	Jaroslav Havlíček	1944	Novel of unhappy love
Písně kosmické	Cosmic Songs	Jan Neruda	1878	Poetry by famed essay writer (→ fejetony)
Písně otroka	Songs of a Slave	Svatopluk Čech	1894	Anti-Austrian poems
Po nás ať přijde potopa!	After Us the Deluge!	František Gellner	1901	Poems of an anarchist
Postřižiny	Cutting It Short	Bohumil Hrabal	1976	Autobiographical novel about author's parents
Povídání o pejskovi a kočičce*	All about Doggie and Pussycat	Josef Čapek	1929	Children's classic with illustrations by the author
Povídky malostranské*	Prague Tales	Jan Neruda	1878	Stories about inhabitants of Prague's Little Quarter
Povídky z jedné a druhé kapsy*	Tales from Two Pockets	Karel → Čapek	1929	Detective stories
Reportáž psaná na oprátce*	Report from the Gallows	Julius → Fučík	1945	Diary of communist imprisoned by Nazis
Romance pro křídlovku	Romance for the Flugelhorn	František Hrubín	1962	Romantic poetry
Romeo, Julie a tma*	Romeo, Juliet and Darkness	Jan Otčenášek	1958	Novel of Jewish girl in hiding during WWII
Rozmarné léto	Capricious Summer	Vladislav Vančura	1926	Stylistically innovative novel of quiet town visited by a magician
Ruce	Hands	Otakar Březina	1901	Poetry

Czech Title	English Title	Author	Date	Notes
Saturnin*	Saturnin	Zdeněk Jirotka	1942	Humoristic bestseller
Sbohem a šáteček	Farewell and a Headscarf	Vítězslav Nezval	1934	Modernist poetry
Sekyra*	The Axe	Ludvík Vaculík	1966	Novel by a dissident author
Série C-L	C-L Series	Eduard Fiker	1958	Detective story
Slezské písně	Silesian Songs	Petr → Bezruč	1903	Proletarian poetry; required reading under communism
Smrt krásných srnců	Death of Lovely Roebuck	Ota Pavel	1971	Stories about the author's Jewish family before and during war
Soukromá vichřice	Private Whirlwind	Vladimír Páral	1966	Racy sixties bestseller
Splav	The Weir	Fráňa Šrámek	1916	Romantic poetry
→ Staré pověsti české*	Old Czech Legends	Alois → Jirásek	1894	Classic retelling of national myths
Svatý kopeček	Sacred Mound	Jiří Wolker	1921	Poetry
Študáci a kantoři	Students and Teachers	Jaroslav Žák	1937	Classic humor about student life
Tankový prapor*	Tank Battalion/ Republic of Whores	Josef Škvorecký	1954	Novel about absurdity of army life in 1950s
→ Temno	Darkness	Alois → Jirásek	1915	Good Czechs against bad Catholics
Torzo naděje	A Torso of Hope	František Halas	1938	Poetry to help nation through Munich
Toulky českou minulostí	Rambles through the Czech Past	Petr Hora (Hořejš)	1985	Widely read historical essays
Třináctá komnata	Thirteenth Chamber	Vladimír Neff	1944	Historical novel
Tyrolské elegie	Tyrolian Elegies	Karel Havlíček Borovský	1870	Satirical, anti-Austrian poems
Ustláno na růžích	A Bed of Roses	Jindřiška Smetanová	1966	Stories from Prague's Little Quarter
Utrpení knížete Sternenhocha*	Sufferings of Prince Sternenhoch	Ladislav Klíma	1928	Avant-garde novel
Valčík na rozloučenou*	The Farewell Party	Milan Kundera	1976	Magical realist novel
Válka s mloky*	War with the Newts	Karel → Čapek	1936	Classic science fiction
Záhada hlavolamu	The Mystery of the Brain Twister	Jaroslav → Foglar	1941	Popular children's literature
Zahrada	The Garden	Jiří Trnka	1962	Children's literature

Czech Title	English Title	Author	Date	Notes
Zbabělci*	The Cowards	Josef Škvorecký	1958	The end of WWII through the eyes of a teenager
Žert*	The Joke	Milan Kundera	1967	Novel about consequences of Stalinism on personal relationships

Source: František Honzák et al. *Fakta do kapsy* I. Praha: Libri, 2001.

the current Czech Republic with his brother Lech who continued on to found the Polish nation, while a third brother, Rus, stayed behind in Russia. Even in myth, Čech's exploits are not substantial. He appears to have done little more than settle his tribe in an area in central Bohemia around the mountain → Říp and proclaim it a rich land overflowing with milk and honey. See also → Libuše.

Čechy (Bohemia). A term used to refer to the western half of the Czech Republic. Together with Moravia (→ *Morava*) and Silesia (→ *Slezsko*) it forms one of the three historic regions of the Czech kingdom. Though *Čechy* is used to refer to only one part of the country (and so people may say they are going on vacation *do Čech* or to Bohemia), the word *Čech* (Czech) is only occasionally used to refer to residents of that part of the country. Virtually all citizens of the country consider themselves Czechs. The distinctions are actually simpler in German which uses the word *tschechisch* to refer to the Czech people and *Böhmen* to refer to the territory where Czechs have lived (along with Germans, Jews, Gypsies, and others). While the word *bohém* is used in Czech to refer to artists living nontraditional lifestyles, it is not usually associated with the country itself.

céčka (C's). A fad item that overwhelmed the country in the early eighties. School kids collected C-shaped pieces of plastic called *céčka*—they came in different sizes and colors—and hung them on their belts or around their necks. The fad was even immortalized in a popular song, "He/She's collecting C's," by the king of Czech disco, Michal David.

Other collectibles under communism were beer coasters, flags and insignias from state-owned enterprises, and pictures of famous singers and actors.

Čedok (Československá dopravní kancelář/ Czechoslovak Tourist Agency). Čedok was founded in 1920 as independent Czechoslovakia's first travel agency. It had already established itself as a synonym for travel when it was seized by the Nazis in 1939 and nationalized by the communists in 1948. Its name survived though, and it was Čedok that took most Czechs on their first trips outside of the country in the era of what was called "collective recreation" after the war. These foreign excursions, however, were largely confined to the Black Sea coast of Bulgaria (→ *Bulharsko*) and, for the more privileged, to Yugoslavia's (→ *Jugoslávie*) Adriatic. All trips out of the country required a special → *výjezdní doložka* (exit visa permit) and *devizový příslib* (secured sum of foreign currency) that were given only to the politically reliable. It was at this time that Czechs developed their habit—still in force today—of bringing all possible necessities with them on trips, lest they have to buy expensive and unfamiliar foreign goods. Perhaps the greatest lifestyle change for Czechs since the fall of communism is the opportunity to travel abroad freely. Within two years of the fall of communism, Čedok, once synonymous with foreign travel, had hundreds of new competitors in the travel agency business including the new goliath Fischer.

černé divadlo (black light theater). A type of theater where actors are rendered invisible by black light and black costumes and carry or wear florescent objects which, when manipulated, give the illusion of effortless, weightless movement. Combined with music and clever choreography, black light theater can produce a disconcerting, magical impression. Though it originated in the Orient, *černé divadlo* found a European home in Prague in the 1950s. Its popularity there was a result of the general popularity of theater (→ *divadlo*) and Prague's reputation as a city of magic and the occult (→ *Praha*). Today the city is home to several black light theaters which mainly compete for tourist dollars.

černí baroni (black barons). The black barons, also known as *PTPáci* (an abbreviation of *Pomocný technický prapor* or Auxiliary Technical Battalion), were members of an army unit formed in 1950 and filled with individuals labeled enemies of the regime. Because they were intellectuals (→ *inteligence*), priests, members of the bourgeoisie (→ *buržoazní původ*), or aristocrats (hence the name, → *šlechta*), they were not allowed to serve in ordinary military units or carry weapons. Instead, they were given extended terms of service of four years or more and forced to do hazardous hard labor in mines or factories. Since they received no remuneration, their status is best likened to slaves and they were treated accordingly; many died and the rest left service with their health broken. Their fate thus became symbolic of the wanton destructiveness of the communist regime. Miloslav Švandrlík wrote a classic novel (entitled *The Black Barons*) which made their experiences the pretext for low humor satirizing the army. After the fall of communism, the book became a popular film, though otherwise the black barons received little official acknowledgment much less compensation for their suffering.

Černý Petr (Black Peter). A popular children's card game similar to Old Maid, except that players try not to get stuck with the Black Peter card. The phrase has thus become attached to anyone suffering from bad luck. One of Miloš Forman's best films is named after the game.

česká kotlina (Czech basin). A geographic term used to refer to the fact that the Czech lands are almost completely surrounded by mountains and thus form a basin or valley. This geography has offered them protection from enemies—Czechs have not suffered the way that Poles have—and arguably influenced their character. In particular, it has enabled Czechs to see themselves as one big family where, as Kundera points out, any success of one Czech is a success for all Czechs, and any failure a disappointment to all Czechs.

Česká otázka (The Czech question). For nineteenth-century Czech intellectuals, the Czech question was the role the Czechs were to play in the world. Was the Czech nation a relic of the past, destined to be swallowed up by the Germans and Russians? Or was it capable of making real contributions to world history? One of the most influential answers to the question, but not the only one, was in → Masaryk's *The Czech Question*. He argued that there was a real Czech essence that could be found in the medieval Hussite (→ *husité*, → Hus) and Brethren (→ *Jednota bratrská*) religious orders who had advanced the global cause of humanism and universal brotherhood. It was these contributions that had been embodied by the National Revival (→ *Národní obrození*) and constituted the *raison d'être* of the Czech nation. Masaryk's answer to the Czech question thus helped both to justify the resurrection of Czech culture and inspire Czechs to take the next step towards building their own state.

Česká republika (Czech Republic). The official name of the country since the breakup (→ *sametový rozvod*) of Czechoslovakia (→ *Československo*) in 1992. It thus succeeded former names like the Czechoslovak Federative Republic (1990–1992), the Czechoslovak Socialist Republic (1960–1989), and the Czechoslovak Republic (1918–1939, 1945–1960). Many citizens find the designation *Česká republika* a mouthful and so use the short form → *Česko*.

české baroko (Czech baroque). A unique architectural style that emerged in the Czech lands in the seventeenth century. The Czech version of the baroque style added to its European counterpart greater forcefulness and complexity. It came to dominate the country during the Counter-Reformation as the Habsburgs rebuilt the country in the Catholic image (→ *jezuité*). Despite its foreign roots, Czech baroque is what gives the country's cities their distinctive feel of mystery and magic. Among the most important artists working in the style were Jan Blažej Santini-Aichel and Kilian Ignaz Dientzenhofer. Interestingly, the mansions of the new postcommunist elite (→ *fialové sako*) are built in a gaudy style that has come to be called *podnikatelské baroko* (businessman's baroque).

České Budějovice. Large city in southern Bohemia (→ *Čechy*) that is most famous for giving its name to Budweiser beer (→ *pivo*), Budvar in Czech. Its brewery has fought a long-running trademark battle with the American beer that took its name, though the Czech brand has roots in the thirteenth century, a full six centuries before Anheuser-Busch was born. The city is also known for its large town square.

Česko (Czechia). A word invented after the breakup of Czechoslovakia (→ *Sametový rozvod*) to refer to the Czech Republic. Many Czechs, especially intellectuals, claim that it rings false in their ears, but it is far easier to say than the clumsy official name, the Czech Republic (→ *Česká republika*), and therefore is in widespread use.

Československá církev (Czechoslovak Church). Founded in 1920 by renegade Roman Catholic priests, the Czechoslovak Church was a reaction to Catholicism's (→ *katolická církev*) association with the Habsburg Empire, and an attempt to create a home-grown, national church. The new church held mass in the vernacular, allowed priests to marry, and reached back to the Hussite (→ Hus, → *husité*) tradition. Popu-lar during the First Republic (→ *První republika*), the church is today very much a minority confession, having lost its battle against both general irreligiosity and three centuries of state Catholicism.

Československo (Czechoslovakia). Though most Westerners see Czechoslovakia as a natural political formation and Czechoslovak as a national identity, the political fates of Czechs and Slovaks (→ *Slovensko*) had been separate since the Great Moravian Empire (→ *Velkomoravská říše*) of the ninth century. While Czechs had been independent or ruled benignly from Vienna, Slovaks never had their own state and suffered under the heavy thumb of the Hungarians. Their union in Czechoslovakia after World War I was a product both of the Czech National Revival (→ *Národní obrození*), which saw Czechs and Slovaks as two parts of the same nation, and the necessity of creating a majority Slav state large enough to compete with its neighbors. The designation of Czechoslovak was quickly accepted by many Czechs, though the majority of Slovaks felt slighted by it and were more likely to see themselves as Slovaks than Czechoslovaks. This Slovak inferiority complex (they would blame Pragocentrism) erupted during World War II, when Slovaks allied with the Nazis to secure an independent state, and again during the Prague Spring (→ *Pražské jaro*), which Slovak political leaders used to gain more autonomy. These recriminations came to the surface after the Velvet Revolution (→ *Sametová revoluce*), which soon gave way to the Velvet Divorce (→ *Sametový rozvod*) and the end of Czechoslovakia in 1992. While many Czechs feel nostalgic for the old days of the federation, the vast majority have reconciled themselves to their new, smaller state.

Český ráj (Czech Paradise). Nature reserve northeast of Prague (→ *Praha*). Lush forests, dramatic sandstone rock formations, and hidden castles (→ *hrady a zámky*) make this area one of the most popular destinations for Czech vacationers (→ *Klub českých* *turistů*) and a true Czech paradise. It was once the stomping grounds of the romantic poet Karel Hynek → Mácha.

češství (Czechness). Unlike most Eastern European countries, Czechs do not wear their nationalism on their sleeves. While pride in being Czech is widespread, there is little overt feeling of being better than other nations, except perhaps for their poorer Eastern neighbors. The lack of a desire to conquer or more negatively defend themselves against conquerors has been rationalized as the positive trait of pacifism (→ *holubičí povaha*). Hard work (→ *práce šlechtí*) and dependence on their own talents (→ *zlaté ručičky*) are seen as the main ways to distinguish themselves and keep Czech culture alive. Cynics though note that Czechs are forever finding ways to bend the law to their purposes or subvert it with → Švejkian playing dumb. Most Czechs are aware of the fragility of their position, surrounded as they are by a sea of Germans, and describe themselves in terms of smallness (→ *malý český člověk*). Indeed, one famous writer asked rhetorically, "What does the Czech nation need most?" and answered, "Ten thousand Don Quixotes." As far as culture goes, it is unequivocally the language (→ *čeština*) which is the core around which the nation revolves. As a result, anyone who speaks native Czech is regarded as a brother regardless of his place of birth. Likewise, writers and poets are seen as the bearers of national heritage and hold a permanent place in the country's pantheon (→ *inteligence*, → *umělec*). Socially, a strong feeling of egalitarianism (→ *rovnostářství*) and lack of respect for elites characterize most Czechs. This is manifested both in the provincial (→ *maloměšťáctví*) roots of the country's culture as well as in the national trait of envy (→ *závist*). In the past, the iconic image of the country was peasants dressed in folk costumes (→ *kroj*) singing folk tunes (→ *lidovka*) and dancing in the village (→ *vesnice*) square. Today, however, most Czechs see themselves as liberal, educated Europeans living in a modern, advanced society. In any case, a strong sense of Czechness is an unsurpassed

virtue and selling out to foreigners, leaving the country, or forgetting one's roots is seen as the greatest betrayal of the Czech cause.

čest práci (honor to labor). A standard greeting under communism. It was most enthusiastically used by party members and enterprise management, but was required of all workers. It was often shortened to simply *čest* (honor) and followed by the appellation → *soudruh* (comrade). In reality, the communists borrowed the phrase from their archenemy, the millionaire shoemaker → Baťa.

čeští letci (Czech fighter pilots). After the Czechs surrendered to the Nazis at the start of World War II, many pilots in the well-trained Czech army managed to escape to England where they joined the RAF and fought to liberate their homeland. Despite their heroism, they were tortured and imprisoned after the war because of their dedication to democratic ideals and first-hand knowledge of the West.

čeština (Czech language). Czech is a part of the family of Slavic languages that includes Polish, Russian, and Serbo-Croatian, among others. Though not mutually intelligible (except for Czech and Slovak), these languages share many word stems and grammatical constructions, much like the Romance languages. Czech, along with its cousins, has a reputation for difficulty due to the large number of declinations and conjugations. The long sequences of consonant letters (→ *strč prst skrz krk*) and difficult to pronounce letter → *ř* are also offputting to foreigners. On the other hand, Czech is largely phonetic, simplifying the problem of spelling, and has only three verb tenses. Czech almost disappeared as a written language under Habsburg rule, when all intellectual and official communication took place in German, and Czech was relegated to the lower orders. It was early nineteenth-century linguists like → Dobrovský and → Jungmann who began the revival of the Czech language by codifying its rules and creating scores of new words (→ *Národní obrození*). Due to the efforts of these patriotic intellectuals, Czech was turned from a language of illiterate peasants (it even lacked a word for industry) into a modern tongue. Interestingly, the language was revived as much through original literature as through multilingual dictionaries and translations of foreign classics where the translator had to fill in gaps of words that did not exist in Czech. Later, in a movement known as purism, some tried, with only partial success, to purge the language of foreign, mainly German, borrowings. Because of the small number of native speakers and the few characteristics distinguishing them from their neighbors, Czechs remain extremely devoted to their language. This manifests itself in sensitivity over correct writing (→ *pravopis*, → *vyjmenovaná slova*) and speaking (→ *spisovná čeština*). Many worry today that the language is being corrupted by mobile phones and e-mail (which do not support several distinctively Czech letters) and commercial television (where announcers use sloppy pronunciation). On the bright side, most Czechs believe their language is immensely difficult and are willing, as the scholar Jungmann claimed, to accept as Czech anyone who speaks native Czech, gypsies (→ *cikán*) excepted.

čestný pionýrský (Pioneer's honor). Just as the Pioneers (→ *Pionýr*) replaced the boy scouts (→ *Junák*) under communism, so did this phrase become the Czech version of scout's honor. Children licked the index and middle fingers on their right hand and raised them aloft when repeating this oath. The equivalent of "Cross my heart and hope to die" meanwhile is *Na mou duši, na psí uši, na kočičí jazýček* (On my soul, on a dog's ears, on a cat's tongue).

chalupa (country house). Originally the term for an old farm house, *chalupa* now refers more to vacation homes in the country. They are essentially larger versions of the → *chata* (cottage) with more amenities like electricity and indoor plumbing. While cottages are left empty in the winter, *chalupy* are suitable for long-term living and many retire to them. Owners invest considerable resources in outdoing their neighbors in the size and luxury of their country homes. Common ornaments include collections of painted ceramic dwarves and miniature concrete castles.

Charta 77 (Charter 77). Dissident movement founded in 1977. In the years after the Soviet invasion (→ *srpnová invaze*), brutal repression forced Czechs to resign themselves to cooperation with the new normalization (→ *normalizace*) regime. The arrest of members of The → Plastic People of the Universe music group in 1976, however, provided the stimulus for Václav → Havel and others to found a movement for the protection of civil rights. Taking inspiration from the government's signature on the Helsinki Final Act, a small group of dissidents (→ *disident*) issued the *Charta 77* calling for the regime to enforce its own laws protecting freedom of expression. The government responded with a massive crackdown, imprisoning the dissident leaders and launching a counter-petition known as the *anti-Charta*. Though well known in the West, repression made the *Charta* largely invisible within the country, and it was only able to attract 2000 official members. Nevertheless, these members included many of the country's leading lights such as the philosopher Jan Patočka (who died during an interrogation), the writers Ludvík Vaculík and Pavel Kohout, and the actor Pavel → Landovský. Opinions differ on *Charta 77*'s significance, with supporters calling it a bastion of hope in the darkness of normalization, and critics seeing it as a small ghetto-like organization that had little influence on public events. Chartists went on to take leading roles in the overthrow of the regime (→ *Sametová revoluce*) and continue to receive respect today while playing a progressively smaller role in politics.

chata (cottage). Despite their low incomes, most every Czech has access to a summer cottage. These cottages are often little more than small one- or two-roomed wooden structures without electricity or running water. Their spare accoutrements include beat-up furniture, a ceramic stove, a radio, and a nearby outhouse (called a *kadibudka*). Despite their humble furnishings, cottages are beloved by Czechs who generally spend every free minute there. Friday afternoons are legendary for the traffic jams outside of major cities as everyone heads for the countryside. This makes trying to do business on the eve of a weekend a futile endeavor. Cottages are often located in close proximity to each other in *chatové oblasti* (cottage reservations) in areas like → *Vysočina*, → *Šumava*, and → *Český ráj*. Though the cottaging craze has old roots, its boom years were the seventies and eighties, when the communists made materials available to the masses or turned a blind eye to theft, and Czechs put their → *zlaté ručičky* (golden hands) to good use. Time at the cottage is put to a variety of uses. Both men and women spend much of their energy on fix-up jobs and gardening (→ *zahrádkářská kolonie*)—several magazines are devoted exclusively to *chataření* (cottaging). Other pastimes are hiking in the woods (→ *Klub českých turistů*) and gathering mushrooms (→ *houbařství*), blueberries, and raspberries. It is also common to invite friends and sit around a fire roasting sausages (→ *špekáček*) and singing songs, or to take a trip to the pub (→ *hospoda*) in the nearest village.

chlebíčky (open-faced sandwiches). *Chlebíčky* are miniature slices of bread topped with various lunchmeats, cheeses, and mayonnaise-based salads (→ *vlašský salát*). They are an essential part of office birthday and retirement parties as well as New Year's Eve (→ *Silvestr*) celebrations. Because the sandwiches are also served at art openings and other events favored by celebrities, the postcommunist cream of society has come to be called *pojídači chlebíčků* (sandwich eaters). The sandwiches can be bought at specialized stores as well as in self-serve restaurants, but are just as frequently prepared at home.

chmel (hops). Hops is the fuel that powers the Czech nation. Since time immemorial hops has been cultivated on the fields of western Bohemia and then processed into beer (→ *pivo*). The hops from Žatec (Saaz in English) is so prized that it is exported to some of the best breweries in Germany and America (including Sam Adams). Many Czechs have personal experience picking *chmel* from participating in annual work brigades (→ *brigáda*). These brigades hold a special place in the hearts of Czechs as they were one of the first times they were both old enough to be interested in the opposite sex and far away from their parents' gaze. It is for this reason that one of the most beloved Czech films, → *Starci na chmelu* (The Hops Pickers), takes place during a hops brigade. Given the place of beer in Czech culture, it is no surprise that *chmel* is often called *zelené zlato* (green gold).

Chodsko. Rural area in southeastern Bohemia (→ *Čechy*). Inhabitants of Chodsko are traditionally known for their independence and fighting abilities. From the fourteenth to seventeenth century, villages in the region received privileges from the crown including personal freedom and limited self-government in exchange for their service as border guards. When these rights were restricted in 1692, the Chod people revolted. Reputedly bearing shields with the head of dog—immortalized in Alois → Jirásek's novel *Psohlavci* (The Dog Heads)—they fought valiantly under the leadership of Jan Sladký Kozina, but were ultimately subdued. Most associate the region with its folkloric traditions, especially its folk costumes (→ *kroj*) and the playing of bagpipes (→ *Švanda dudák*). The writer Božena → Němcová lived for a short time in Chodsko and made friends with the local inhabitants while collecting folk tales and songs.

chozrasčot (cost accounting in a self-supporting unit). One of the few Russian words (→ *ruština*) to enter the Czech lexicon during communism. Considered a brilliant reform of the socialist economy in the seventies and eighties, *chozrasčot* only meant that enterprises should cover their own costs rather than having losses paid for by the government. While this sounded suspiciously like capitalism, the Russian term helped mask its reactionary meaning. Like all reforms under the communist regime, *chozrasčot* was never followed through and ended a failure.

Číhošťský zázrak (Číhošť miracle). In 1949, during mass at a small church in the town of Číhošť, a cross on the altar moved several times from side to side, apparently of its own accord. This so-called miracle was in fact engineered by the communists, who tortured the local priest until he admitted to faking it himself. The incident served as the pretext for a series of trials (→ *politické procesy*) against Church dignitaries (→ *katolická církev*) and the liquidation of the monastic orders.

cikán (Gypsy, Roma). Originally from India and speaking a language related to Sanskrit, Gypsies or Roma have lived in the Czech lands since at least the fifteenth century, earning their living as tinkers, musicians, and thieves. While most native Czech Gypsies were exterminated in the Holocaust, their population expanded markedly when many Slovak Gypsies were resettled in the vacated Czech borderlands after the war and made to stop their wandering ways. Under communism, Gypsies worked mainly in construction and sanitation, though since the Velvet Revolution (→ *Sametová revoluce*) many have found themselves unemployed and turned to petty crime. Very few have moved into the middle class or educated professions and most live in predominantly Gypsy parts of cities. The census places them at less than one percent of the Czech population, but the actual number is likely far higher. The word *cikán* carries negative connotations in Czech, though even some Gypsies use it. The politically correct word is *Rom* (Roma in English) which means man or person in the Roma language. Most Czechs profess an open dislike of Gypsies and many will regale foreigners with stories of their bad experiences. A typical conversation sounds something like this: "I'm not a racist. I have no problem with Africans, Indians, or Chinese. But Gypsies are

another story." They will then proceed to relate how they were mugged, attacked, or harassed by Gypsies. The most popular legends describe how Gypsies build large campfires in the middle of their state-owned apartments. More recently, this racism has turned violent with skinhead groups attacking Gypsies. Gypsies for their part are reluctant to assimilate into the majority. Nevertheless, they have been immortalized in popular folk songs like "*Černý cikán*" (The Black Gypsy) or "*Cikánka*" (The Gypsy Girl) and are a permanent part of Czech culture.

cimbál. Folk music genre. *Cimbál* music is so named for the instrument at its center, the *cimbál* (hammered dulcimer in English) a flat, stringed instrument that looks a little like a zither. The music is characteristic of the Carpathian mountain region, which includes portions of Hungary, Slovakia, Romania as well as the Moravian half of the Czech Republic. In addition to the *cimbál*, a typical band features violins, a viola, a contrabass, and a clarinet. Traditionally, the music was played at weddings, funerals, and holidays with songs tailored to the mood of each occasion. Though it was ultimately pushed aside by brass-band music (→ *dechovka*), *cimbál* made something of a comeback in the 1950s and today is featured in pubs and restaurants as well as at folklore festivals. The music is frequently associated with the strong emotions of Gypsies (→ *cikán*) and Moravians (→ *Morava*).

Cimrman, Jára. Fictional Czech genius and polymath who reputedly lived at the beginning of the twentieth century. Cimrman was first introduced on a radio show in the late sixties and soon became the subject of a series of ever-popular plays by Ladislav Smoljak and Zdeněk Svěrák. Though Cimrman himself never appears in these plays, expert Cimrmanologists lecture on his many achievements in the fields of science, sport, pedagogy, literature, and art and then perform a play purportedly written by him. In one popular example, Cimrman rewrites the classic fairy tale

"Mr. Tall, Mr. Wide, and Mr. Sharp-Sighted" (→ *Dlouhý, široký a bystrozraký*) as "Mr. Tall, Mr. Wide, and Mr. Near-Sighted." In general, the plays are a masterful send up of and homage to Czech nationalism and the Czech place in the world, right down to Cimrman's name which is the Czech phonetic spelling of the German name Zimmermann. Cimrman is a typical → *malý český člověk* (little Czech person), who through pluck, skill, and persistence makes his mark on the world, though the world pays him no mind. The plays have inspired a Cimrman cult and spawned thousands of amateur Cimrmanologists who contribute to the myth.

Cirkus Kludský (Kludský Circus). Founded by Czech native Antonín Kludský and run with the help of his twenty sons, the Kludský Circus became the most popular circus in the Czech lands and one of the largest in Europe in the late nineteenth and early twentieth century. The circus disappeared under communism—its main replacement was the Berousek family circus—but was renewed by the Kludský family after 1989. It was one of the inspirations for Eduard Bass's widely-read novel and later popular television series, *Cirkus Humberto*, which detailed the adventures of a fictional family circus.

ČKD (Českomoravská Kolben-Daněk/ Kolben-Daněk Machinery Works). An enormous industrial firm founded in 1926 (though its roots go back to 1871). ČKD was formed from the merger of three separate companies of both Czech and German ownership, hence the hyphenated name. Producing turbines, locomotives, and streetcars, the firm was first a symbol of the growing industrial power of Czechoslovakia between the wars and then a symbol of socialist ideals when it was nationalized after the war.

Člověče, nezlob se (I'm Sorry, Man). The country's most popular children's board game. Similar to the American game "Sorry," players move around the board by rolling dice and sending others back to their home base. Mc-

Donald's has recently featured it on billboards in an effort to Czechify their image. Another commonly sought out toy is the building blocks that go by the name Merkur.

Co Čech, to muzikant (Every Czech a musician). Common phrase that testifies to the important place of music in Czech life. The bright side of this tradition is the rich history of music in the Czech lands. This includes not only classical music (→ Smetana, → Dvořák, Janáček), but also folk music and dances. The national song, the → polka, found its best-known expression in Jaromír Vejvoda's → "*Škoda lásky*" which was translated into English as the "Beer Barrel Polka." Another reference point is the play *Strakonický dudák* (→ *Švanda dudák*) about a poor bag-piper from south Bohemia (a region with Celtic roots) who dreams of fame and fortune. Proof of Czechs' musical prowess is that two-thirds of musicians and half of bandleaders in the Austrian Military Orchestra were Czechs. This talent is now a product of the excellent musical education that begins as early as nursery school (→ *Lidová škola umění*). Most Czechs can sit around a campfire or in a bar and sing the night away with both folk (→ *lidovka*) and popular melodies. Every Czech even chooses a song he wishes to be played at his funeral (→ *pohřeb*). Another side of the Czech love of music is summed up in the phrase "*Já nic, já muzikant*" (Me nothing, me musician) and refers to the national tendency to avoid taking responsibility or standing up to oppressors (→ *holubičí povaha*). Today Czech musicality can be seen in the enormous popularity of musicals—both foreign and domestic—that have made Prague into a second Broadway.

country. Word used to refer to country and western music, a popular genre among Czechs. Country music originally gained popularity through the → *tramping* movement, but it ultimately caught on among the wider public, perhaps because of its associations with the West (→ Vinnetou). Aficionados of the form have gone so far as to wear cowboy hats and display the old Confederate flag. The Czech Republic today boasts a prolific country music scene (→ Mládek), radio stations playing only country music, and even several Wild West theme parks.

ČSAD (Československá státní autobusová doprava/Czechoslovak Bus Transport Company). For any Czech living outside of major cities, buses run by ČSAD have been their essential link with the larger world. Numerous daily links connected even the most isolated villages (→ vesnice) with regional hubs, the same buses carrying both commuters to work and children to school. Budget woes and a recent car boom, however, have led to a decline in the number and frequency of routes much to the chagrin of many villagers. Signs for ČSAD bus stops can be seen on the side of most roads.

čtvrtá cenová skupina (fourth price category). Under the planned economy of communism, all restaurants and pubs (→ hospoda) were placed into four price categories. These categories were based on such amenities as the presence of tablecloths, the number of menu items and alcohol offerings, and the quality of lavatories. Since prices were centrally-planned, they also determined how much the establishment could charge. The lowest of the categories and therefore the cheapest was the fourth. Despite their dire conditions, pubs in this category were widely sought out by students and intellectuals for their authentic and lively atmosphere. Research has shown that the fourth category outdid and outdoes all of the others in the quantity of alcohol consumed.

cukrárna (sweetshop). In the past when every shop closed from noon on Saturday until Monday morning, sweetshops stayed open seven days a week to supply gifts for traditional Sunday afternoon visits to grandparents or friends. To foreigners, the *cukrárna* looks like a combination of ice-cream store and coffeehouse where customers can sit down to eat on the spot or pick the sweets they wish to take home and have them wrapped up in paper. Most Czechs have a favorite *zákusek*

(sweet) from a selection of classics, all named for their shape, like *větrník* (pinwheel), *trubička* (little tube), *indiánek* (little Indian), *špička* (little point), *štafetka* (little baton), *věneček* (little wreath), and *rakvička* (little coffin). The morbid names are parodied in Juraj Herz's classic film, *The Cremator of Corpses*, where the title character offers guests either a little wreath or a little coffin. Like Viennese sweets, most are made of a pastry topped or filled by a dollop of whipped cream.

čundr (overnight hike). A weekend trip to the countryside with a small backpack and a few friends. A *čundr* is something more than a walk and something less than a camping trip. After a day of hiking, the participants often end up in a countryside pub (→ hospoda) or around a fire where they sing songs (someone always brings a guitar) until they fall asleep under the heavens (*pod širákem*). A necessary complement to a *čundr* is the layered wafer called *Tatranky*, whose loads of calories are guaranteed to give the *čundrák* (hiker) enough energy to get over the next hill. These hikes are popular with all age groups and in the past were the weekend activity *par excellence*.

Cyril (827–869) **and Methodius** (825–884). Brothers known as the apostles of the Slavs. Born in Thessalonica, Cyril and Methodius were invited to the Great Moravian Empire (→ Velkomoravská říše) to help christianize its Slavic inhabitants. Though not the first to proselytize in the Czech lands, Cyril and Methodius were the most successful. They translated the liturgy into the Slavonic tongue and created an alphabet for that language which in modified form is used today in Russia and known as Cyrillic. Though associated with the Orthodox Church and harassed by German bishops, Cyril and Methodius are credited with having catholicized the Czechs and Slovaks. They are also associated with the church of → Velehrad where they converted the leader of the Great Moravian Empire and are celebrated in a national holiday on July 5.

D

D1. The name of the country's main superhighway that connects Prague to Brno. Built in the seventies, D1 was the first major multilane road in the country and cut a line through the heart of Prague thanks to the Nusle Bridge. Instead of paying tolls, cars on D1 need to sport a certain freeway sticker on their windshield. Special police spotters with binoculars observe traffic for those without stickers and send out patrols to fine them. The main job of policemen, however, is to stand on the side of the road and conduct spot checks where they inevitably find an obscure violation of some technical norm. The dearth of cars in the country, at least until recently, means that most Czechs are poor drivers. They think nothing of passing on two-lane roads or backing up over long distances if they miss a turn.

DAMU/FAMU (Theater and Film Faculties of the Academy of Performing Arts). The training grounds of the country's artistic elite (→ *umělec*). Czech students apply not just to a university, but to a particular department or faculty, and since their founding in the early postwar era, the drama and film faculties have been one of the most popular choices. For a period in the sixties, DAMU and FAMU were among the strongest departments of their type in the world. The film school, FAMU, trained not just the greats of the Czech New Wave (→ *Nová vlna*), but even many celebrated directors from Yugoslavia and elsewhere. DAMU has similarly contributed to the country's rich theater scene (→ *divadlo*). Though normalization

(→ *normalizace*) took its toll on the teaching corps and nepotism has always been a problem, graduates of both faculties continue to dominate the country's stage and silver screen.

David, Michal (1960). Singer/songwriter. David became famous in the early eighties by producing Czech-inflected versions of Italian pop music. His hits like "Nonstop" and "Don't Hint" topped the hit parade at the time and were played constantly in discotheques. Though most acknowledge that his music is pure fluff, happy memories of a youth spent listening to his songs allowed David to make a comeback in the late nineties. David also composed a children's theme song to the → Spartakiáda gymnastics exhibition.

dechovka (brass band music). No Czech wedding (→ *svatba*), funeral (→ *pohřeb*), or ball (→ *ples*) is complete without a heavy dose of brass band music. It is said that the style originated with soldiers who brought their marching music home from the Napoleonic wars and were able to buy newly affordable instruments. Bands playing *dechovka* were subsequently formed, both by entire villages as well as occupational groups like miners, veterans, postmen, and railway workers. Their repertoire is made up mostly of marches, waltzes, → polkas, and mazurkas. The most famous bandleader and composer was undoubtedly František Kmoch (1848–1912), whose group became the model for others and whose works became standards in the genre. His music was such a symbol of Czechness that the wartime biopic about Kmoch, *To byl český muzikant* (That Was a Czech Musician), provoked anti-German riots. The genre continues to expand today with groups constantly coming up with new hokey compositions celebrating their local communities. Frequent competitions—including one called Kmoch's Kolín—give these bands an opportunity to show their stuff. Public opinion polls have found that three-quarters of Czechs express positive views towards *dechovka*, but it is most popular among the middle-aged and residents of villages. Communist leaders (themselves mostly older men) heavily promoted the genre, and brass bands like Moravanka used to play frequently on television or at state celebrations. One of the most popular television programs of the seventies and eighties, *Let's Meet at the Music*, featured elderly couples dancing to *dechovka*. Today brass band music evokes a mix of feelings ranging from nostalgia and nationalist pride to embarrassment at its amateurism to nausea at its ubiquity.

Děda Mráz (Grandfather Frost). The Russian version of Santa Claus (→ *Vánoce*). Like Santa, *Děda Mráz* has a long white beard and red suit, but in the Russian version he travels with a snow maiden instead of reindeer. The figure was forcibly imported to Czechoslovakia after the communist takeover. In 1952, then president Antonín Zápotocký alerted children that → *Ježíšek* (baby Jesus) who had traditionally brought them presents had grown up and turned into *Děda Mráz*. Despite heavy propaganda, the tradition never did catch on. Today *Děda Mráz* survives only in the lyrics to the Czech version of "Jingle Bells" and in the cult Russian film → *Mrazík*.

defenestrace (defenestration). The act of throwing someone out of a window. Defenestration is a tradition in the Czech lands thanks to two famous incidents. In 1419, Hussites (→ *husité*) protesting their persecution by the Catholic Church (→ *katolická církev*) threw seven members of the town council out of a window of the Prague New Town Hall and

on to a phalanx of pikes below. Again, in 1618, members of the Czech estates rebelling against the increasingly powerful Habsburg monarchy threw two of the king's vice-regents from a window of the Prague Castle, though this time the throwees landed safely on piles of refuse (→ *Třicetiletá válka*). A third case that might squeeze into the category is the liberal Foreign Minister Jan Masaryk, who was found dead below the window of his apartment soon after the communist putsch in 1948. It is still unclear whether he committed suicide or was pushed by communist agents. While this tradition of throwing people from windows may provide psychological satisfaction, it testifies to a nation not entirely comfortable with normal politics.

dekrety na byty (apartment leases). Among the first victims of communist rule were private landlords who, as exploiters of the working man, were quickly relieved of their property holdings. The result was that most urban citizens became tenants of the state. As part of the communist guarantee of housing to all, these tenants received *dekrety* (decrees) which gave them certain rights over their apartment. For example, it was almost impossible to evict the holder of a *dekret* and the apartment could be passed down to the holder's children or relatives. This led to enormously complicated exchanges for those who wished to change apartments—one had to find others who would trade their apartment for one's own. New *dekrety* could be obtained only after moving up a long waiting list—many couples got married or had babies to speed up the process—paying a bribe (→ *protekce*), or taking a job in an undesirable part of the country. The general shortage of apartments and a ban on buying or selling *dekrety* gave rise to a large black market. Indeed, both these restrictions and a black market still exist today as approximately a third of Czechs continue to hold leases on state-owned apartments.

dělník (worker). The Czechs are one of the few Eastern European nations with a genuine working class that predated communism

(→ *komunismus*). Indeed, it was partly due to the strength of industrial workers that communism found fertile roots in the country. Needless to say, workers' interests were put first under communism—their wages were equal to those of professionals and their children found more doors open to them. Indeed, in the fifties it was common to say, "Show me your hands," with the implication that only those with calloused hands could rightfully claim to be workers and receive priority. Though the working class has been left behind in the move to capitalism, it continues to be seen as the salt of the country. In a recent poll, manual laborers were chosen as the most trusted profession, above even doctors and professors, and far ahead of the reviled aristocracy (→ *šlechta*). See also → *Jsem horník a kdo je víc.*

Den osvobození (Liberation Day). Under communism, May 9, the last day of World War II in Europe, was an important holiday featuring parades of the latest military hardware. It was also a day to pay tribute to the Red Army for its role in liberating Czechoslovakia. Since the fall of communism, the holiday has been moved to May 8 (the day of the official surrender, rather than the day that fighting ended in Prague) and renamed Victory Day to de-emphasize the role of the Russians.

Destinová, Ema (1878–1930). Nestled between Austrian and Germany, it is no surprise that Czechs caught the opera bug. Their greatest soprano and thus a national hero was Ema Destinová. She was good enough to sing at the Metropolitan Opera with Caruso, but she was also a Czech patriot, who sacrificed her career to return to her country during World War I. Her opposition to the Austrians—she sang the soon-to-be national anthem → *"Kde domov můj"* to conclude a concert during the war—gave her life a legendary quality. Her activities during the war even inspired a biopic in the 1970s that was greeted with applause by audiences who equated her efforts to resistance against communism. During her own life, however, she never received the complete acceptance of the Czech cultural elite. She was not offered a permanent place in the National Theater (→ *Národní divadlo*), a typical punishment for Czechs who are more successful abroad than at home. Jarmila Novotná (1907–1994) was the country's other great soprano; like Destinová, she also helped to fight against dictatorship, in her case by singing in America (→ *Amerika*) during World War II.

Dietl, Jaroslav (1929–1985). In the seventies and eighties, Dietl wrote dozens of television series which helped Czechs endure that gloomy period. His most famous work was the series → *Nemocnice na kraji města* (Hospital on the Edge of Town)—a sort of Czech *St. Elsewhere*—that was good enough to play on West German television. However he was not above serving the communist regime as well. His series *Okres na severu* (Northern District), for example, described the reconstruction of a historic city center to fit socialist ideals of beauty and efficiency, while *Žena za pultem* (The Woman Behind the Counter) followed a grocery store clerk who worked according to socialist ideals of efficiency. Like all good writers for television, his work is marked by memorable characters, strong pacing—it was said that he could dramatize the telephone listings—and compelling moral dilemmas. His influence on viewers was so great that they often confused fiction and reality. When the grandfather character in his series *Three Men in a Cottage* got married, the actor playing him received thousands of letters of congratulations. Despite his close relations with the communists, many of Dietl's shows remain beloved to this day.

Dikobraz (The Porcupine). Satirical magazine published under communism. Its most noteworthy content was political cartoons depicting bloodthirsty imperialists, greedy capitalists, and local counterrevolutionary forces, but more prosaic and earthy jokes made up the bulk of each issue. It paled in comparison with unofficial political humor at the time, which turned the tables on communist leaders.

diktát (dictation). One of the most common school exercises in Czech language classes. The teacher reads aloud a short essay or feuilleton (→ *fejeton*) and students are required to copy it down to the letter. These dictations are then graded according to strict rules. Even one mistake or *hrubka* (a missing comma, accent mark, or capital letter is enough) can lower one's grade from an A (better known as a 1) to B (or 2) (→ *vysvědčení*). Students have the most difficulty choosing the right form of the "ee" sound which can be written as both *i* and *y* (→ *vyjmenovaná slova*). Given that the Czech language is largely phonetic, it is hard for English speakers to grasp why students need this weekly exercise, though the Czech obsession with spelling (→ *pravopis*) explains part of it. The actor and writer Zdeněk → Svěrák (→ Cimrman) currently hosts a television show called *Diktát* which is simply that: he dictates a passage and then analyzes common mistakes.

disident (dissident). Dissidents in the sense of citizens of a totalitarian regime fighting for civil and political rights first appeared in the Czech context (the word comes from Russian) after the Soviet invasion in 1968 (→ *srpnová invaze*). The few brave individuals who stood up against the repressive normalization regime (→ *normalizace*) were mainly writers, artists, scientists, and former politicians who had participated in the Prague Spring (→ *Pražské jaro*). Their activities included public demonstrations, open letters, and petitions, as well as the production of → *samizdat* and the holding of secret lectures, discussions, and even theater performances in private apartments. The first dissident organization, however, was not formed until 1977, when Václav → Havel and others founded → *Charta* 77. The *Charta* united individuals of widely diverse political affiliations—from communists to Catholic conservatives—and life experiences, from former government ministers to former political prisoners. What held them together was a belief in human rights and democracy, and opposition to communist dictatorship. The government, however, unleashed campaign after campaign against them, reducing their numbers through harassment, imprisonment, and forced emigration. Despite their evident courage, the role of dissidents in bringing down the communist regime is widely debated today. While most recognize their heroism, others criticize their isolation from society or their failure to come to terms with the postcommunist democracy. Some of the ill will may be due to the fact that most Czechs collaborated with the old regime.

divadlo (theater). It is hard to overemphasize the place of theater in the Czech national consciousness. Theater was at the heart of the National Revival (→ *Národní obrození*) in the nineteenth century as dramatists like Josef Kajetán Tyl and even puppeteers (→ Kopecký) helped to create a sense of Czechness with their traveling theaters. Their plays often portrayed clever and talented Czechs outwitting their German or Germanized Czech neighbors. While Tyl and others like him had to roam the countryside to spread Czech theater, the founding of the → *Národní divadlo* (National Theater) in Prague in the 1880s finally provided an arena for Czech playwrights to make a "real" living. Probably the most popular plays to come out of the National Theater were melodramas, comedies, or musicals set in provincial villages (→ *vesnice*), seen as the heart and soul of the Czech nation. Among the classics of Czech theater from this era are → *Lucerna*, → *Maryša*, and → *Naši furianti*. During the interwar period, it was the slapstick comedy of Vlasta → Burian and the political musicals of the *Osvobozené Divadlo* (The Liberated Theater) created by → Voskovec & Werich which captured the popular imagination. Even after the advent of film and television, theater remained at the heart of Czech cultural life with theater groups like *Činoherní Klub* (The Actors' Club), *Divadlo ABC*, and → *Divad-*

lo Na zábradlí giving the world plays by the likes of Karel → Čapek, Václav → Havel, and Pavel Kohout. One specificity of the Czech lands is the plethora of *autorská divadla* (author's theaters) devoted almost solely to the work of their founders (→ Cimrman, → Semafor). Another is the repertory theaters, which instead of putting on one play at a time, constantly keep half a dozen productions ready for performance (one consequence is heavy reliance on prompters). Though there is a certain snobbishness attached to the theater, it is a snobbishness that extends deep into society, as performances sell out all over the country. Given theater's influence, it was natural that actors, playwrights, and directors played an important role in overthrowing the communists (→ *Sametová revoluce*).

Divadlo Na zábradlí (Theater on the Balustrade). A theater founded by the psychologist Ivan Vyskočil and the singer/writer Jiří Suchý in 1958. Its first performance was the musical *Kdyby tisíc klarinetů* (If a Thousand Clarinets), which signaled the end to the cultural wasteland of the fifties. It tells the story of soldiers who find their weapons magically transformed into musical instruments. After Suchý left to found → Semafor, the theater moved away from its cabaret origins and became home to incisive, satirical, and existentialist work. Its small stage and narrow seating area, still intact today, emphasized contact between the performers and the audience. Under the direction of Jiří Grossman, the theater was the main showcase for Václav → Havel's work including plays like *Vyrozumění* (The Memorandum) and *Zahradní slavnost* (The Garden Party) in the sixties, and Havel was for a time the theater's dramaturge. In the seventies and eighties, the theater became a refuge for numerous film directors, most famously Evald Schorm, who were banned from making films. The theater survived into the nineties, with Grossman returning as artistic director, though personal conflicts led to the founding of the more commercial Theater without a Balustrade.

Dívčí válka (War of the Maidens). Legend has it that after the death of → Libuše at the dawn of Czech history, womenfolk began to be oppressed by their men and rebelled by moving into their own castle, Děvín. Led by a woman named Vlasta, they then proceeded to set traps for and murder their menfolk. In one particularly memorable episode, a beautiful girl named Šárka was bound to a tree as a lure for passing knights who were duly slaughtered. The country's first king, Přemysl (→ *Přemyslovci*), ultimately got his act together and put down the rebellion, setting the stage for a patriarchy that lasts to this day. Though some Czech men are *pod* → *pantoflem* (hen-pecked; literally "under the slipper"), they steadfastly refuse any whiff of women's work (i.e., cleaning, washing, cooking) and expect to be waited on even as their wives have to earn a living at work. Women seem to have borne the burden well and are among the most beautiful in Europe (with numerous supermodels like Pavlína Pořízková, Eva Herzigová, and Tereza Maxová) until all this activity causes them to age prematurely. The one sign of gallantry in Czech males is their duty to enter any public place in front of female companions to shield them from prying eyes and flying beer bottles.

Dlouhý, široký a bystrozraký (Mr. Tall, Mr. Wide, and Mr. Sharp-sighted). Popular fairy tale (→ *pohádka*). The three title characters use their amazing gifts—Mr. Tall can stretch to unimaginable heights, Mr. Wide can expand his girth, and Mr. Sharp-sighted can see over enormous distances—to help a prince rescue his chosen bride from an evil warlock. A popular play of the Jára → Cimrman Theater is a parody of the fairy tale entitled *Mr. Tall, Mr. Wide, and Mr. Shortsighted*.

Dobrovský, Josef (1753–1829). Philologist and historian. Called by → Masaryk the first world-class Czech in modern times, Dobrovský attained fame with his spirited defense of the Czech language (→ *čeština*) delivered to the Habsburg emperor. Among his scientific achievements were explicating and setting grammatical rules for Czech and showing how new words could be created. Though he did not share the romanticism of the next generation of national awakeners (→ *Národní obrození*, → Jungmann) and fell into disfavor for showing the falsity of the Kingscourt Manuscript (→ *Rukopis královédvorský*), Dobrovský's contribution to the revival of the Czech language and literature was foundational and without an equal.

dobrý den (good day). A substantial degree of formality still persists in Czech society. Strangers, acquaintances, and elders are not addressed with the informal "hi" (in Czech *ahoj* or *čau*), but rather with *dobrý den*. Children are taught from an early age to immediately greet everyone they meet with this phrase, and even adults continue to use it when entering a store, seeing a neighbor in the stairwell, and even passing strangers in less crowded areas. It is likewise considered polite to say goodbye when leaving a shop.

do prdele (up yours). The most common Czech curse (besides → *hovno* or shit), it literally means "to the ass," but is probably better translated as "fuck" or if prefaced by *jdi* (go) as "fuck you." Just as English-speakers often catch themselves before cursing and say "darn" instead of "damn," so do Czechs replace "*do prdele*" with the meaningless "*do prčic*." The custom has inspired a yearly hike (→ *Klub českých turistů*, → *čundr*)—attended by several thousand—to the town of Prčice (*do prčic* can be interpreted as "to Prčice").

Domácí kuchařka (Home Cookbook). Published in 1826 by the patriot Magdaléna Dobromila Rettigová, this collection of traditional recipes was one of the first products of the National Revival (→ *Národní obrození*) to have an influence beyond intellectuals and actually penetrate into ordinary homes. In a series of works teaching women how to cook, sew, and behave, Rettigová played a key role in spreading Czech culture and enabling the masses to see themselves as Czechs. Her cookbook includes the precursors to such Czech comfort foods as → *vepřo-knedlo-zelo* and → *svíčková*.

domovní důvěrník (concierge). For the approximately thirty percent of Czechs who lived in state-owned apartments during communism, *domovní důvěrníci* served as something like landlords. Anyone with a complaint about their neighbors playing loud music or water dripping through their ceiling went to the *domovní důvěrník*, who would speak to the offending party or somehow find a repairman (a difficult task before 1989). *Domovní důvěrníci* also served a political function: they were often members of the party and reported suspicious activity (e.g., visits by foreigners) to the police and made sure that tenants put out the required decorations (i.e., Soviet flags) in their windows on national holidays (→ *1. máj*, → *VŘSR*). For this reason *domovní důvěrníci* were both hated and feared. In return, however, they often received free use of an apartment and the minor pleasure of acting as lords over their neighbors.

dožínky (harvest festival). One of many names for traditional festivals celebrating the harvest. After the harvest had been gathered, villages held celebrations (→ *zábava*) with food, music, and dancing. In some places, the local landlord or the best reaper was awarded a wreath woven from grain. As the country industrialized, folk traditions like *dožínky* became virtually extinct.

držet palec (to keep one's fingers crossed; literally "to hold one's thumb"). The Czech equivalent of keeping one's fingers crossed for someone is to hold one's thumb inside the fist or, especially among children, to make two fists (*držet pěsti*). Actors meanwhile are not told "to break a leg" but to break their necks (*zlom vaz*).

Dukelský průsmyk (Dukla Pass). Occupying a strategic location between Slovakia and Poland, Dukla Pass was the site of a gruesome battle on the Eastern Front in World War II. When Soviet forces along with Czech and Slovak units led by future president Ludvík → Svoboda tried to take the pass in October 1944, they became sitting ducks for Nazi soldiers who held the high ground on both sides of the narrow gap. The bloody battle in which scores of allied soldiers died meant one of the first tastes of liberation for Czechoslovakia. The communists immortalized the victory in the so-called "Valley of Death," lionizing its participants and renaming streets, buildings, and sports teams (→ Dukla Praha) in its honor. The name Dukla thus became synonymous with the heroic fight of communists against fascism. The pass itself was turned into a memorial and battlefield park and became a frequent destination of school fieldtrips. Despite its importance to Czechs and Slovaks, most military historians do not consider it a key battle of the war.

Dukla Praha. As the team representing the Czechoslovak army, Dukla was the perennial champion of the domestic soccer league under communism. The concept of an army team was imposed—like so much else—after 1948 according to the Soviet model. This led to the formation of Dukla Praha in football and the no less successful Dukla Jihlava in hockey. These teams could essentially pick and choose players they wanted, offering them nominal employment in the army, higher salaries, a winning team, and the opportunity to play in international competition. It was these advantages that led many fans to hate the team (much as the Yankees are hated in America). The success of Dukla Praha was incontrovertible, though, as they won seven league titles in ten years in the fifties and sixties. The team was also home to the first Czech named European player of the year, Josef → Masopust. After 1989, Dukla Praha's fortunes declined and they dropped into the second division. Even today, however, many of the country's Olympic stars, such as decathletes Tomáš Dvořák and Roman Šebrle, train with Dukla Praha.

Dušičky (All Souls Day). November 2 is observed throughout the country as All Souls Day. Families visit the graves of their deceased and lay a wreath and light candles

(→ *pohřeb*). Czechs go to the cemetery not just on *Dušičky*, but also on Christmas (→ *Vánoce*) and the birthday and nameday (→ *jmeniny*) of the departed.

Dvořák, Antonín (1841–1904). Classical music composer. If → Smetana is the country's nationalist composer, then Dvořák is its great romantic. His *Slavonic Dances, New World Symphony* (written while he was head of the National Conservatory of Music in New York), and the opera → *Rusalka* all tug at the heartstrings of Czechs. Typically Czech in his music are the strong, hummable melodies that most can recognize instantly. Like his compatriots → Smetana and Janáček, Dvořák drew heavily from traditional Czech folk songs (→ *lidovka*) and was a devoted patriot. However, he never achieved the public veneration of Smetana because of opposition from the communist Minister of Culture Zdeněk Nejedlý, who believed Dvořák to be lacking in nationalist feeling. Indeed, despite his fame and popularity, Prague still has no statue of Dvořák.

Dvorský, R.A. (1899–1966). Band leader. With his band, the Melodymakers, Dvorský popularized swing music in the thirties and stands as a symbol of the bourgeois First Republic (→ *První republika*). His sound and style began enjoying a revival in the nineties under the influence of the singer Ondřej Havelka, who leads a band called the Melody Boys.

dvůr (yard, courtyard). Along with the kitchen, the center of Czech domestic life. The courtyards in the middle of apartment blocks traditionally buzz with activity. Tenants hang their laundry and beat their carpets; children run around and play; women sit on benches and gossip, while men tend to small garden plots (→ *zahrádkářská kolonie*).

37

E

Ema má mísu (Ema has a bowl). The first complete sentence in what used to be the most widespread children's primer. It is followed by the similarly funny-sounding *Máma má maso* (Mother has meat) and *Ó, my se máme* (Oh, what a good time we are having). Under communism, even first-grade textbooks were not immune from ideological indoctrination, with later chapters teaching children about Labor Day (→ *1. máj*) and the struggle for world peace.

ententýky (eeny-meeny-mainy-mo). The Czech version of the children's counting out game. In its entirety, the rhyme goes as follows: "Ententýky, two blocks, the devil flew away from the streetcar without a hat and barefoot and hurt his nose. There was a bump as big as all of Africa. En ten ven, it's that one, that one has to drop out." The rhyme was composed by the famous poet František Hrubín.

Erben, Karel Jaromír (1811–1870). Writer and collector of fairy tales. Erben is the Czech version of the Brothers Grimm and was in fact inspired by them to roam the countryside gathering oral tales. His collections of traditional Czech folk tales (→ *pohádka*) are read with relish by all Czech children and even some adults. Among those which have become classics are → *Smolíček Pacholíček*, Stump Boy (→ *Otesánek*), and the talented threesome Mr. Tall, Mr. Wide, and Mr. Sharp-sighted (→ *Dlouhý, široký a bystrozraký*). Erben is equally remembered for his poetic cycle *Kytice* (Bouquet of Flowers),

which tells horrifying stories of simple villagers who come into contact with supernatural beings and suffer terrible ends.

evangelík (Protestant). Members of all sects of Protestantism are known as evangelicals, regardless of whether they proselytize. While they are a minority among Czech believers, they continue to feel that their faith is closest to the Czech spirit. See → *Československá církev*.

Evropa (Europe). Even if the European Union is not overly popular, the designation European emphatically is. Most Czechs are proud to call themselves Europeans—in distinction to the non-European Russians—and see it as an indication of their high level of civilization and culture, as well as their country's supposedly pivotal role in European history. Indeed, many are offended if not properly recognized as Europeans. Czech geographers often place the country in the exact center of Europe (→ *střední Evropa*), noting that Prague is far west of Vienna (→ *Vídeň*).

exil (exile). One of the consequences of frequent foreign rule is that many great Czech figures have had to live in exile. The first wave of emigrants were the nobility and religious scholars who were forced to leave the country after the defeat at White Mountain (→ *Bílá hora*). In the nineteenth century, Czechs joined many Europeans in immigrating to the United States, especially to the Midwest and Texas where Czech communities still exist. The next great surge of emigration came after the communist takeover (→ *Vítězný únor*) in 1948 and again after the Soviet invasion (→ *srpnová invaze*) in 1968. These latter-day émigrés were demonized by the communists, and even ordinary Czechs have not welcomed them home with open arms, seeing them as having had it easy while those who stayed home had to suffer.

F

fasovat (to receive work accessories). Word used to describe the distribution of supplies to workers in certain professions. Under communism, many employees received work accessories at the beginning of every month. Manual laborers were given the abrasive soap known as Solvina and office workers received writing implements or notebooks. In a quasi-legal, but widespread practice, these items were often taken home. A good job was thus one that allowed workers to receive ample quantities of work materials.

fejeton (feuilleton). A newspaper article that is a blend of creative writing and political commentary and usually printed on the back page of the newspaper. It differs from a standard op-ed piece by drawing on personal experience and telling a story that de-livers a payoff at the end rather than the beginning. Since the days of Jan Neruda who defined the genre in the nineteenth century, it has been favored by many of the country's best writers. Between the wars, the regular feuilletons of Karel → Čapek in → *Lidové noviny* were reason enough to buy the paper. The art, of course, deteriorated under the rigid press censorship of communism, but writers like Ludvík Vaculík managed to distribute critical and incisive feuilletons through the → *samizdat* system. Today bookshops are jammed full of collections of feuilletons by the country's writers and journalists.

Ferda Mravenec (Ferda the Ant). Popular cartoon character created by the artist Ondřej Sekora. Ferda's humorous adventures in the world of insects first appeared in the

Favorite Books

The following list is the result of a readers' poll conducted by Czech libraries. Readers were asked to name their favorite book, and over 93,000 readers sent in their choice. The results attest to the fact that Czech tastes in literature are not different than those of other countries—forty-four of the top two hundred choices in Great Britain also appear in the Czech top two hundred. The one surprise was the popularity of the writer Lenka Lanczová who writes novels for teenage girls.

RANK	TITLE	AUTHOR	NATIONALITY	VOTES
1	Harry Potter	J.K. Rowling	English	6979
2	Lord of the Rings	J.R.R. Tolkien	English	2697
3	The Bible			1996
4	Saturnin	Zdeněk Jirotka	Czech	1888
5	The Grandmother	Božena → Němcová	Czech	1082

Rank	Title	Author	Nationality	Votes
6	The Egyptian	Mika Waltari	Finnish	895
7	The Little Prince	Antoine de Saint-Exupéry	French	832
8	Anybody Can Do Anything	Betty MacDonald	American	686
9	Egg and I	Betty MacDonald	American	673
10	The Children of Noisy Village	Astrid Lindgren	Swedish	662
11	The Mole's Adventures (→ Krteček)	Zdeněk Miler	Czech	647
12	The Good Soldier → Švejk	Jaroslav → Hašek	Czech	600
13	River God	Wilbur Smith	English	577
14	Ferda the Ant (→ Ferda Mravenec)	Ondřej Sekora	Czech	529
15	Robinson Crusoe	Daniel Defoe	English	526
16	Fast Arrows	Jaroslav → Foglar	Czech	483
17	Boys from the Beaver River	Jaroslav Foglar	Czech	445
18	The Alchymist	Paulo Coelho	Brazilian	404
19	We Children from the Zoo Station	Christiane F.	German	404
20	There Were Five of Us (→ Bylo nás pět)	Karel Poláček	Czech	402
21	All about Doggie and Pussycat	Josef Čapek	Czech	371
22	Bouquet of National Legends	Karel Jaromír → Erben	Czech	358
23	The Sign of Gemini	Lenka Lanczová	Czech	356
24	Johnny's Journey (→ Honzíkova cesta)	Bohumil Říha	Czech	347
25	Mammoth Hunters	Eduard Štorch	Czech	336
26	Memento	Radek John	Czech	335
27	Dášeňka: The Life of a Puppy	Karel → Čapek	Czech	332
28	Fairytales	Božena Němcová	Czech	329
29	The Hobbit	J.R.R. Tolkien	English	325
30	The Famous Five	Enid Blyton	English	308
31	It	Stephen King	American	296
32	The World According to Garp	John Irving	American	293
33	Mach and Šebestová	Miloš Macourek	Czech	291
34	Three Comrades	Erich Maria Remarque	German	291
35	Kája Mařík	Felix Háj	Czech	289
36	Dune	Frank Herbert	American	284
37	Fireflies (→ Broučci)	Jan Karafiát	Czech	267

Rank	Title	Author	Nationality	Votes
38	The Return of Hyman Kaplan	Leo Rosten	American	252
39	Mystery of the Brain Twister	Jaroslav Foglar	Czech	246
40	→ Vinnetou	Karl May	German	245
41	Bed Full of Roses	Lenka Lanczová	Czech	238
42	Robin	Zdena Frýbová	Czech	231
43	1984	George Orwell	English	230
44	Saddle Girl Club	Bonnie Bryant	American	224
45	Mikeš the Cat	Josef → Lada	Czech	212
46	The Master and Margarita	Mikhail Bulgakov	Russian	210
47	Jane Eyre	Charlotte Brontë	English	206
48	Quo Vadis	Henryk Sienkiewicz	Polish	205
49	Les Misérables	Victor Hugo	French	204
50	Gone with the Wind	Margaret Mitchell	American	195

Source: *www.mojekniha.cz*

newspaper → *Lidové noviny* in the thirties. With the coming of communism, however, Sekora's hard-working ant helped to propagate the new collectivist order. Ferda thus worked to fulfill five-year plans (→ *pětiletka*) and fought against pests planted by the imperialist enemies (→ *mandelinka bramborová*). These transgressions, however, have not diminished his or Sekora's popularity.

fialové sako (purple jacket). Slang term for postcommunist businessmen. The new entrepreneurs who emerged after the fall of communism were immediately recognizable for their new styles as much as their wealth. In contrast to the poorly fitting black or grey suits of communist administrators, their wardrobes ranged across the rainbow, including the legendary purple sport jacket, a style borrowed from neighboring Bavaria. Though many businessmen built their fortunes on shrewdness and skill, a good number took advantage of weak legislation to strip old companies of their assets (→ *tunelování*) or used old connections (→ *protekce*) to profit from enterprise privatization (→ *kupónová privatizace*). Members of this new class quickly jumped to the top of the social ladder and became lifestyle pioneers. They adopted habits common in the West but unknown in the East, like playing golf, drinking cocktails, eating out, and smoking cigars. With their new-won wealth they also built luxurious and tasteless mansions in a style that came to be called *podnikatelské baroko* (businessman's baroque, → *české baroko*).

Foglar, Jaroslav (1907–1999). The author of dozens of books for young boys and girls that remain popular to this day. His most famous series is known by the title *Rychlé šípy* (Fast Arrows). It follows a group of five upstanding boys who form their own club and stumble on all sorts of adventures. One of the characters, Mirek Dušín, has become a synonym for a goody two-shoes in Czech. Foglar's aim in the books was to give children a model that would guide them to their own creative activity. Thus, for example, he created a set of tasks for children known as → *bobříky* (little beavers). One of his best known inventions was the *ježek v kleci* (hedgehog in a cage)— a spiked wooden ball that through careful manipulation has to be removed from its cage without breaking any of the parts. These can be bought in souvenir shops around Prague. Foglar was also indelibly linked to the scouting movement (→ *Junák*), repressed under the communists in favor of the Pioneers (→ *Pionýr*), and led his own troop for over sixty years. Under communism, Foglar's books were frowned upon, but children still passed around dog-eared copies to their best friends. Since the fall of communism, his entire oeuvre has been republished in new editions.

Fond solidarity (Solidarity Fund). Workers picking up their paycheck under communism often found small sums deducted from their pay to go towards a Solidarity Fund. These monies went to support communist rebel movements or oppressed peoples. This was one of many ways that the old regime was able to requisition free labor from its citizens (→ *Akce Z*, → *pracovní sobota*). Under the old regime, Czechs had frequent exposure to the world's downtrodden in the national media as well as through encounters with foreign exchange students from these same countries (→ *Vietnamec*).

fotbal (soccer). Though Czechs may be more successful at hockey (→ *hokej*), it is soccer, as in the rest of the world, that is the real game of the people and is played most intensively. The country is home to nine national leagues stretching from the first division Gambrinus League to the lowest rungs of village amateurism, where matches are followed by beer drinking among players who range from teenagers to grandfathers. Memorable moments in Czech soccer history include two second place finishes at the World Cup (1934 and 1962), the exploits of František Plánička, Pepi → Bican, Josef → Masopust, and, most of all, Tonda → Panenka's penalty shot to win the European Championship in 1976. In 2003, Pavel Nedvěd became the second Czech (the first was Masopust) to win the Golden Ball as Europe's player of the year. Except for the manufactured rise of → Dukla Praha under the communists, the first league has always been dominated by traditional rivals → Sparta and Slavia with other teams only occasionally challenging their hegemony. Unlike in America where sports matches are family affairs, Czech soccer and hockey spectators consist almost entirely of adult men who enjoy getting drunk, screaming obscenities, and brawling with fans of the opposition.

Franz Joseph (1830–1916). The long-reigning emperor of the Austro-Hungarian Empire. Like Victoria for the English, Franz Joseph presided over the peaceful and prosperous second half of the nineteenth century, ruling from 1848 until his death. Though no great fan of Czechs—he stubbornly refused to extend them the privileges granted to the Hungarians—his benign neglect permitted the growth of Czech national culture and laid the basis for Czech independence after World War I. As leader of a large multiethnic empire—known as the *C. a K. Monarchie* or Imperial and Royal Monarchy—he would begin public proclamations with the words "*Mým národům*" (To my nations). Franz Joseph's habit of waking early led him to impose the same burden on all his subjects, a legacy that persists today with many Czechs arriving at work by 6 o' clock. Another legacy of the emperor was a tradition of Byzantine bureaucracy that has been just as enduring (→ *razítko*). Portraits of Franz Joseph—with his big bushy mustache and erect military posture—are still a potent visual reminder of the days of Austrian rule, for which many Czechs retain an only semi-ironic nostalgia.

Fučík, Julius (1903–1943). Communist journalist and martyr. Between the wars, Fučík was a communist activist and editor of the party newspaper → *Rudé právo*. A member of the resistance (→ *odboj*), he was arrested and murdered by the Nazis, but managed to write a diary of his detention which compatriots smuggled out of prison. His notes were later turned into the book *Reportáž psaná na oprátce* (Report from the Gallows) that describes his own heroism in the face of torture, and the cowardice of those who betrayed him. With the help of the book, which became required reading (→ *povinná* *četba*) for all elementary school students, the communists turned him into a larger-than-life martyr, a required prop in all communist countries. Czechoslovakia was littered with Julius Fučík parks, streets, and cultural centers in an attempt to make people identify communism with opposition to fascism. Recent scholars have found that the communists edited his manuscript, eliminating some of the less heroic passages. Fučík's prewar paean to the Soviet Union, "In the Land Where Tomorrow Already Means Yesterday," inspired people to joke that today must be the day before yesterday. Another object of mirth was Fučík's widow Gusta, who was regularly trotted out at public events.

Changes in Street Names Since 1989

After the revolution in 1989, Czechs quickly moved to change the names of streets, parks, squares, and metro stops. The following table documents a few of these changes in major cities across the country. One of the more interesting is the change from streets celebrating the Bolshevik Revolution (named November 7 Street, → VŘSR) to those celebrating the Velvet Revolution (named November 17 Street, → *Sametová revoluce*) merely by adding a single number.

CITY	FORMER NAME	CURRENT NAME
Tábor	Lenin Square	T.G. Masaryk Square
	Leningrad Street	Petersburg Street
	Zápotocký Street	F. Křižík Street
	Gottwald Street	Budějovice Street
Strakonice	Lenin Street	Factory Street
	Fučík Street	Želivský Street
	Peace Square	Friendship Square
Třeboň	Fučík Square	T.G. Masaryk Square
České Budějovice	Žižka Square	Přemysl Otakar II Square
	Red Army Boulevard	Rudolf Boulevard
	Peace Boulevard	Prague Boulevard
	Victorious February Street	Opletal Street
Vysoké Mýto	Trade Union Street	Resistance Fighter Street
	November 7 Street	November 17 Street
Prague	Moscow Station	Angel Station
	Lenin Station	Dejvice Station
	Gottwald Station	Vyšehrad Station
	Youth Station	Pankrác Station
	Lenin Boulevard	Europe Boulevard
	Kremlin Street	Lithuania Street
	State Security (SNB) Street	Vršovice Street
	Kalinin Boulevard	Seifert Boulevard
	Defenders of Peace Boulevard	Milada Horáková Boulevard

City	Former Name	Current Name
Prague	Red-Armadiers Square	Palach Square
	Antonín Zápotocký Square	Winston Churchill Square
	Lenin Square	Victory Square
Brno	Victory Boulevard	Masaryk Boulevard
	Gagarin Street	Kobližná Street
	Choráz Street	Jesuit Street
	February 25 Square	Cabbage Market
	Soviet Heroes Square	Grain Market
	Klement Gottwald Boulevard	Cejl Boulevard
	V.I. Lenin Boulevard	Baron Kounicá Boulevard
Brandýs nad Labem	Red Army Boulevard	Kralovicka Boulevard
Plzeň	Sverdlovsk Alley	Freedom Alley
	Antonín Zápotocký Bridge	General Patton Bridge
	Charkov Embankment	English Embankment
	May 1 Boulevard	Klatovy Boulevard
	Moscow Boulevard	America Boulevard
	Julius Fučík Boulevard	Cardinal Beran Boulevard
	Marx Boulevard	Eduard Beneš Boulevard
	Engels Street	Majer Street
	Lenin Street	Hus Street
	Leningrad Street	Masaryk Street
Ostrava	Dimitrov Street	Railroad Station Street
	Gottwald Boulevard	October 28th Boulevard
	Komsomol Street	Scout Street
	Stakhanovites Street	Mezi Domky Street
Olomouc	Lenin Boulevard	Freedom Boulevard
	Red Army Square	Lower Square
	Peace Square	Upper Square
	People's Militia Boulevard	Student Boulevard
	Liberation Boulevard	Masaryk Boulevard
Trutnov	Soviet Street	Czech Street
	Gottwald Square	Krakonoš Square

Source: *Lidové Noviny*, 17 November 1999.

G

gadžo (non-Gypsy). Roma or Gyspy (→ *cikán*) word meaning one who is not a Roma. It is thus similar to the Yiddish *goy* or the English gentile, except that it means non-Gypsy instead of non-Jew. Indeed, there are numerous similarities between Gypsies and Jews from bans on intermarriage and ritual eating codes to victimization by the Nazis. *Gadžo* is the only word from the Roma language that most Czechs know.

Golden Kids. Musical supergroup of the late sixties. Made up of three good-looking and talented stars—Marta Kubišová, Václav Neckář, and Helena Vondráčková—the Golden Kids seemed destined to dominate the pop charts for the next decade. Their interpretations of Western top forty hits fit Czech musical tastes to a tee. Instead, Kubišová opposed the Soviet invasion (most famously in the song → "*Modlitba pro Martu*"/A Prayer for Marta) and was banned for the next twenty years. Neckář and Vondráčková meanwhile made their peace with the new leaders and remained pop icons throughout the seventies and eighties. In the early nineties, the group reunited for a number of sold out concerts and brought back memories of hope from the late sixties (→ *Pražské jaro*).

golem. A mythical figure supposedly created by the Rabbi Loew in the sixteenth century to protect the Jews (→ *Žid*) of Prague from pogroms. Resembling a half-formed human, the golem was made from the clay of the → Vltava River and animated through Kabbalah. Variations on the tale see the golem escaping control of its master (or an apprentice) and wreaking general havoc. Though it has served as the inspiration for numerous literary works, including a popular film celebrating nuclear power, and is commonly associated with Prague, the golem's main life has been as a tourist draw for Prague's Jewish quarter. Indeed, the image of Prague as a city of magic, superstition, and alchemy, is as much a creation of foreign observers as a deeply felt part of Czech culture.

gothajský salám (Gotha salami). The cheapest deli meat on sale at grocery stores. A combination of unknown parts of the pig, Gotha salami is a popular lunch choice for workers who buy 10 decagrams along with several rolls (→ *rohlík*). Slightly higher priced, but equally popular sliced meats are *Junior*, *Poličan*, *Vysočina*, and Hunter's Salami (*Lovečák*). All are handed to the customer wrapped in thin, brown paper.

Gott, Karel (1939). Pop singer. There is no better known Czech (among Czechs that is) over the last forty years than Karel Gott. Nicknamed the Sinatra of the East, Gott has attracted fans with an operatic voice, a saccharine repertoire, and perfectly preserved good looks. He has repeatedly won every award a Czech singer can win (most famously the → *Zlatý slavík* twenty-two times between 1963 and 1991). His renditions of songs like "*Lady Carneval*" and "*Kdepak ty ptáčku hnízdo máš?*" (Where Is Your Nest, My Little Bird?) or translations of "Pretty Woman" and "Love

Me Tender" are indelibly written in the collective unconscious of all Czechs, and played almost constantly on Czech radio. He is also the source of pride for his popularity—albeit mainly among older women—in West Germany. Across the socialist bloc, he is remembered for his rendition of the theme song to a popular animated cartoon, *Včelka Mája* (The Little Bee Maja). Despite his kowtowing to the communist regime and a preference for eighteen-year-old girlfriends, Gott remains the most popular celebrity in the country bar none, and is the most frequent headliner in the country's tabloid press.

Gottwald, Klement (1896–1953). The first communist leader of Czechoslovakia. Born in Moravia (→ *Morava*) to an unmarried working woman, Gottwald came into public view as the leader of the Czechoslovak Communist Party (→ KSČ) between the wars. His achievement was in purging the party of all independent thinkers and along with his henchmen—known as the Karlín Boys—turning it into an unquestioningly loyal minion of the Soviet Union. How far he went can be seen in his famous speech to parliament in 1929 when he declared, "We are the party of the Czechoslovak proletariat and our highest staff is Moscow. And we go to Moscow to learn, you know what? We go to Moscow to learn from the Russian Bolsheviks how to wring your necks. And you know that the Russian Bolsheviks are masters of that." After spending the war in Moscow, Gottwald returned to lead the Communist Party to an electoral victory and finally a putsch in 1948. His speech to a large crowd on Wenceslas Square (→ *Václavské náměstí*) on February 25, 1948 was one of the key moments in Czech history and celebrated as a holiday (→ *Vítězný únor*) under communism. As the head of government and the communist party, Gottwald became the most powerful man in the country and used his power to liquidate all rivals, potential rivals, and even innocent bystanders. He also became the object of a cult of personality with his face postered across the country, and the city

of Zlín (→ Baťa) renamed → Gottwaldov after him. Besides being a habitual drunk, he was reputedly suffering from the advanced stages of syphilis when he took power. In one of the few cases of poetic justice in Czech history, he died after catching pneumonia at the funeral of Stalin, thus remaining faithful to his master to the end. Attempts to preserve his body in a mausoleum at the national memorial on Vítkov Hill (→ Žižkov) in Prague turned out badly (Czechs never mastered the art like the Russians) and he had to be cremated in 1962.

Gottwaldov. The Moravian (→ *Morava*) town of Zlín was renamed Gottwaldov by the communists in honor of the first communist president Klement → Gottwald. The town was chosen because of its large shoe factory, considered a major site of worker exploitation (→ Baťa). Its name was changed back to Zlín after the fall of communism.

granát (garnet). This fiery red precious stone has long been mined around the town of Turnov in eastern Bohemia and has thus become a favorite of both Czechs and foreign tourists.

guláš (goulash). Borrowed from Hungarian cuisine, this thick meat stew full of onions, tomatoes, and garlic has been adopted wholeheartedly by Czechs. It takes many forms—Szeged goulash, for example, adds pork and cabbage to the recipe—but it rarely reaches the degree of spiciness of its Hungarian cousin.

gymnázium (high school). Though almost all Czechs attend high school, only a minority are selected for college-preparatory *gymnázia* where study consists mainly of the liberal arts. Admission depends on grades, results on an entrance exam, and, previously, the political record of one's parents. Most other students go to specialized high schools with a focus on subjects like textiles or electronics (called by the shortened *průmyslovka* or industrial school), health sciences, economics,

School-leaving Exam (→ *maturita*)

The following lists show the subjects of the required school-leaving exam from the mid-eighties and in comparison, subjects from April 2003. They come from the Slovanské náměstí → gymnázium in Brno. The questions were passed out to students before the exam and each student randomly drew one theme on which he or she was quizzed by their teacher and a school inspector.

	School-leaving Exam Topics in History (1980s)	
1.	a.	Class and economic foundations of Renaissance culture abroad and at home, new perspective on life, new style of life
	b.	Beginnings of the workers' movement in Austria before World War I
2.	a.	Origins and evolution of utopian and scientific socialism, influence on the international workers' movement, contemporary significance of Marxist-Leninist ideology
	b.	The Internationals and the international workers' movement
3.	a.	World War I—causes, consequences, significance of → VŘSR (Great October Socialist Revolution), crisis of the capitalist system
	b.	The battle of Czechs and Slovaks for independence—the contradictory positions of the bourgeois politicians and the workers' movement, the significance of VŘSR for the origin of the Czechoslovak Republic
4.	a.	The first and second industrial revolutions—new class-divided society
	b.	Main characteristics of imperialism—the highest stage of capitalism, territorial division of the world before World War I, colonialism
5.	a.	From the beginning of the workers' movement in Russia to the bourgeois democratic revolution of 1905/07, causes and consequences of its defeat
	b.	V.I. Lenin—the man and the work, his influence on the workers' movement in Russia and on the international workers' movement
6.	a.	Great October Socialist Revolution—historic watershed in the evolution of humanity, establishment of the dictatorship of the proletariat in Russia
	b.	Battle for the political character of the First Republic (→ *První republika*)—the origin of the Communist Party of Czechoslovakia (→ KSČ)
7.	a.	Origin, class basis, and character of fascism in Italy and Germany, aggressive plans of the fascist states
	b.	Czechoslovak Republic between the wars—battle of the Communist Party of Czechoslovakia for the rights of workers in a period of economic crisis
8.	a.	Building of socialism in Russia after the defeat of intervention and domestic counterrevolution
	b.	Paris commune—first dictatorship of the proletariat, lessons for the international workers' movement
9.	a.	The second phase of World War II—the Soviet Union's major share in the defeat of fascism, postwar arrangement of Europe, the origin of the worldwide socialist system
	b.	Czechoslovak resistance during World War II—two centers of foreign resistance, domestic resistance under the leadership of the Communist Party of Czechoslovakia, Slovak national uprising (→ SNP) and the May Uprising (→ *Květnové povstání*) in relation to the liberation of the Czechoslovak Republic

10.	a.	Betrayal by the Czechoslovak bourgeoisie and their allies—politics of the Western states and the position of the USSR. Munich (→ *Mnichov*), the complete destruction of the Czechoslovak Republic
	b.	Beginnings of World War II—causes of its origin, character, evaluation of its status at the end of the first phase
11.	a.	Causes of the transition from the primitive communal order to the slave order, significance of work for the physical and mental evolution of man, production and social relations, religious ideas, gradual and uneven evolution in the period of classless society
	b.	Prehistoric settlement of our territory—main developmental stages, most significant cultures and archeological finds, economic and social changes, arrival of the Slavs
12.	a.	Origin and building of the worldwide socialist system, Comecon, Warsaw Pact, alliance with the Soviet Union
	b.	Liberation of the Czechoslovak Republic by the Red Army, transition from the national democratic revolution to the socialist revolution 1945-48
13.	a.	Main characteristics and beginnings of the feudal order in Europe—origins of feudal diffusion, significance of Christian ideology and Church organization in the life of early feudal society
	b.	First state formations on our territory—evolution, causes, and consequences of their downfall, relations with the Byzantine and East Frankish Empires
14.	a.	Origins of the culture of antiquity—ancient methods of production, slaveholders' democracy, the contribution of ancient culture
	b.	Historic evolution of Brno—center of the workers' movement in Moravia, oldest settlement, origin of the city, first manufactures, battles of the proletariat, Josef Hybeš, the newspaper *Rovnost*, liberation, the city under socialism
15.	a.	Class character of the culture of early and developed feudalism in our country and abroad, influence of the Church on the creation of a world view and mass opinion
	b.	The Czech state under the Luxembourgs
16.	a.	Stabilization and expansion of feudal monarchies in the period of developed feudalism—England, France, Spain, Germany in the period of developed feudalism
	b.	Origin and development of the Czech feudal state under the Premyslids (→ *Přemyslovci*)
17.	a.	Hussite revolutionary movement—program, supporters, significant centers, individuals, propagation abroad, causes of defeat (→ *husité*)
	b.	Reformation in Europe—goals, representatives, consequences
18.	a.	Growth of temporal powers of the Church, its ideological influence, battle over investiture
	b.	Causes and aims of the Hussite revolutionary movement—social contradictions in the Czech lands, criticism of the Church and the social order, activities and significance of the speeches of Master Jan → Hus
19.	a.	Culmination of the opposition of Czech towns and non-Catholic nobility to the violent Habsburg government and the consequences of the defeat for the Czech nation
	b.	Causes, course, character of the Thirty Years' War (→ *Třicetiletá válka*) and its influence on conditions in Europe

20.	a.	Government of → Jiří z Poděbrad—his peace project and its modern realization
	b.	Establishment of the Habsburgs on the Czech throne, their attempted Catholicization, Germanization, and centralized, absolutist government
21.	a.	Most significant bourgeois revolutions in Europe and their influence on the development of the capitalist order
	b.	Origin, evolution, and role of towns from feudalism to the modern day
22.	a.	Transition from guild small-scale production to capitalist large-scale production, causes of stagnation, transition periods, beginnings of factory production
	b.	Economic and social changes during the enlightened absolutism of → Maria Theresa and reforms during the reign of Joseph II
23.	a.	Building of socialism in Czechoslovakia after Victorious February (→ *Vítězný únor*), main tasks of socialist construction, 16th Congress of the Communist Party of Czechoslovakia
	b.	Second period of the general crisis of capitalism—contradictions in the postwar world, peace movements, military-political groupings, peaceful coexistence of the two world systems, Helsinki, Stockholm, Belgrade, peace proposals of the 26th Congress of the Communist Party of the Soviet Union
24.	a.	Territorial evolution of the Czech state—use of maps from the oldest settlements up to the present day
	b.	Class and economic foundations of the baroque abroad and at home, the baroque and the Catholic Counter-Reformation
25.	a.	First bourgeois democratic revolution in France and its influence on political developments in Italy and Germany
	b.	Constitutional battles of Czechs and Slovaks in the revolutionary year of 1848

School-leaving Exam Topics in History (April 2003)

1.	Evolution of human society in primeval times
2.	Ancient Middle Eastern states
3.	Ancient Greece
4.	Ancient Rome
5.	Cultural legacy of antiquity
6.	Beginnings of the Middle Ages in Europe
7.	Slavic affairs in early medieval Europe
8.	Europe from the 12th to the 15th century
9.	The Czech state during the reign of the last Premyslids (→ *Přemyslovci*) and the Luxembourgs
10.	Position of the Church in the Middle Ages and the reform movement
11.	Europe and the world at the start of modern times
12.	Origin of the Habsburg confederation and its development to the middle of the 17th century
13.	Development of Europe after the Thirty Years' War (→ *Třicetiletá válka*)
14.	First great modern revolutions in Europe and America

15.	Survey of cultural development from the beginning of the Middle Ages to the 15th century
16.	Survey of cultural development from the 15th century to contemporary times
17.	The French Revolution and Napoleonic wars
18.	Europe in the first half of the 19th century
19.	The revolutionary year 1848 in Europe
20.	Main outlines of development in Europe and the world in the second half of the 19th century
21.	Developments in the Czech lands in the second half of the 19th century
22.	World War I
23.	1919-1929 in Europe and the world
24.	Origin and development of Czechoslovakia to 1929
25.	Russian Revolution, origin and development of the USSR to World War II
26.	Global economic crisis and the fight against fascism in the 1930s
27.	World War II
28.	Situation in the Czech lands during World War II
29.	Main outlines of development in the world after 1945
30.	Main outlines of development in the Czech lands after 1945

pedagogy, or art. Both *gymnázia* and specialized high schools conclude with a school-leaving exam (→ *maturita*), a necessity for getting into college. Teachers at these schools are addressed as *profesor* and in the past actually engaged in real scholarship. For the less talented are *učiliště* (trade schools) each producing a specific occupational category like waiter, chef, hairdresser, plumber, gardener, locksmith, shop assistant, and, the lowest of the low, bricklayer.

The most desirable of these schools used to be the car repair trade school, which under communism enabled its graduates to earn high incomes through kickbacks. After the first year of study, these schools often send students out to work every other week. *Učiliště* grant their graduates a *vyuční list* (vocational diploma) rather than a *maturita*. Bribes (→ *protekce*) often help students get into *gymnázia* or more desirable trade schools.

H

Habsburkové (Habsburgs). Nationalist mythology has it that for three hundred years Czechs languished under Habsburg rule. In fact, this exaggerates the suffering of Czechs. For much of their time under Habsburg rule, Czechs merely desired more autonomy, not complete independence. While unsympathetic to Czech nationalism, the Habsburgs did designate the Czechs lands the industrial center of the empire and it is hard to imagine the Czech lands prospering more outside of the monarchy. Habsburg rulers like → Maria Theresa, Joseph II, and → Franz Joseph loom large in Czech history and are not viewed negatively today.

Haná. A region known as the breadbasket of the Czech Republic. Centered around the Moravian town of → Olomouc, the territory of Haná consists mainly of fields of grain. The large estates of its landowners were forcibly nationalized by the communists in the forties and fifties and turned into collective farms (→JZD). Haná's inhabitants are known for their distinctive speaking style—called *hanáčtina*—which replaces short e's with long ones, and for their conservative ways. The agrarian roots of the region can be seen in the mythic figure of → *Král Ječmínek* (King Barley).

hantec. A regional dialect associated with the Moravian (→ *Morava*) town of → Brno. It likely originated from lower-class, thieves' slang, but eventually became a source of pride for denizens of the country's second city. It mainly consists of borrowings from German like *šalina* for *tramvaj* (streetcar) and *retich*

instead of WC, as well as invented words like *rola* for trainstation, *brzda* for bread, and *škopek* for beer. It also includes unique grammatical constructions like the word *su* in place of *jsem* (I am), which appears in the popular bumper sticker *Já su z Brna* (I'm from Brno). Hantec was popularized by the strongman Franta Kocourek and his mentally challenged sidekick Rudy Kovanda, who are celebrated annually in Brno. Dictionaries of Hantec can be found in any Moravian bookstore.

Hanzelka and Zikmund. World travelers. Jiří Hanzelka (1920–2003) and Miroslav Zikmund (1919) gained fame in the forties and fifties for a series of journeys they made across Africa, Asia, Latin America, and Oceania in a silver car manufactured by the Czech Tatra company. Their articles, books, and films portraying these exotic regions made a splash with the Czech public which was then getting used to living behind barbed-wire borders. Indeed, as a small country, Czechs have traditionally looked to travelers to find out how they are viewed in the world. Later banned from publishing for their opposition to the Soviet invasion, Hanzelka and Zikmund continued writing in → *samizdat* while remaining widely recognized for their accomplishments.

háro (long hair). As in the West, long hair became popular among Czech non-conformists in the late sixties. However, it remained anathema to the guardians of public morality—they liked to say "long hair, short intellect"—who would march young men with long hair to the nearest barbershop for a forced trim. Meanwhile, women were forced to make do with only one commercially available artificial hair color—a sort of henna—which was thus ubiquitous until the fall of communism.

Hašek, Jaroslav (1883–1923). Author of *The Good Soldier → Švejk*. Hašek was not just a talented writer, but also a Czech icon in his own right. He spent much of his time frequenting Prague's many pubs where he planned what Czechs call *mystifikace* (hoaxes). Thus, for example, as editor of the magazine *Svět zvířat* (The World of Animals), Hašek created brand-new animals or plagiarized articles directly from German magazines. In 1911, he and a group of friends founded a political party with the ironic name "Party for Moderate Progress within the Bounds of the Law," though he later served as a commissar in Russia during the Bolshevik Revolution. Publication of *The Good Soldier Švejk* made him famous, but it did not change his hard-living ways. Whether getting drunk in bars or scrambling to make money, Hašek's larger-than-life persona made him the patron saint of all Czech beer drinkers and jokers.

Hašler, Karel (1879–1941). Composer of patriotic and popular melodies beloved to this day. Like George M. Cohan, his closest American counterpart, Hašler began as an actor and vaudevillian, but later turned to writing popular songs. The best known is his sentimental ode to Czechness, "*Ta naše písnička česká*" (Our Czech Song), whose text says that when Czech music dies, then the Czech nation will perish (→ *Co Čech, to muzikant*). His compositions became folk hymns and were published in volumes entitled "Old Prague Songs." His popularity was so great between the wars that a manufacturer of menthol candies called them *Hašlerky* and used the slogan "Hašler coughs, nothing to fear/Hašlerky will cure him." The lozenges can still be found on supermarket shelves today. Hašler himself died in a Nazi concentration camp after being arrested for ignoring warnings not to perform patriotic and anti-Nazi songs. After the war, the communists ignored his achievements because of his many songs hailing → Masaryk and the legionnaires (→ *legionáři*) and making fun of the inter-war communists.

Havel, Václav (1936). Playwright, dissident (→ *disident*), and president. Havel was born into one of the country's most influential families. His uncle Miloš had built the → Barrandov Studios and his father was part owner of the Lucerna Theater. This bourgeois background meant that his opportunities after the communist takeover were limited. Left with little chance to study or get ahead in any career, Havel became interested in the theater scene and found his métier in writing powerful absurdist plays like *Zahradní slavnost* (The Garden Party) or *Vyrozumění* (The Memorandum) that played at the Theater on the Balustrade (→ *Divadlo Na zábradlí*). He gained worldwide renown for cofounding the dissident movement → *Charta 77*, and spent several terms in prison for speaking his mind. In a famous essay entitled "The Power of the Powerless," Havel argued that the everyday compromises of greengrocers (that is, ordinary people) kept the regime afloat and advocated "living in truth" as a means of opposition. Come the revolution, Havel's moral integrity made him an obvious choice for president and the slogan "*Havel na → Hrad*" (Havel to the Castle) was chanted at demonstrations. Many remember his first days as president, when he continued dressing in jeans and sweaters or ill-fitting suits (he memorably appeared in pants several sizes too small), and invited Frank Zappa and Lou Reed to visit him at the castle. While few challenge his achievements as a dissident, his twelve years as president were marked by political controversies over his interventions into policy and personal ones over his marriage to a film star. Nevertheless, he is destined to go down in the pantheon of Czech heroes.

Havířov. In their drive to fashion a brand new society, the communists even dared to construct entire cities from scratch. Such was the

Czech Presidents

This table tries to capture more how the public views the former presidents of Czechoslovakia and the Czech Republic than their actual historic contributions. More detailed information about many of them is available in the main text of the dictionary.

PRESIDENT	TERM	
Tomáš G. → Masaryk	1918–1935	The first, longest-serving, and most esteemed president. The standard against which all presidents are measured.
Edvard → Beneš	1935–1938 1945–1948	As one of the founders of independent Czechoslovakia, the long-serving foreign minister was a natural choice to succeed his close ally Masaryk. Though a consistent democrat who had the country's best interests at heart, Beneš's reputation has been damaged by his decisions to surrender to the Nazis without a fight (→ *Mnichov*) and to accept the communist putsch in 1948 (→ *Vítězný únor*). A new law honoring his memory was controversial both at home and in Germany.
Emil Hácha	1938–1945	A puppet in the hands of the Nazis, Hácha died in prison after the war and is little remembered today.
Klement → Gottwald	1948–1953	Long-time leader of the Communist Party and first worker's president of Czechoslovakia, Gottwald was known for his fiery speeches and inelegant ways.
Antonín Zápotocký	1953–1957	The most folksy of the communist presidents and thus somewhat of a people's favorite despite his brutal rule. Born to a prominent Social Democratic politician and raised in the working class town of → Kladno, Zápotocký trained as a stonecutter and spent part of the war in a concentration camp before working his way up the communist hierarchy.
Antonín Novotný	1957–1968	Schooled as a mechanic, Novotný was an uncharismatic leader who was carried along by the events of the sixties (→ *Pražské jaro*) until they finally overwhelmed him. Rumor had it that he was voted the world's best-looking head of state.
Ludvík → Svoboda	1968–1975	A legendary war hero whose tacit support helped the communists take power in 1948. His popular autobiography, *From Buzuluk to Prague*, described the long fight to liberate Czechoslovakia during World War II. In and out of favor in the fifties and sixties, by the time he became president—largely as a symbol of national unity after the Soviet invasion—Svoboda was already on his last legs. He is the only one of the communist leaders to remain popular today.
Gustáv → Husák	1975–1989	The first and only Slovak to be named president. Though jailed as a bourgeois nationalist by the communists, Husák was rehabilitated in time to lead the hardliners in their repression after the Soviet invasion. Even when Svoboda was president, Husák held the real reins of power. Many remember the death of his wife Viera in a helicopter crash.

| Václav → Havel | 1989–2003 | The dissident leader memorably began his presidency with a speech that told citizens their country was not flowering. Czechs also remember the flood pants he wore during his inauguration, and his speech impediment. |

origin of Havířov, a city of 100,000 in northern Moravia, which was planned from start to finish to house workers from the nearby coal mines. Indeed, its name means "Miners' Town." To the dismay of many of its residents, it was built in line with the then dominant concrete and collective-living esthetic of its communist founders. See also → *Jsem horník.*

Havlíček Borovský, Karel (1821–1856). Journalist, writer, and patriot. Inspired by the National Revival (→ *Národní obrození*), the young Havlíček moved to Prague to write for and edit the newspaper *Národní noviny* (National News). Always a sharp-tongued satirist, he criticized those who would speak about their love for the nation, but not act on it. He stayed true to his ideals when he persisted in his attacks on Austrian rule even after the crackdown of 1848 (→ *Bachův absolutismus*). While virtually all others stayed silent, Havlíček continued publishing despite having to close his newspaper, leave Prague, and face several trials. In December 1851, he was finally sent into exile and spent the next three years in Brixen in the Austrian Tyrol where he wrote satirical and political works. He returned home to Bohemia to find that his wife had died just days before and most of his former friends would have nothing to do with him. His health broken, Havlíček died soon after. At his funeral, Božena → Němcová memorably laid a crown of thorns on his head. He remains a symbol of bravery and, like Jan → Hus, of the necessity of speaking the truth regardless of the consequences. After World War II, the town of Německý Brod (German Ford) was renamed Havlíčkův Brod (Havlíček's Ford) in his honor.

Hej, mistře! (Hey, Master!). Christmas (→ *Vánoce*) mass written by the composer Jakub Jan Ryba (1765–1815). It has achieved widespread popularity by combining the distinctively Czech characteristics of strong melody, colloquial language, and pastoral content, and is played every Christmas.

hejkal (bogeyman). Strange sounds heard when walking in the forest are blamed on the mythical creature called *hejkal*. Summer camp counselors often use *hejkal* to scare their charges.

hejtman (regional governor). A traditional term to refer to regional governors. It has recently been revived after a territorial reorganization of the country.

Heydrichiáda. Name given to the Nazi reprisals that followed the assassination of Reichsprotektor Reinhard Heydrich (→ *Protektorát*) by Czech partisans during World War II. The most visible part of the *Heydrichiáda* was the complete liquidation of the town of → Lidice, but punishment extended to all levels of Czech society and led to the almost complete end of rebel activity in the country.

hezky česky (nicely Czech). Rhyming phrase that is used to describe something that is both Czech and is nicely done. It may be used in reference to a turn of phrase or a great accomplishment.

hloupý Honza (Stupid Jack). A stock figure in Czech fairy tales (→ *pohádka*). Honza is not the brightest bulb in the box, but somehow manages to succeed in the end. Some in fact liken him to → Švejk, whose lack of intelligence likewise did not stand in the way of outwitting his betters. Frequently Honza is portrayed as not stupid, but lazy. In the tale's most popular version, Honza is roused out of bed by his mother and forced to make his way in the world. He eventually wins half a kingdom by making a princess laugh, though he declines to marry her and loses his reward on the way home. In still other tales he is a wiseguy who gets away with impudence. He might be taken as the prototype of the provincial Czech mentality (→ *maloměšťáctví*).

Hody hody doprovody (Feasts, feasts, parades). Nursery rhyme recited on Easter (→ *Velikonoce*). Its text continues, "Give me a painted egg/if you don't give me a painted one/give me at least a white one/the hen will bring you another." The rhyme refers to the practice of whipping women with a → *pomlázka* in return for a colored egg. Eggs of course symbolize fertility and resurrection.

hokej (hockey). Though usually thought of as a sport confined to the great white north, hockey has found a welcoming home among Czechs. As early as the turn of the century, Czechs were playing and winning at hockey, perhaps thanks to the country's many ponds (→ *rybník*). By the forties, they were among the best in the world, winning silver at the Olympics in Saint Moritz and gold at the next year's world championships. It was then that their dreams went to pieces. Just before setting off for the 1950 world championships, most of the team was arrested and jailed for reputedly planning to defect. Many suspected that the Russians were behind the arrest, for with the Czechs out of the way, the Soviet team began to win gold. The irony is even more bitter because Czech players taught the inexperienced Russians how to play the game. Matches between the two sides became even more hard fought after the Soviet invasion in 1968. At the next year's world championships—originally to have been held in Prague but moved to Sweden—Czechoslovakia beat the Soviet Union, twice, unleashing chants of "*Vy nám tanky, my vám branky*" (You send us tanks, we send you goals) and causing demonstrations in Prague and the stoning of the Aeroflot office. As evidence of the political importance of hockey, these riots led to the unseating of Dubček as general secretary and the introduction of

normalization (→ *normalizace*). Only in the eighties was a select group of Czechs allowed to join the NHL (previously they had to defect through Yugoslavia) and prove their ability against the rest of the world. The Velvet Revolution (→ *Sametová revoluce*) finally led to a Czech invasion of foreign leagues in America, Sweden, and even Russia (→ Jágr). Though the national team won numerous world championships, it was not until 1998 in Nagano that they finally broke through to win Olympic gold and temporarily relieved the country's citizens of their post-revolution depression. That victory is now the subject of an opera entitled *Nagano*.

Holík, Jaroslav (1942). Along with his younger brother Jiří, Jaroslav Holík was one of the stars of Czech hockey (→ *hokej*) in the sixties and seventies. Disdaining the finesse style of most Czech hockey players, Holík was instead a banger and fighter. His temper was not just confined to the rink and as a result, he frequently found himself in trouble with the authorities who did not want players to be too independently minded. Jiří was the opposite of his brother, a pure skater at left wing. Particularly memorable were the Holíks' duels with the Russians, especially at the world championships in 1972. They also captured numerous league titles playing together for the army team Dukla Jihlava (→ Dukla Praha). Jaroslav remains as explosive today, coaching the national under-21 team, and rooting for his son Robert, a star for the New Jersey Devils.

holubičí povaha (dove-like character). There is a common belief among Czechs that they are a peace-loving people. Its roots are likely in the country's long-running weakness, which makes attacks on its powerful neighbors an impossibility. Despite several military triumphs, → Žižka's armies in the Middle Ages and the legionnaires (→ *legionáři*) come to mind, for most of their history, Czechs tended to roll over at the first sign of opposition, most tragically when they surrendered to the Nazis without a shot in 1938 (→ *Mnichov*). The same goes for life under foreign occupation—whether Austrian, German, or Russian—when violent resistance was almost unknown. One joke tells of a meeting between a Czech and a Yugoslav after World War II. The Yugoslav says, "Whenever we saw a Nazi, we slit his throat." The Czech replies, "We would have liked to as well, but in our country it was not allowed." Despite its consequences, Czechs continue to make a virtue out of necessity, and see pacifism as an essential and positive element of their national character. More hard-nosed observers, however, worry about the psychological consequences of not fighting for their freedom, but rather having it fall into their laps (→ 28. *říjen*, → *Sametová revoluce*).

Homolka. A fictional family at the center of three films (the first entitled *Ecce homo Homolka*) by the director Jaroslav Papoušek. They are typically Czech in their deep self-absorption, frequent battles over trivial matters, and cowardice in the face of the strong. In a classic scene from the first part of the trilogy, the Homolkas are enjoying a summer day by lounging in the woods. When they hear a woman calling for help, they do what any Czech would in the same situation: they pack up their things and leave as quickly as possible.

Honzíkova cesta (Johnny's Journey). A children's book written by Bohumil Říha in the fifties which was required reading for elementary school pupils from the time of its publication until the fall of communism. The story centers on young Honzík, who takes a trip from Prague to visit his grandparents in the countryside. His grandparents naturally work on a collective farm (→ JZD) and show Honzík the joys of collectivization, telling him how much better they live now than under the old masters. Whenever Honzík points to something, we learn that it is not just a horse or rooster or kitchen, but a collective farm horse, rooster, or kitchen. Honzík also gets into his share of

trouble, but is always bailed out by a friendly Pioneer (→ *Pionýr*). Emphasizing observation in place of action, *Honzíkova cesta* typifies the opposite pole to the adventure literature of → Foglar. Though the book is essentially socialist realism (→ *budovatelský*, → *sorela*) for children, it was beloved for its happy tone and the winning innocence of the title character. It has recently been bowdlerized of its communist sections and reissued.

Horáková, Milada (1901–1950). Social democratic politician and martyr. Though for most of the world, the symbol of the communist show trials (→ *politické procesy*) of the fifties is the Jewish communist leader Rudolf → Slánský, for Czechs it is Milada Horáková. Between the wars Horáková was a lawyer, member of parliament, and crusader for human rights. She was part of the Czech opposition (→ *odboj*) to the Nazis—a member of the board of the resistance organization "We Will Remain Faithful"—and as a result was arrested and imprisoned for the duration of the war. After the war, she continued her uncompromising stands by opposing the communists and was again arrested and tortured. Horáková refused to go along with the communist show trial and in a highly publicized case against "Horáková and Company" was sentenced to death. Despite international calls for her release, with Einstein among others pleading for her life, she was hanged in 1950 and received justice only after the fall of communism. Her body, which was cremated and scattered to the winds by the communists, has recently been symbolically reburied in the national pantheon → *Slavín*.

hospoda (pub). The churches of the Czech nation. Just about every street corner in the country is home to a pub; even villages with a few dozen residents have at least one. A typical pub has long wooden tables where everyone has a seat. This encourages strangers to sit together and engage in the habit of *tlachání* (chattering). Pubs are also usually well-lit and lack loud music. The drink of choice naturally is beer (→ *pivo*), though shots of harder alcohol (→ *rum*) are common as well (mixed drinks are almost unknown). Many in fact choose pubs by the brand of beer on tap. When ordering, an extended index finger means an order of two beers, while the thumbs up is used for only one. More often empty mugs are replaced with full ones automatically. Pubs typically carry names that begin with the preposition *u* which roughly translates as "at the sign of." Thus there is the writer → Hrabal's haunt *U zlatého tygra* (At the Sign of the Golden Tiger), → Hašek's favorite *U kalicha* (At the Sign of the Chalice), and Prague's oldest pub, now a tourist trap, *U Fleků*. Neighborhood pubs often have regulars, called by the German term *štamgasti*, whose personal mugs rest on a special shelf. Finally, no *hospoda* is complete without thick cigarette smoke and surly waitresses.

houbařství (mushrooming). A popular pastime among Czechs of all ages is mushrooming or combing the forest floor for mushrooms. Practiced mushroomers can return from a morning's work with several basketfuls. Though Americans tend to avoid the sport because of the dangers of poisoning themselves, most Czechs are experts on the difference between *jedlé* (edible), *nejedlé* (inedible), and *jedovaté* (poisonous) mushrooms. Only a handful of people die each year, but professionals and helplines are always on hand to help in identification. Mushrooming reaches high season in late August and September, but any rainfall will bring out mushroom hunters early the next morning. The mushrooms collected are most commonly dipped in batter and fried, or made into mushroom goulash (→ *guláš*) or mushroom soup. The poisonous *muchomůrka* (toadstool) has inspired a popular children's book about a sad toadstool who wishes mushroom hunters would pick her.

hovno (shit). A fundamental concept in the Czech vocabulary. Not only is it by itself the most common swear word, but it also figures in oft-repeated phrases like "*Stojí to za hovno*" (It's worth shit) and "*Je to na hovno*" (It's for shit), meaning that something is worth-

less or useless. Gentler souls replace hovno with *houby* or mushrooms. Equally abused is the verb "*srát*" (to shit) which with a variety of prefixes can express just about any strong emotion. Czechs, however, consider it unhygienic for a toilet and bathtub to be located in the same space and thus put them in separate rooms.

Hrabal, Bohumil (1914–1997). Popular writer. Hrabal's earliest stories appeared at a dismal time for Czech literature, when socialist realist aesthetics (→ *budovatelský*, → *sorela*) dictated inspiring stories about heroic partisans and valiant workers. Hrabal instead wrote about simple people living ordinary lives, and wrote about them in a language that sounded like the way people actually talked, with all its vulgarisms and colloquial phrasings. One of his most famous books, *Obsluhoval jsem anglického krále* (I Served the King of England), thus tells the rags to riches to rags story of a hotel waiter riding the vicissitudes of twentieth-century Czech history. Several of his works, including *Ostře sledované vlaky* (Closely Watched Trains), are better remembered for their poetic film adaptations in the hands of the director Jiří Menzel. Hrabal was as well known for his personality as for his books. He was a constant presence in Prague's pubs (→ *hospoda*), where he did much of his writing, and he took care of dozens of stray cats. His death, after falling out of a hospital window, led Czechs to remember their tradition of defenestration (→ *defenestrace*).

Hrad (Castle). While castles (→ *hrady a zámky*) are ubiquitous on Czech territory, all mentions of "the Castle" refer to the Prague Castle. Set on a hill above the → Vltava, the Prague Castle became the country's seat of government in the ninth century, replacing → Vyšehrad. Since then, Castle Hill (known as *Hradčany*) has been home to princes, kings, Holy Roman Emperors, and presidents. Its most distinctive monument is the gothic St. Vitus Cathedral—begun in the fourteenth century, but only finished in the twentieth—

that is home to Prague's bishop, as well as the royal crown jewels (→ *koruna*) and the relics of the Czech patron saints (→ Svatý Václav). The Castle was also the inspiration of Kafka's book of the same name. Since independence in 1918, it has been the official residence of the country's president and has become so identified with the office that protestors during the Velvet Revolution (→ *Sametová revoluce*) shouted "→ *Havel na Hrad*" or "Havel to the Castle." Supporters of the president are thus sometimes referred to as the castle bloc.

hrady a zámky (castles and châteaux). There are probably few countries more densely populated by castles and châteaux then the Czech Republic. Just about every city and small town boasts a monument to the days of hereditary rule. The difference between a *hrad* and a *zámek* is that a castle was built with defense in mind and is thus heavily fortified and usually located in a place that is difficult to assail, most frequently a hilltop. A chateau, by contrast, served as a living space for an aristocratic family and was surrounded by parks or gardens. Both types exist in a range of styles, though the main castle-building period was in the thirteenth century, while chateaux did not come about until the Renaissance. Castles and chateaux became state property after the World War II when the communists evicted all the country's aristocrats and nationalized their land. Many *hrady* and *zámky* are thus open for public tours during castle season, which lasts from April 1 to October 1, and often feature medieval swordfights or puppet shows. They are a popular destination for those on a weekend hike (→ *čundr*). The most visited castles include → Karlštejn, Český Krumlov, and the Prague Castle, which is referred to simply as the Castle (→ *Hrad*). Václav → Havel's weekend cottage was ironically called *hrádeček* or little castle. Well-known chateaux are Červená Lhota and Hluboká. Since 1989 many aristocratic families (→ *šlechta*) have tried to recover their old estates, and the state has obliged if they are willing to invest in their upkeep and keep them open to tourists (→ *restituce*).

Hrušínský, Rudolf (1920–1994). Film and theater actor. If Czechs were to choose the best actor of the century, the nod would most likely go to Rudolf Hrušínský. Hrušínský used his broad face, hangdog eyes, and gravelly voice to lend an air of quality to any production in which he appeared. His first major role was as → Švejk, whose good-natured idiocy he rendered perfectly in two classic films from the fifties. His oeuvre, however, ranges widely—from comedy to drama to horror. Among his most memorable performances are as the Nazi collaborator Kopfrkingel in Juraj Herz's *Spalovač mrtvol* (The Cremator of Corpses), the quarantined patient Prepsl in Karel Kachyňa's *Pozor, vizita* (Attention, the Doctor Is Coming), and in numerous films by Jiří Menzel such as *Rozmarné léto* (Capricious Summer), *Slavnosti sněženek* (Snowflake Celebration), and *Vesničko má středisková* (My Sweet Little Village). His opposition to the communists limited his opportunities in the seventies and eighties, but after the revolution he was elected to the Federal Assembly. The Hrušínský name lives on after his death, as his two sons and grandson have taken on starring roles.

Hujer. Character from the popular seventies film *Marečku, podejte mi pero* (Mareček, Please Pass Me a Pen) whose name has become a synonym for an ass-kisser. In the film, which pokes fun at the plight of factory-workers having to go to night school, the character Hujer tries to butter up his teachers by bringing them fruit from his garden and learning the assignments by heart. Such character traits were encouraged under communism where what mattered was not what you knew, but whose boots you were willing to lick.

Hus, Jan (1371–1415). Priest and religious reformer. Though centuries of Austrian rule have made them a Catholic people (→ *katolická církev*), Czechs of all faiths and non-faiths continue to worship their own proto-Protestant reformer, Jan Hus. A follower of the teachings of the English theologian John Wycliffe, Hus used his pulpit in the Bethlehem Chapel to fight against the selling of indulgences, champion biblical over Church authority, and preach in the vernacular. He also managed to find time to reform Czech spelling (he added the upside-down carets above certain consonants to replace two consonants, → ř instead of rz, for example). Hus's sermons eventually attracted the attention of the Church hierarchy which forbade him to preach and then summoned him to Konstanz—the Emperor guaranteeing his safety—to defend his teaching. Despite a brilliant defense, the Church reneged on its word and had him burned at the stake. Today Hus is viewed as a symbol of truth against power, one of the underlying motifs of Czech history in its classic rendering. The Church's refusal to apologize for its treatment of him until 1999 is a prime reason why Czechs have little patience for papists. Adding to his appeal, Hus was something of a Czech nationalist, while the Catholic Church helped the Habsburgs to rule the country.

Husák, Gustáv (1913–1991). The leader of Czechoslovakia in the seventies and eighties. Called by Milan Kundera the "president of forgetting," Husák took power after the Soviet invasion and came to symbolize the bleak period known as normalization (→ *normalizace*). His rule was characterized by the utter destruction of Czech culture: intellectuals lost their jobs and rigid censorship was imposed on all media. He also placed a vice on politics with only the most craven opportunists holding high positions. In exchange, he offered Czechs Western-like consumption habits, with supplies of meat and materials for cottages (→ *chata*) becoming plentiful. It came as somewhat of a surprise that the job of normalizing the country would fall to Husák, for he himself had been a victim of communist party purges in the fifties and had served time in jail for his purportedly Slovak nationalist views. By the time he became first secretary (→ ÚV KSČ), however, he was a pure Czechoslovak down to his unique way of speaking that mixed the

Poll to Choose the Greatest Czech

These are the results of a poll asking Czechs to choose the greatest Czech in history. A similar poll in 1978 produced a very different ordering with Klement Gottwald on top, followed by Ludvík Svoboda, and "Representatives of the Bourgeois Czechoslovak Republic" in third place.

RANK	PERSON
1	Tomáš G. → Masaryk
2	→ Karel IV
3	Jan → Hus
4	Václav → Havel
5	J. A. → Komenský
6	Jan → Žižka
7	Jan → Palach
8	Edvard → Beneš
9	Emil → Zátopek
10	Ludvík → Svoboda
11	Bedřich → Smetana

Source: *Mladá fronta Dnes*, 16 April 2003.

Czech and Slovak languages. Husák was replaced just before the revolution and died almost concurrently with the regime he helped to build. His name lives on today in the phrase *Husákovy děti* (Husák's children), which is used to refer to the large generation born in the seventies under the influence of his pro-natalist policies.

husité (Hussites). Followers of the religious reformer Jan → Hus. The Hussite movement initially began with Hus's criticisms of such Church abuses as selling indulgences. His message, however, soon spread from Prague to the countryside where folk preachers added a chiliastic vision to his criticisms. Hussitism began to represent a return to the original word of God and among its demands was adoption of communion in both kinds (with both wine and bread). Hus's death at the hands of the church gave a strong impetus to the movement and in 1420 radical Hussites founded a new community in Tábor. The city was soon transformed into an armed military camp, and under the leadership of Jan → Žižka, its *polní vojsko* (field army) turned back crusade after crusade seeking to destroy it. Hussitism, however, was damaged by internal struggles, with extremists like the Adamites (who went around naked and helped to give the term Bohemian its figurative meaning) disrupting the movement's initial unity. The Tábor-based radical Hussitism was defeated in 1434 at → Lipany, though the ideology survived until → *Bílá hora* (there was even at one point a Hussite King, → *Jiří z Poděbrad*). As a result of Hussitism, nearly three-quarters of Czechs were Protestants before the brutal Habsburg-led Counter-Reformation stamped out nearly all traces of the faith and forced its adherents to leave the country. The leaders of the National Awakening (→ *Národní obrození*) celebrated the Hussites, with considerable distortions, as the model of a humanist, democratic Czech ideology. The atheist communists likewise lionized the Hussites, though they twisted their message into one of social equality and revolution. Lost in the attempts to make history serve present ends were the primarily religious motivations of the original Hussite movement.

I

igelitka (plastic bag). Like many useful items under communism, plastic shopping bags were hard to come by; even grocery stores did not supply them. As a result, people horded quality bags—indeed, anything that was potentially useful was stored away for a rainy day—and even washed and hung them out with the laundry. Plastic bags themselves were a late innovation, arriving only in the eighties. Before then, people would carry their groceries in bags made of netting.

inteligence (intelligentsia). Czechs have long put enormous faith in their intellectuals. The pronouncements of artists, writers, and thinkers are sought out and listened to at all important and unimportant moments in the life of the country. This position was earned by the nineteenth-century intelligentsia of the National Revival (→ *Národní obrození*) for their role in creating Czech identity. On the other hand, intellectuals were among the strongest supporters of the communists who took over the country in 1948 (→ *Vítězný únor*), though some eventually wised up and formed the core of the dissident (→ *disident*) movement which helped to overthrow that regime.

inženýr (engineer). Title granted to graduates of a technical university. Recipients of an engineering degree are addressed formally as *pane inženýre* (Mr. Engineer) and display the initials *Ing.* in front of their name. The title was common under communism when liberal arts were played down and universities mandated to train technicians for building the new industrial paradise. Because so many people were forced into technical fields to get a university education, it is not unusual to see engineers working in fields as diverse as theater, advertising, and politics. At the same time, by the late eighties, the title came to be associated with an ambitious and opportunistic class of yuppies who would do anything to get into college and get ahead.

J

Jáchymov (Joachimstal). Spa and mining town in northern Bohemia. If Czech history had taken a different path, the town of Jáchymov might be known for its natural springs and beautiful spas or as the place where the word "dollar" originated—silver coins known as *Joachimsthalers* and later simply *tolars* were produced there. Instead, uranium was discovered in Jáchymov (the Curies got their supplies there), and during the fifties and sixties, political prisoners were sent to the mines in Jáchymov to excavate fuel for the Soviet nuclear program. Conditions in the mines were horrific and thousands died under the brutal work regime or from radiation sickness, making the town a symbol of the brutality of the old regime.

jací jsme (what we are like). The issue of "what we are like" is one that continually occupies Czech thinking. Uncertain about their own position in the world and their contribution to human civilization, Czechs often ask themselves what they amount to as a nation. Newspaper columns frequently analyze how Czechs are perceived by foreigners, and visitors to the country can expect to be asked what they think of Czechs. The most famous meditation on this theme was the journalist Ferdinand Peroutka's book, entitled *Jací jsme*. Ordinary people inevitably answer the question positively with reference to the musical and literary contributions of Czechs and to their golden hands (→ *zlaté ručičky*). It is only intellectuals who occasionally bemoan national traits like envy (→ *závist*) and provinciality (→ *maloměšťáctví*)

and would rather see the country melt into the sea of the European Union. See also → *Česká otázka*, → *češství*.

Jágr, Jaromír (1972). Hockey (→ *hokej*) player. Jágr had the good fortune to come of age as a player just after the revolution when Czechs could finally sign freely with foreign teams. Before 1989, only a few select players were allowed to spend the tail end of their careers playing in the NHL or Scandinavian leagues, though others fled the country through Yugoslavia to test their skills abroad. After signing with the Pittsburgh Penguins, the burly right-winger became one of the NHL's leading goal scorers and a perennial all-star. Jágr remained true to his native country, wearing the number 68 in remembrance of the Soviet invasion (→ *srpnová invaze*) and bringing his mother to Pittsburgh to serve him home-cooked Czech food (→ *jídlo*). He also boasted a perfect mullet, the preferred haircut of Czech athletes. As the most successful Czech abroad and one of the richest, Jágr is the idol of Czech boys and women, though he was only the most visible of an enormous wave of hockey stars including Dominik Hašek, Robert → Holík, Patrik Eliáš, and Milan Hejduk who entered the league after 1989. Indeed, nearly eighty Czech players suited up for NHL squads in the 2001–2002 season, and their exploits are recounted daily in local newspapers.

Jak na Nový rok, tak po celý rok (As on New Year, so for the whole year). Folk superstition that whatever happens on New Year's

Day is an omen for the rest of the year. As a result, Czechs wear new clothes, clean the house, make certain to have money in their pocket, and try not to argue or get angry on January 1. Many also eat bean soup for luck—the beans representing coins. The president traditionally gives a state of the nation address on New Year's Day. Of course, for most Czechs, recovering from their hangover takes precedence over all of these activities.

Jak svět přichází o básníky (How the World Loses Its Poets). Released in 1982, this film became an unexpected hit for its realistic portrayal of two high-school friends, Štěpán and Kendy, searching for love and meaning. It was so popular, especially among more sensitive souls, that it produced four sequels—all with titles featuring the word "poets"—following the friends through medical school and adulthood.

Jan Novák. The most typical Czech name, a sort of John Smith. The name Novák (also Novotný or Nový) originally referred to a person who was newly settled in a region (from the Latin *novus* or new). Other common surnames refer to a person's status—Svoboda (Freeman, i.e., not a serf) and Dvořák (large landowner, from the Czech for courtyard);

occupation—Krejčí (Tailor), Sedlák (Farmer); personality—Šťastný (Happy), Smutný (Sad), Veselý (Merry); or national origin—Němec (German), Polák (Pole). The country also has its share of funny-sounding last names such as Skočdopole (Jumpintothefield) or Nejezchleba (Donteatbread). Surnames became widespread in the early nineteenth century—before then people rarely left their village and so rarely encountered strangers—and were introduced by fiat in the modernizing reforms instituted after Napoleon's invasion. During the National Revival (→ *Národní obrození*) many German names were Czechified—Zimmermann became → Cimrman and Schneider turned into Šnajder. Over time tastes in given names have changed (though more for women, than men who still like to name sons after themselves). Earlier generations tended to stick with traditional Czech names (Václav, Vojtěch) and biblical names (Marie was by far the most common among women). Parents at the time also tended to choose a name without regard to the child's sex and thus names appeared frequently in both masculine and feminine forms—Petr/Petra, Jan/Jana, and even Vlasta/Vlasta. After World War II, there was a fascination with Russian names—Boris, Igor, Vladimír, Táťana—while in the eighties, biblical names

Most Common Czech Names

The first table lists the most common boys', girls' and last names in the first years of the twenty-first century. English translations and the most common short forms of these names (→ *zdrobnělina*) are listed in parentheses. The following two tables track changes in common first names over time. See the entry → Jan Novák for more detailed information about Czech naming practices.

	Boys' names	Girls' names	Last names
1	Jiří (George) (Jura, Jirka)	Marie (Maruška, Mařenka, Majka)	Novák (New One)
2	Josef (Pepa, Pepík, Jožka)	Jana (Janička, Janinka)	Svoboda (Freeman)
3	Jan (Honza, Jenda, Jeníček)	Anna (Anička, Anča)	Novotný (New One)
4	Petr (Petřík, Petříček, Péťa)	Eva (Evička)	Dvořák
5	Jaroslav (Jarda, Jarek, Jaroušek)	Hana (Hanička, Hanča)	Černý (Black)

Boys' names	Girls' names	Last names
6	Pavel (Pavlík, Pavlíček)	Věra (Věruška, Věrka)	Procházka (Walker)
7	Miroslav (Mirek, Mireček)	Lenka (Magdalena) (Lenička, Lenča)	Kučera (Curly Hair)
8	František (Franta, Fanouš, Fana)	Alena (Alenka, Alča)	Veselý (Merry)
9	Martin (Martínek)	Jaroslava (Jarka, Jaruška)	Horák (Highlander)
10	Zdeněk (Sidonius) (Zdeněček)	Ludmila (Lída, Liduška, Míla)	Němec (German)
11	Václav (Wenceslas) (Vašek, Venca, Venda, Vašík)	Petra (Petruška, Peťka)	Pokorný (Humble)
12	Tomáš (Tomášek)	Kateřina (Katka, Káča, Káťa)	Pospíšil (Hurried)
13	Karel (Kája, Karlíček)	Helena (Helenka, Helča)	Marek
14	Milan (Milánek)	Lucie (Lucka, Lucinka)	Hájek (Thicket)
15	Michal (Míša, Michálek)	Zdeňka (Sidonie) (Zdenička, Zdena)	Král (King)
16	Vladimír (Vláďa)	Jitka (Judith) (Jituška)	Jelínek (Little Deer)
17	Ladislav (Láďa, Ládíček)	Jarmila (Jarmilka, Jarka, Jarča)	Růžička (Little Rose)
18	Stanislav (Standa, Stáníček)	Martina (Martinka)	Beneš
19	Lukáš (Lukášek)	Jiřina (Georgina) (Jiřinka, Jiřka)	Fiala (Violet)
20	David (Davídek)	Božena (Thea) (Boženka, Božka)	Sedláček (Peasant/Farmer)
21	Antonín (Tonda, Toník, Toníček)	Ivana (Jane) (Ivanka, Iva)	Zeman (Yeoman/Squire)
22	Roman (Románek)	Veronika (Verča, Verunka)	Doležal
23	Jakub (James/Jacob) (Kuba, Kubíček)	Michaela (Míša, Michalka)	Krejčí (Tailor)
24	Radek (Radeček)	Vlasta (Patricia) (Vlastička)	Kolář (Wheelwright)
25	Ondřej (Andrew) (Ondra, Ondráš, Ondrášek)	Monika (Monička, Monča)	Navrátil (Returned)

Source: Ministry of Interior website (www.mvcr.cz); own research

	Most Common Girls' Names			Most Common Boys' Names		
	Daughters	Mothers	Grandmothers	Sons	Fathers	Grandfathers
1	Tereza	Jana	Marie	Jan	Petr	Josef
2	Kateřina	Lenka	Anna	Jakub	Jiří	Jiří
3	Michaela	Petra	Jana	Tomáš	Pavel	Jan
4	Nikola	Martina	Věra	Martin	Martin	František
5	Kristýna	Hana	Eva	Michal	Jan	Jaroslav

	DAUGHTERS	MOTHERS	GRANDMOTHERS	SONS	FATHERS	GRANDFATHERS
6	Veronika	Eva	Ludmila	Lukáš	Jaroslav	Václav
7	Lucie	Monika	Jaroslava	Filip	Miroslav	Miroslav
8	Anna	Ivana	Zdeňka	Dominik	Tomáš	Karel
9	Barbora	Pavla	Hana	Petr	Josef	Zdeněk
10	Adéla	Jitka	Alena	Jiří	Milan	Ladislav

Source: Czech Statistical Office website, *www.czso.cz*

became popular. Today, traditional Czech names have given way to more unusual (from a Czech perspective) names associated with Western countries—e.g., Nikola, Denisa, Kristýna. Several names are so common that they have developed their own nicknames— Jan becomes Honza, Josef becomes Pepa. Middle names are rare and limited to religious Catholics. Naming practices are further regulated by the state. Czechs need special permission to give their children names not on the government's list of officially approved names. See also → *jmeniny*.

Jánošík (1688–1713). The Slovak Robin Hood. Jánošík came from a small Slovak village and originally fought against the Habsburgs with the rebel leader Rákóczi. During these battles, he became acquainted with forest robbers (*zbojníci*) and soon a leader or *kapitán* of a group of these brigands. According to legend, he took from the rich and gave to the poor and fought for the rights of the common man. Later folk tales and songs endowed him with extraordinary strength, bravery, and guile. When he was finally captured by the authorities, he refused to divulge the names of his comrades and received the most painful form of death sentence—hanging by a rib until he died. And this all before the age of twenty-five. Slovak partisan units during World War II called themselves the Jánošík Brigades, and Slovaks (→ *Slovensko*) are sometimes referred to by Czechs as *Jánošíci*.

Jar. Popular brand of dish washing soap. The name is now a synonym for any dish washing soap so much so that women send their husbands to buy "Jar" rather than soap.

jarmark (fair). Village and small town festivities. Especially → *pouť*, as well as major holidays like Christmas (→ *Vánoce*), are inevitably accompanied by commercial fairs called *jarmarky*. Temporary wooden shacks are set up on the town square for craftsmen, merchants, and bakers to sell their wares—iron candlesticks, wooden toys, pictures of saints, or gingerbread treats. Today these traditional sale items have been joined by cheap clothing and electronic trinkets often imported from Vietnam (→ *Vietnamec*).

Jednota (Unity). The name of the main chain of grocery stores under communism. A typical branch had only two aisles, and though its shelves were usually full, the selection was dismal. Sauerkraut and other preserved vegetables (→ *zavařeniny*) were plentiful, but fresh produce was hard to come by. Milk, interestingly, was sold in plastic bags. Only in the run-up to Christmas (→ *Vánoce*) did generally unavailable items like oranges and bananas appear and even then only in limited quantities. Hours used to be limited from 7 to 5 on weekends and to noon on Saturday. As in all shops, one employee stands guard in the back to prevent shoplifting. Today the successors to Jednota (which still exists in many villages) are rapidly losing business to larger and cheaper supermarkets even though they retain the advantage of convenience.

Jednota bratrská (Union of Brethren). Protestant sect founded in 1457. Inspired by the teachings of Petr Chelčický, a student of Jan → Hus, members of the *Jednota* espoused a religion rejecting violence and material profit and emphasizing education and diligence.

Though small in number, the group inspired or attracted the intellectual leaders of the time. It was members of the *Jednota* who produced the most important translation of the Bible into Czech, the → *Bible kralická*. The flower of the sect was the pedagogue and thinker, Jan Amos → Komenský, who along with the remainder of the Brethren was forced to flee the country after → *Bílá hora*. The teachings of the *Jednota* survived this exile and even spread to other countries, before returning to the Czech lands as the Evangelical Brotherhood Church and the Unity of Czech Brotherhood in the nineteenth century. Despite the attempt of patriots to associate these Protestant sects with true Czechness, they have yet to attract more than a handful of followers away from the dominant Catholic faith (→ *Katolická církev*). It is, however, widely believed that the Brethren helped give birth to the democratic, humanist traditions which characterize the Czech nation (→ *Česká otázka*).

Ještěd. This thousand meter tall mountain in northern Bohemia is better known as the site of a hotel/television transmitter voted by architects and critics as the Czech building of the century. Built on the mountain's summit, the structure rises up in a graceful hyperbolic curve to form a dewdrop-shaped crown to the mountain.

ježibaba (witch, hag). To scare Czech children just mention *ježibaba*. She is the long-nosed, pointy-chinned witch (*čarodějnice*) who shows up in many Czech fairy tales (→ *pohádka*). What she likes above all is to lure children into her house and cook them up for dinner. The word comes from the verb *ježit* (to bristle) and the short form for grandmother *(bába)* and thus means a bristling old hag. In fact, the *ježibaba* character was probably imported from Russia where she is known as *baba Yaga*.

Ježíšek (baby Jesus). Not Santa Claus, but *Ježíšek* is the deliverer of Christmas (→ *Vánoce*) presents to children. On the evening of December 24, kids are bundled out of the

living room so *Ježíšek* can lay his gifts under the tree. He is usually portrayed as an infant, though occasionally Santa Claus-like figures can be seen. Before Christmas, people wish each other a *bohatého Ježíška*, or a rich baby Jesus. See also → *Děda Mráz*.

Ježíšmarjá (Jesus and Mary). While *Ježíšmarjá, pane bože* (good lord), and *krucifix* are the most common oaths in Czech and can be heard in the mouths of everyone from kindergarteners to retirees, their religious meaning is lost on most Czechs. A combination of forced catholicization, industrialism, and communsim have made the large majority into confirmed materialists who see little use for religious ritual. This, however, has not stopped them from embracing new-fangled spiritualisms like psychotronics.

jezuité (Jesuits). As elsewhere in Europe, so in the Czech lands the work of the Counter-Reformation fell to the Jesuits. And because Protestantism had become so entrenched among Czechs, their task required the use of considerable force. The most infamous of these Jesuits was the fanatical preacher Antonín Koniáš who burned over 30,000 Czech books and wrote a key to recognizing heretical errors. In the eyes of later national awakeners, the Jesuits were thus cast as the main villains (→ *temno*) in Czech history, imposing foreign customs over naturally Czech traditions. In place of democracy came hierarchy, in place of freedom, subjugation. Yet, revisionist historians have pointed to their key role in national development. Not only did they alter the landscape with their religious architecture (→ *české baroko*, → *boží muka*) and establish many beloved folk traditions (→ *betlém*), but they also set up an estimable system of schools that contributed in no small measure to the relative prosperity of the Czech lands.

jídlo (food). While it is beer (→ *pivo*) that gives them their identity, food is just as close to Czech hearts. Devotion to traditional recipes is high. Experimentation has long been frowned upon and with the exception of → pizza few foreign foods have penetrated Czech cuisine. The oldies but goodies are pork or beef, accompanied by dumplings (→ *knedlík*) or potatoes (→ *brambory*), and topped with sauce (→ *omáčka*) or sauerkraut (→ *zelí*). Only rarely do they contain any spices. The main meal of the day is served at lunch—and thus eaten in cafeterias or pubs—with breakfast and dinner often consisting of rolls (→ *rohlík*) with yogurt and cheese. All meals are consumed as quickly as possible; children are taught not to speak during meals. Hospitality, however, is important and guests often find themselves overwhelmed with food.

Jiránek, Vladimír (1938). The country's most loved cartoonist. His strips are easily recognized by the spare pen strokes used to create an array of confused, cynical characters, usually representing ordinary Czechs overwhelmed by their country's history. Under communism, Jiránek's work appeared in the satirical weekly → *Dikobraz* (Porcupine) and since the revolution in newspapers like → *Lidové noviny* and *Mladá fronta*. He is as well known for his bedtime cartoon (→ *večerníček*) *Bob and Bobek* about two rabbits, the younger of which dislikes getting up in the morning because it is still night for him.

Jirásek, Alois (1851–1930). The novels, plays, and writings of Alois Jirásek helped to create and popularize the standard interpretation of Czech history. Jirásek's → *Staré pověsti české* (Old Czech Legends) introduced the Czech masses to a panoply of legendary medieval figures first described in Cosmas's twelfth-century chronicles (→ Kosmas). Though the historian František Palacký was the first to lionize the brave Hussite warriors (→ *husité*) fighting against the enemies of the Czechs, it was Jirásek's novels like *Proti všem* (Against All) which fixed these images in the Czech mind forever and made national heroes of Jan → Hus, Jan → Žižka, and Prokop Holý. It was Jirásek himself who created the picture of Habsburg rule after White Mountain (→ *Bílá hora*) as a period of → *temno* (darkness) in his novel of the same name. Jirásek

Old Czech Legends
(→ *Staré pověsti české*)

These are the contents of Alois → Jirásek's classic compilation of ancient Czech legends.

Old Czech Legends
Forefather → Čech
Forefather Krok and his Daughters
Bivoj
→ Libuše
→ *Přemyslovci*
Libuše's Prophecies
The War of the Maidens (→ *Dívčí válka*)
Křesomysl and Horymír
The Lucan Wars
Durynk and Neklán
Legends of Christian Times
King Svatopluk of Moravia (→ *Morava*)
King Barley (→ *Král Ječmínek*)
The Banner of St. Wenceslas (→ Svatý Václav)
The Story of Bruncvík
The Abbey Treasure
Tales of Old Prague (→ *Praha*)
Old Prague
Zito the Magician
King Wenceslas IV
The Old Town Clock
Dalibor of Kožojedy
Tales of the Ghetto
Melancholy Places
The House of Dr. Faustus
Some Myths of the Middle Ages
→ Žižka
The Miners of Kutná Hora
The White Lady (→ *Bílá pani*)
The Rose Clearing
Divine Retribution
→ Jánošík

Ancient Prophecies
Sybil's Prophecy
The Blind Youth's Prophecy
The Prophecy of Havlas Pavlata
Other Prophecies
The Knights of → Blaník

also established the accepted version of the National Revival (→ *Národní obrození*) as a reawakening of democratic traditions in novels like *F.L. Věk* (later made into a popular television series). He even lived long enough to see his ideals fulfilled in the birth of independent Czechoslovakia and served in its parliament. Like Walter Scott for the Scots or Henryk Sienkiewicz for the Poles, Jirásek gave his people a vision of a heroic, chivalrous past that they continue to savor.

Jiří z Poděbrad (1420–1471). Known as the Hussite (→ *husité*) king, Jiří had actually fought at → Lipany on the side of the moderate Hussites. In the anarchy that followed the battle, he managed to reunite the country, finding common ground with the Catholics; for his efforts, he was elected king, the first from the local nobility since the Premyslids. Under increasing pressure from the Church (→ *katolická církev*), which wanted him to renounce communion in both bread and wine, Jiří tried to defend his kingdom by forming an alliance of sovereign European states that Czechs often call a precursor to

the United Nations. His reign was later celebrated by patriots during the National Revival (→ *Národní obrození*).

Jitex. Clothing line. Manufactured in the town of Písek, Jitex was the best-known clothing brand under communism. Men's suits, however, were ordered from and associated with the clothing factory in the Moravian town of Prostějov. While the communists made some effort to follow Western trends, selection was highly limited so that it was not uncommon to run into others wearing the exact same clothes.

Jízda králů (Ride of Kings). Traditional folklore festival held in the region of → Slovácko, especially the village of Vlčnov. Each year, a young boy around the age of ten is chosen as king. On the day of the celebration he is dressed in women's clothes and paraded through town on a horse with a rose in his mouth. He is accompanied by ministers and criers who beseech onlookers for contributions with clever rhymes and the phrase, "For the king, good woman, for a poor, but honest king." Though the origins of the ride are obscure, speculation centers around the Hungarian king Matthias Corvinus, who had to disguise himself as he retreated home after a lost battle.

jmeniny (name day). Besides their birthday, every Czech also celebrates a name day, the day in the Church calendar when the saint bearing their name is honored. Rather than

Communist Slogans

Under communism Czechs were surrounded by propagandistic slogans—in their schools, workplaces, and even apartment buildings. The following table reproduces some of the best known.

Učit se, učit se, učit se—V.I. Lenin	Learn, learn, learn—V.I. Lenin
Lidé, bděte—Fučík	People, be alert—Fučík
Se Sovětským svazem na věčné časy a nikdy jinak	With the Soviet Union for all time and never otherwise
Mír dětem celého světa	Peace to children of the whole world
Republice více práce, to je naše agitace	More work for the Republic, that's our propaganda

Závěry V. sjezdu splníme	We will fulfill the conclusions of the Fifth Congress
Sovětský svaz (Sovětská žena) náš vzor	The Soviet Union (Soviet woman), our model
Pětiletka naše cesta do socialismus	The five-year plan, our path to socialism
S komunisty do lepších časů	With the communists to better times
Sláva rudé armádě	Hurrah to the Red Army
→ Jsem horník a kdo je víc	I am a miner and who is more
Kupředu, zpátky ni krok	Forward, not one step back
Dále a směleji vpřed k vybudování socialismu	Further and more boldly forward towards the building of socialism
Se Sovětským svazem za trvalý mír ve světě	With the Soviet Union for lasting peace in the world
Ameriku dohoníme a předhoníme	We will catch up to and surpass America
Kapitalismus je metla lidstva	Capitalism is the scourge of humanity
Kdo nejde s námi, jde proti nám	He who is not with us is against us
Kdo nepracuje ať nejí	He who doesn't work shouldn't eat
Když se kácí les, lítají třísky	When you cut down a forest, the chips fly
V čele s KSČ za nová vítězství socialismu	With the KSČ in the lead for new victories of socialism
Překročíme plán	We will exceed the plan
Ten kdo stojí na chodníku, ten nemiluje republiku (miluje Ameriku)	He who stands on the sidewalk does not love his country (loves America)
Prací posílíme mír	With work we strengthen peace
Buduj vlast, posílíš mír	Build your homeland and you strengthen peace
Ser rychle, posílíš mír	Shit quickly and you strengthen peace

use the term name day, Czechs usually refer to it simply as *svátek* (holiday) as in "It's your holiday today." On these holidays, women usually receive flowers from friends and co-workers, and men may get a small flask of rum. Florists in fact usually feature signs alerting customers to the name being celebrated that day. Almost every day of the year, except certain national and religious holidays, is associated with a particular Czech name (→ Jan Novák). March 19, the name day of Joseph, traditionally the most common name, was popularly known as International Men's Day (→ MDŽ) and marked by heavy drinking in the country's pubs.

Jsem horník a kdo je víc (I'm a miner and who is more). An oft-repeated slogan under communism. It was supposed to express the equality of all working people, but it turned out that miners were more equal than others. They received higher pay, better housing, and more generous pensions. Whether this compensated for the dangers of working as a miner under a regime that cared little for occupational safety is another question. Indeed, the state had to offer special benefits to induce workers to come to mining centers like → Ostrava and Ústí nad Labem. It was also mining, especially in the uranium mines of → Jáchymov, that was the most common punishment for political prisoners. More generally, communists were enthusiastic sloganeers; inane sayings like Lenin's "Learn, learn, learn" or "With the Soviet Union for Eternity" graced every public building.

Jugoslávie (Yugoslavia). The most popular vacation destination for Czechs. Yugoslavia was sought out for its beautiful beaches and islands, now almost entirely in the possession of Croatia. Under communism, few received permission (→ *výjezdní doložka*) to visit the country because of its more open borders and the consequent fear that they would flee to the West. Today, however, hordes of vacationers take buses or cars on the ten- to fifteen-hour trip to the Adriatic coast. Typically, they pack food for their entire stay and subsist on powdered soups, cured sausage, and beer. While Czechs have little comprehension of the violence (→ *holubičí povaha*) that destroyed Yugoslavia, Westerners persist in confusing the two countries.

Junák (Boy Scouts). Borrowing from the British model, Antonín Svojsík founded the Czech version of scouting in 1911, just two years after the original. Called either *Junák* (a word meaning brave youth) or *skauting*, the boy scouts achieved widespread popularity during the First Republic (→ *První republika*). The movement was harassed under the communists, who dismissed it as a bourgeois relic, and tried to replace it with the Pioneers (→ *Pionýr*). Scouting has experienced a revival since the fall of communism and children dressed in green uniforms and brown kerchiefs are again a common sight.

Jungmann, Josef (1773–1847). Philologist, translator, and national awakener. During a conversation in his university years, Jungmann realized that he could not find the appropriate Czech words to express his thoughts. He thus made up his mind to both learn and develop his mother tongue. While prior supporters of the Czech language (→ Dobrovský) had assumed it to be a language of the common folk, Jungmann was determined to produce a language capable of great art and science. He contributed to this goal—through translations of great literary works like Milton's *Paradise Lost* — histories of Czech literature, and a five-volume Czech-German dictionary. He also cofounded national organizations and the first scientific journal in Czech. Jungmann was a true patriot in his devotion to the Czech cause and, along with → Dobrovský and → Palacký, one of the key figures in the National Revival (→ *Národní obrození*).

JZD (Jednotné zemědělské družstvo/Standard Farming Cooperative). The Czech version of the Russian *kolkhoz*, this was the name of all the collective farms (i.e., virtually all farms period) in the country under communism. Land reform had started even before the putsch, but it was left to the communists to expropriate small farmers (they had repeatedly promised to leave them alone) and make collectivization complete. The process is best depicted in Vojtěch Jasný's film *Všichni dobří rodáci* (All the Good Countrymen) where the communists use any means possible—from persuasion to threats to violence—to force farmers to give up their land. Most Czechs spent at least part of their youth on JZDs as part of student brigades (→ *brigáda*) for collecting the year's harvest of hops (→ *chmel*) or potatoes. Today, faded JZD signs can be seen across the countryside. See also → *Starci na chmelu*.

K

kádrový spis (personnel file). The communist state kept personnel files on all of its citizens. These files included not just information about education and work experience, but also about family members—whether they were workers or bourgeoisie—trips abroad, and political activities. This information played a key role in all aspects of life. People who found the doors to education, work, and travel closed to them knew that it was all a result of their bad *kádrový spis*, a flaw that could be overcome only with great difficulty.

kalich (chalice). Symbol of the Hussite movement (→ *husité*). The chalice stood for the Hussite belief that communion should be taken in both kinds—in bread and wine. It can still be seen today adorning Protestant churches.

kapr (carp). The main course of the traditional Christmas (→ *Vánoce*) dinner is slices of carp dipped in bread crumbs and deep fried. In the weeks before the holiday, the streets are lined with large tubs full of the fish. Customers pick out the one they like and either have it killed on the spot or take it home to swim around in their bathtubs. The fish themselves are raised in the ponds (→ *rybník*) of south Bohemia that were specially built for fish-farming centuries ago. Though it is not viewed as the tastiest fish by Westerners (it likes to wallow in the mud), Czechs see carp as a delicacy, not least because, as a landlocked country, fish retain an exotic, holiday feel. On the other hand, its many small bones lead to crowded emergency rooms on Christmas Eve.

Karel IV (Charles IV) (1316–1378). Medieval Czech king and Holy Roman Emperor. Karel IV is widely considered the greatest leader in the country's history. The son of Jan of Luxembourg and the Czech princess Eliška Přemyslovna, Karel was originally raised in Bohemia until his father took him away to the French court for education. After reaching maturity, he became king of the Bohemian crownlands, taking over a country in a desolate state. His energy and initiative led him to embark on a project of reconstruction that produced such monuments as Charles University (the first university in Central Europe), Charles Bridge, the New Town of Prague (centered on Charles Square), the castle → Karlštejn, the spa town (→ *lázně*) of → Karlovy Vary (Carlsbad), and considerable improvements to the Prague Castle (→ *Hrad*). Upon being named Holy Roman Emperor, he earned the enduring respect of Czechs for his decision to center the empire in Prague and to use Czech (→ *čeština*) as the language of state. Karel IV also paid tribute to his Premyslid (→ *Přemyslovci*) forebearers, naming his son Václav and beginning his coronation procession at → Vyšehrad. The combination of devotion to all things Czech, immense leadership skills, and a palpable material legacy gave him rights to the title *otec vlasti* (father of the homeland).

Karlovy Vary (Carlsbad). The best-known Czech spa (→ *lázně*). Legend has it that its springs were discovered by → Karel IV during a deer hunt, and the town now carries his name. Its golden age as a spa town, however, began in the seventeenth century when it caught the fancy of the Viennese court. The local Dr. David Becher came up with new spa cures—for example, drinking the waters in addition to bathing in them—and it was his family who gave the world the drink → Becherovka. With its long colonnades, manicured walking paths, and frilly architecture, Karlovy Vary set the style for other Czech spa towns. Its Grandhotel Pupp is considered the country's most luxurious hotel.

Karlštejn. A castle (→ *hrady a zámky*) built outside of Prague by the Holy Roman Emperor → Karel IV in the fourteenth century. Its original purpose was to hold the imperial crown jewels (→ *koruna*), but political turmoil meant that they never stayed there for long. Legend has it that Karel IV forbade women to spend the night in the castle. This legend became the subject of a nineteenth-century play, *Night in Karlštejn*, about Karel's wife who disguised herself as a man in order to overturn the ban. The play has since become a favorite of community theaters (→ *ochotnické divadlo*) and was later transformed into a popular musical film. Karlštejn is considered one of the most beautiful of the country's castles and every year welcomes over 300,000 visitors, the majority of them Czechs.

katolická církev (Catholic Church). Despite a love-hate relationship with the Church, Czechs were and remain a Catholic people. They were christianized in the ninth century by the Greek brothers → Cyril and Methodius. Unlike the Russians and Eastern Slavs, however, the Czechs did not reject the pope and remained within the Catholic Church. The Hussites (→ *husité*) made large inroads into this tradition, but the Habsburgs imposed a strict re-Catholicization, which saw the near eradication of Protestantism and the building of hundreds of churches (→ *české baroko*). It was then that the faith inculcated itself into the daily life of the masses as rituals like pilgrimages (→ *pout*) and nativity scenes (→ *betlém*) gained great favor. The Church

was, however, permanently tainted by its association with foreign oppressors. The communist regime tried to stamp out religion by sentencing priests to labor camps, nationalizing Church property, and punishing those who attended mass regularly (→ *Číhošťský zázrak*). Despite the harassment, churches remained open and christenings continued to be performed, though only state-licensed priests were allowed to preach. By the seventies, the Church had largely ceased to put up active resistance to the communists and even disciplined its own dissident members. The eighties and nineties saw a slight revival in belief, but communism and modernization had taken their toll. Today over forty percent of the country confesses to atheism, one of the highest percentages in the world. Further evidence of disbelief is that most Czechs remain opposed to restitution of Church property seized by the communists. Catholicism is strongest in the rural areas of south Moravia (→ *Morava*), especially around the pilgrimage church of → Velehrad.

kavárna (coffeehouse, café). Czechs are typical Central Europeans in their love of coffeehouses. Coffee arrived in the Habsburg Empire, of which the Czechs were then a part, when the Ottomans were repulsed at the gates of Vienna in 1683 and left behind sacks of coffee beans. By the late nineteenth and early twentieth century, the coffeehouse had become the center of intellectual life in a region of the world teeming with would-be intellectuals. Circles of like-minded thinkers would meet daily at particular cafés to drink espresso, read the newspapers, and argue over ideas. One of the more illustrious was the Café Arco where the German-Jewish writers of Prague, including Franz Kafka, congregated. The best-known Czech café is Slavia with its beautiful views of the → Vltava and the National Theater (→ *Národní divadlo*). For over 120 years, Slavia has served as a meeting point for artists, writers, and later dissidents; illustrious patrons would hold court at their personal tables. The communists criticized coffeehouses as breeding grounds for social parasites whom they often referred to negatively as *kaváren̆ští intelektuálové* (coffeehouse intellectuals); they instead preferred pubs (→ *hospoda*) and large cafeterias. Only recently have classic cafés opened in something near their former splendor as espresso machines replace the formerly ubiquitous Turkish coffee and its indissoluble grounds.

Kavčí hory (Jackdaw Mountains). A common shorthand for the studios of the main public television station, Czech Television, which moved to these hills in Prague in 1979. Czech Television began broadcasting in 1959, but Czechs had to wait until 1970 for a second channel and until 1975 for color broadcasts. The limited offerings before 1989 included the daily propaganda that passed for news as well as hagiographic portraits of soldiers, policemen, politicians, and workers. Viewers, however, sought out a number of well-made dramatic series—for example, → *Nemocnice na kraji města*—and films and detective shows from Western Europe. The lack of options, however, did not stop television watching from becoming the prototypical pastime of the seventies and eighties. The fall of communism brought a sea-change: the private television station Nova, owned by the American magnate Ronald Lauder, quickly became the dominant force in the market, offering viewers American sitcoms like MASH, South American telenovelas, and low-brow domestic variety shows.

"Kde domov můj" (Where Is My Home). Written in 1834 by the dramatist Josef Kajetán Tyl and the composer František Škroup for the patriotic operetta *Fidlovačka* (Shoemaker's Festival), this song became a favorite of Czech patriots and ultimately, in 1919, the national anthem. Its text eloquently evokes the Czech countryside—waters murmuring through meadows and trees rustling on rocky hills. Indeed, Czechs identify their nation with the simple beauties of the national landscape rather than with military glory (like the French) or nationalism (like the Germans). More than pride, the Czech anthem is likely to evoke sadness, tears, and homesickness. It is played at the conclusion of television and radio programming at night as well as on New Year's Eve (→ *Silvestr*). During the existence of Czechoslovakia (→ *Československo*), the plaintive *"Kde domov můj"* was always followed by the rousing Slovak anthem, *"Nad Tatrou sa blýská"* (Lightning over the Tatras).

Kdysi dávno (Once a long time ago). Czech fairy tales (→ *pohádka*) have a large number of ways to express the idea "Once upon a time." The most common is *kdysi dávno*, but other mood setters are *Byl jednou jeden král* (There was once a king) and *Žil byl* (He lived, he was), which send the imagination back into legendary times, or *Za devatero horami a devatero řekami* (Beyond nine mountains and nine rivers), which puts one's thoughts in lands far, far away. An interesting linguistic construction is *Bylo nebylo* (It was and it wasn't) which signals that the tale is set in a world that is and is not our own.

Kladno. Industrial city just west of Prague (→ *Praha*). While Prague is the city of a hundred towers, Kladno is the city of a hundred smokestacks; its flagship enterprise is the enormous steel plant called Poldi. For this reason, it has a tradition of worker militancy and support for left-wing causes, which made it a favorite of the communists. These traditions were described by future president and Kladno native Antonín Zápotocký, in the book *Rudá záře nad Kladnem* (Red Glare Above Kladno), a work that would become required reading for school children. Kladno was as important to the communists for its symbolism as for its reserves of burly workers who could be quickly transported to Prague to put down student demonstrations against the regime.

klekání (evening bell). Church bells are traditionally rung in the evening at 6 o'clock, an event known as *klekání*. Children who do not go to bed on time are threatened with a ghost that is appropriately named the evening ghost or *klekánice*.

Klub českých turistů (Czech Hikers Club). Even the most cursory visit to the Czech countryside will bring one into contact with square-shaped symbols—two white bars framing a red, green, yellow, or blue bar—painted on trees and fence posts. These symbols help mark trails and are the handiwork of the Czech Hikers Club. Since the Club's founding in 1888, members have produced the best set of marked hiking paths in all Europe. They cover 37,000 km and connect just about every village and town in the country, often running through farms and backyards. The Club's services remain heavily utilized today with → *tramping*, and hikers (→ *čundr*) heading to the hills every weekend to explore the countryside or participate in famous hikes like *do Prčic* (→ *do prdele*). The popularity of *turistika* (hiking) rests in the widespread belief of the natural beauty of their own country and a desire to see it up close.

knedlík (dumpling). The main starch in the Czech diet. Though fairly tasteless, dumplings are much beloved for their ability to fill up the stomach and stick to the ribs. They are made from old rolls (→ *rohlík*) along with flour, yeast, milk, and egg, though many buy them premade in grocery stores in the form of a long roll that is then cut into slices. Dumplings are most commonly served with meat and most importantly one of a variety of sauces (→ *omáčka*) like tomato, dill, horseradish, or cream (→ *svíčková*). They also appear with goulash (→ *guláš*), sauerkraut (→ *vepřo-knedlo-zelo*), and are sometimes fried up with eggs and served alone (a sort of French toast). A heavier and more yeasty type of dumpling is filled with fruit, sprinkled with sugar and served as a dessert. Several towns hold dumpling-eating contests—the current record is fifty-nine in an hour (a normal portion is four). It is dumplings that Czechs pine for most when traveling abroad.

knižní čtvrtky (book Thursdays). Because everything was centrally planned under communism, new books arrived in stores only once a week—on Thursdays—and sold out quickly due to low regulated prices. The result was that Czech readers would line up in front of the bookstore early on Thursday morning to get a copy of the latest novel by regime-approved writers like Vladimír Páral or Radek John. Of course, the shelves also remained stacked with six-figure print runs of the collected speeches of Klement → Gottwald or Gustáv → Husák, bought almost entirely for show. Less favored or banned authors in contrast could find their work pulped and were distributed only in → *samizdat*. Much of the best literature thus came from abroad with translations of left-wing authors like Hemingway, Steinbeck, Saroyan, and Heller appearing regularly. In any case, Czechs are avid readers and purchase even relatively obscure poetry in bulk. Today many intellectuals look back wistfully at book distribution under communism, when relatively decent writers could earn good salaries and see their work printed in large quantities, provided of course that they avoided mention of politics. This contrasts with the current situation where royalties are low and print runs small, though the dramatic increase in variety makes it worth the price.

Kocourkov. The fictional town of Kocourkov has come to stand for a place full of foolish, self-important people. The 1930s film → *U nás v Kocourkově* (At Home in Kocourkov) written by Karel Poláček (→ *Bylo nás pět*), for example, describes a village where an escaped convict dupes the town's fatuous citizens into electing him mayor. The current Czech political scene is often likened to Kocourkov.

Kofola. The Czech version of Coca-Cola. Kofola was invented by the communists in 1962 to show consumers that they did not need Western products. It may taste a little sour to those used to the American version, but it still does a passable imitation; the patriotically-inclined even sing its praises. Like Coke, *kofola* carried its own slogan: "There are lots of thirsts, there is only one *kofola*." Though *kofola* disappeared after the Velvet

Revolution in the wave of foreign imports, it is currently enjoying a comeback along with other consumer goods from communism.

koláč (cake/pastry). When children scream for something sweet, they scream for a *koláč*. This usually refers to a circular pastry that is topped with plum jam or cottage cheese. In fairy tales, the *koláč* sometimes has the power to charm and enchant. The common phrase *Bez práce nejsou koláče* translates literally as "Without work there are no *koláč* " and more colloquially as "No pain, no gain."

kolová (bicycle soccer). Czechs are inveterate players of obscure sports. Besides → *nohejbal*, they have also specialized in bicycle soccer, and a distinctively Czech form of handball. All of these sports are organized into leagues and widely followed, not least because Czechs are so successful at them.

Komenský (Comenius), Jan Amos (1592–1670). Theologian and pedagogue. The most famous member of the Protestant sect → *Jednota bratrská* (Union of Brethren), Komenský was one of his era's great humanists and teachers. His most famous work, *The Labyrinth of the World and the Paradise of the Heart*, diagnosed the contemporary world's ills and recommended education as the cure. Indeed, Komenský's most important legacy was his advocacy of liberal education for all citizens. Though he was forced into exile (→ *exil*) after the Battle of White Mountain (→ *Bílá hora*), he continued to write and teach in Poland, England, and ultimately the Netherlands. Czechs revere him not only for these achievements, but also for his undying love of the Czech nation and the homesickness he endured in exile. His lines, "I believe God that after the passing of the storm of wrath, the government of your affairs will again return to you, O, Czech people," are frequently cited, especially in the song "A Prayer for Marta" (→ *"Modlitba pro Martu"*). Towards the end of his life, as the last surviving bishop of the *Jednota*, Komenský turned to revelation and memorably predicted the destruc-

tion of the Habsburg Empire and the final resolution of the Czech question. The date of Komenský's birth, March 28, is now celebrated as Teachers' Day and Komenský himself is referred to as "The Teacher of Nations." Many school facades thus feature a bust of Komenský. As is the case with many of their national heroes, Komenský is believed to be better known outside the country than he actually is, though legend has it that he was offered the first presidency of Harvard University.

kominík (chimneysweep). Chimneysweeps are seen as symbols of good luck. When children run into one, they immediately try to touch one of the buttons on his jacket and then one of their own buttons to bring themselves good fortune.

komunismus (communism). Though often portrayed as a foreign import, communist ideology has strong domestic roots in the Czech lands. The Communist Party (→ KSČ) has fared well in free elections, going all the way back to its founding in the 1920s. Their success drew on both the early development of the proletariat (→ *dělník*) in the heavily industrialized country, and strong traditions of egalitarianism (→ *rovnostářství*) in Czech culture. It was thus no great surprise that, after the betrayal of Munich (→ *Mnichov*), the communists garnered forty percent of the vote in 1946 and took power through more or less legal channels (→ *Vítězný únor*). Though few approved entirely of their brutal methods in the fifties, they were able to draw on enough residual support to hold off de-Stalinization and public dissent longer than other communist states. It required the invasion of the Warsaw Pact forces in 1968 (→ *srpnová invaze*) to finally destroy any illusions about the superiority of communism. Since the Velvet Revolution (→ *Sametová revoluce*), the Communist Party has been able to resurrect itself mainly among senior citizens and others out of work, but the idea of communism has lost almost all of its appeal. This does not mean, however, that people do not retain some good memories of the old regime. In fact, there has been a recent wave of nostalgia for the music of the seventies and eighties. It is worth noting that the system under which Czechs lived from 1948 to 1989 was never called communism, only socialism. The exalted state of communism, according to the country's leaders, would be achieved only at some undetermined point in the future.

A Day in the Life of Socialism

The following are the main events reported in the news on 2 October 1981. They were collected by Jiří Svršek from *Pravda* (Truth), the organ of the Western Bohemian Regional Committee of the Communist Party of Czechoslovakia. They can be found in Czech at *www.natura.eridan.cz/natura/2001/2/20010204.html*

Comradely Discussion

PRAGUE (CPA)—Member of the Presidium and secretary of the ÚV KSČ (Central Committee of the Communist Party of Czechoslovakia), Vasil Biľak, along with the secretary of the ÚV KSČ, Jan Fojtík, yesterday met with the executive secretary of the Presidium of the Central Committee of the Union of Communists of Yugoslavia (SKJ), Trp Jakovlevsky, who is on a friendly visit to the ČSSR. In an open, comradely discussion, they exchanged opinions on dilemmas of current global developments and questions of the further evolution of relations between the KSČ and the SKJ in both countries.

Order of Labor to O. Karban

PLZEŇ (ja)—On the occasion of his sixtieth birthday, the president of the republic awarded the Order of Labor to Oldřich Karban, an employee of the OV (District Committee) KSČ in Domažlice. The high state distinction was given to him yesterday by the leading secretary of the KV (Regional Committee) KSČ, Josef Mevald, in the presence of the chairman of the regional Audit and Control Commission of the KSČ, František Galatík, the leading secretary of the OV KSČ in Domažlice, Karel Krýsl, and the chairman of the regional committee of the Association of Czechoslovak-Soviet Friendship, Jiří Lukavský.

Comrade Josef Mevald expressed profound gratitude to Oldřich Karban for his lifelong devoted and self-sacrificing work for the Communist Party of Czechoslovakia and the socialist community. During his productive life, Oldřich Karban held many responsible party and public functions. He was the leading secretary of the District Committee of the party, a secretary of the District Committee of the National Front, and lastly the chairman of the District Audit and Control Commission of the KSČ in Domažlice.

Over the whole course of his fertile and hard-working life, he remained faithful to Marxism-Leninism, to proletarian internationalism, and to deep friendship with the Soviet Union. Even in the party's most difficult times, he did not disappoint.

Comrade Josef Mevald at the same time thanked the wife of Oldřich Karban, who was also present, for consistently creating a good home life for the demanding and self-sacrificing work of a communist-revolutionary.

All present heartily congratulated Karban on his birthday and on the awarding of the high state honor.

They Did It!

Vřesová (bh)—After several attempts to achieve maximum production, when the weather, operational conditions, and the machines themselves challenged the efforts and class consciousness of the workers, the collective of the technological unit from the February 25th Fuel Combine, syndicate enterprise, Vřesová, achieved a record monthly output of 391,220 m³ of covered earth.

And finally at six o'clock in the morning the representatives of the collective could present the illustrious report to the director of the syndicate enterprise, Com. Eng. Josef Beneš, the chairman of the CZV KSČ, Com. Eng. Budoházy, and the chairman of ZV ROH, Com. Pavel Mašek. Their success was all the more joyous, because it was also a gift to the meeting of the Presidium of the KV KSČ in Plzeň, which met yesterday in Vinitíř.

The record output was attained and is not a reason simply for celebration, but also for reflection on how to further the development of the progressive movement which increases the socialist consciousness of the people and helps them in fulfilling the plan.

Chairman of the FSÚ Named

Prague (ctk)—On the nomination of the government of the ČSSR, the President of the Czechoslovak Socialist Republic, Gustáv Husák, yesterday named Eng. Vladimir Miček chairman of the Federal Statistical Office (FSÚ). At the same time he recalled Eng. Jan Kazimour from that position. That same day, at a gathering of the leading workers of FSÚ, Václav Hůla installed Vladimír Miček in the position of Deputy Chairman of the Government of ČSSR and at the same time assessed the many years of work of the hitherto chairman of the FSÚ.

On the Eve of the GDR State Holiday

Prague (ctk)—On the occasion of the forthcoming state holiday of the German Democratic Republic—the 32nd anniversary of the founding of the GDR—the ambassador of the GDR to the ČSSR, Helmut Ziebart, yesterday met with Czechoslovak and foreign journalists in Prague.

Comrade Ziebart reminded those present that this year's celebrations of the state holiday of the GDR are taking place as more and more attempts are made in Western Europe—in close proximity to the GDR and the ČSSR—to increase tensions in international relations and return to the times of the Cold War. That is why today, more than any time in the past, the main principle of the GDR's foreign policy is the battle for peace and disarmament, for the revival of political dialogue, and the creation of an atmosphere of trust. In this struggle, the GDR closely cooperates with the Soviet Union, the ČSSR, and other states of the socialist community—Helmut Ziebart emphasized.

The GDR celebrates its anniversary as an economically and politically stable state, as a reliable partner of socialist countries—continued the GDR ambassador. In recent years, the GDR has recorded significant economic successes. It raised the living standards of its people and linked the GDR to socialist economic integration.

Bilateral relations between the GDR and the ČSSR have developed dynamically on the basis of an agreement of friendship and aid that was signed four years ago. The decisive impulse emerged from the meeting of comrades Erich Honecker and Gustáv Husák and other high representatives of both countries. We are persuaded that friendly relations between the GDR and the ČSSR and their cooperation with the Soviet Union are bringing significant stimuli for the strengthening of stability in Central Europe. The party and state leadership of the GDR is doing everything it can to further strengthen these ties in the spirit of the traditional friendship of these countries—Helmut Ziebart said in conclusion.

Letters: We Have Faith in the Polish Workers

We, trade unionists, organized in the Union of Workers in Art, Culture, and Community Affairs, are extremely disturbed by news about the distressing situation in neighboring Poland. We resolutely reject the antisocialist conclusions of the "Solidarity" congress, containing a challenge to fight against the principles of socialism, which is a gross interference in the internal affairs of our country.

We also stand behind the working class of Poland, its healthy core, and we believe that under the leadership of its party, the Polish people will defend their historic achievements and that the PPR (Polish People's Republic) will further remain a stalwart member of the socialist community. We believe that the Polish workers will not allow the principles of the Polish socialist state to be eroded.

Participants in the Meeting of Workers in Art, Culture, and Community Affairs in Plzeň.

The Startling Demands of "Solidarity"

WARSAW—The second half of the "Solidarity" congress in Gdańsk continued a discussion about the organization's programmatic resolution. The newspaper *The People's Tribune* yesterday pondered deeply over the content of this document. It is startling, they write, how the programmatic resolution formulates demands and aims of "Solidarity" without taking into account feasibility, and it does so nearly in the form of an ultimatum addressed to the leadership of the PPR.

In reading the chapter entitled "Self-governing Republic," the impression emerges that it is not at all about the Polish People's Republic. The proposals contained in it go beyond the boundaries of the Polish constitution. The conclusion of the document does not offer a compromise, but rather forces the leadership to sign on to obligations flowing from "Solidarity's" own "anticrisis program" and its own form of a so-called "self-governing republic," writes *The People's Tribune*.

Meeting in New York

NEW YORK—The leader of the ČSSR delegation at the 36th Meeting of the General Assembly of the UN, Minister of Foreign Affairs Bohuslav Chňoupek met with his Mozambican colleague Joaquim Albert Chissan. They exchanged opinions on current issues in international politics on the agenda of the General Assembly, especially the difficult situation in Southern Africa, caused by the aggressive politics of South African racists.

The same day Minister Chňoupek met with the minister of foreign affairs of the Republic of Cape Verde Islands, Silvin da Luz.

Invitation to the Delegation

BUDAPEST—At the invitation of the first secretary of the ÚV MSDS (Central Committee of the Hungarian Socialist Workers' Party), János Kádár, and the chairman of the Presidium of the HPR, Pál Losonczi, a party and government delegation of the Angolan People's Republic led by the chairman of the People's Movement for the Liberation of Angola (MPLA), the Labor Party, and President of the Republic, Eduard dos Santos, will arrive in the coming days for an official friendly visit to Hungary, the press agency MTI reports.

A New Partisan Front

SAN SALVADOR—Two partisan fronts in Salvador—the northeastern and southeastern— have joined and a new front under unified leadership controls a large region, especially in the Morazan Departement, the Venceremos transmitter of the Salvadorian patriotic forces announced. According to other reports, partisans have inflicted severe losses on government armies, especially in the eastern part of the country.

Rebel units blocked a strategic highway connecting the Departement San Miguel and Usulatan and also control several sections of the Pan-American Highway. In the San Vicente Departement, partisans carried out a daring attack on a government army barracks.

The So-called Iranian Government in Exile

PARIS—The former Iranian president, Abol Hasan Bani Sadr, and the leader of the opposition organization the People's Mujahadeen, Masud Radzavi, who left Iran in July, yesterday in Paris announced the creation of a so-called Iranian Government in Exile. As Radzavi communicated to Reuters, he himself will hold the function of prime minister in this "government" and Bani Sadr the function of interim "head of state."

Three Iranian military planes yesterday morning attacked oil plants north of the capital of Kuwait, the official Kuwaiti Press Agency KUNA reported. According to these reports, the attack caused a fire in a crude oil storage area about 40 kilometers south of the Kuwait-Iraq border. It did not, however, claim any human lives.

Kopecký, Matěj (1775–1847). Legendary puppeteer who is considered the forefather of the long Czech puppeteering tradition (→ *loutkové divadlo*). In the days when all higher culture was confined to German, Kopecký gave adults and children their first taste of Czech theater (→ *divadlo*) with his traveling puppet shows. Usually portrayed roaming the countryside in a *maringotka* (caravan), Kopecký was just the best known of many puppeteers who put on both emotionally expressive baroque style performances, as well as plays that helped to build a sense of national consciousness.

koruna (crown). The symbol of Czech statehood is the crown of Saint Wenceslas (→ Svatý Václav). The crown was first used for the coronation of → Karel IV in 1347, making it the fourth oldest in Europe. Originally held in the castle of → Karlštejn, the Czech crown jewels are now kept in hiding and only exhibited temporarily on special occasions, which means for one week approximately every five years. Since independence in 1918, the Czech currency has been the *koruna*, which is divided into one hundred *haléřů* (hellers).

Czech and Czechoslovak Banknotes

These are the main banknotes that have circulated on the Czech lands since independence excluding the Nazi occupation. The 100 Kč note from 1920 introduced a tradition of green hundred crown notes and was known as Green Hradčany (Castle Hill), just as later 100 crown notes were known as greens. New notes were introduced through a currency reform in 1953, during which the government confiscated most of the personal savings of its citizens. It was said that by turning the 1971 20 Kč note upside down, one could see the face of popular singer Helena Vondráčková. The 1989 100 Kč note with Klement Gottwald was removed from circulation almost immediately after the revolution in November 1989. When the Czech Republic and Slovakia split in 1993, the countries divided the currency by adding distinctive stamps to the appropriate number of existing notes.

Denomination	Front	Back	Dates of Use
1000 Kč	Woman with globe	Reapers	1919–1937
100 Kč	Slavonic priestess	Peasant women and Hradčany (→ *Hrad*)	1920–1939
5 Kč	Jan Amos → Komenský	State seal	1922–1926
50 Kč	–	Trenčín Castle	1924–1933
500 Kč	Legionnaire	Woman's head, lion, child	1924–1931
20 Kč	Milan Rastislav Štefánik	Alois Rasin	1927–1945
100 Kč	Woman's head	Tomáš G. → Masaryk	1932–1944
1000 Kč	Woman with children	František → Palacký	1935–1944
100 Kč	Woman's head – Young Republic	–	1945–1953
5000 Kč	Bedřich → Smetana	National Theater (→ *Národní divadlo*)	1946–1953
500 Kč	Ján Kollár	Štrba Lake	1946–1953
50 Kč	Milan Rastislav Štefánik	Banská Bystrica	1948–1953
20 Kč	Peasant girl's head	Peasant girl and vase with flowers	1950–1953
25 Kč	Jan → Žižka	City of Tábor	1953–1962
50 Kč	Statues of "Brotherhood"	City of Banská Bystrica	1953–1967
100 Kč	Worker and peasant	Prague Castle	1953–1967
25 Kč	Jan → Žižka	City of Tabor	1958–1971
10 Kč	Peasant child and pioneer (→ *Pionýr*)	Orava dam and factory	1961–1988
100 Kč	Worker and peasant	Charles Bridge and Prague Castle	1962–1993
50 Kč	Russian soldier and partisan	Slovnaft refinery	1965–1991
20 Kč	Jan → Žižka	Žižka at the head of his army	1971–1991
500 Kč	Soldiers	Devín Castle	1973–1993
1000 Kč	Bedřich → Smetana	→ Vyšehrad	1985–1993

Denomination	Front	Back	Dates of Use
10 Kč	Pavel Ország Hviezdoslav	Orava Region	1986–1993
50 Kč	Ludovít Štúr	Bratislava Castle and → SNP Bridge	1987–1993
20 Kč	Jan Amos → Komenský	Tree of Learning	1988–1993
100 Kč	Klement → Gottwald	Prague Castle and Bridge Towers	1989–1989
50 Kč	St. Agnes of Bohemia	Gothic "A" from St. Salvatore Church	1993–
100 Kč	→ Karel IV	Seal of Charles University	1993–
200 Kč	Jan Amos → Komenský	Hands	1993–
500 Kč	Božena → Němcová	Girl's head with flowers and thorns	1993–
1000 Kč	František → Palacký	Eagle, Kroměříž Castle	1993–
5000 Kč	Tomáš G. → Masaryk	Prague buildings	1993–
20 Kč	Přemysl Otakar II	Royal Crown and seal, Golden Bull of Sicily	1994–
2000 Kč	Ema → Destinová	Muse, violin, violoncello	1996–

Source: Jan Bajer *Papírová Platidla Československa 1919–1993, České Republiky, Slovenské Republiky 1993–1999.* Praha: Elektris, 1999.

Kosmas (around 1045–1125). Priest and historian. Kosmas's *Chronika Bohemorum* (Chronicle of the Bohemians) is the first substantial history of the Czech people and the source of many of the legends that form Czech identity. Beginning with the creation of the world and the Tower of Babel, the work moves swiftly on to the arrival of Forefather → Čech, → Libuše, and the origins of the Premyslids (→ *Přemyslovci*), before turning to events more firmly grounded in fact. Relying on literary sources as well as his own fantasy and telling the tale with wit and irony, Kosmas created a history that inspired later chroniclers like Dalimil and → Jirásek and gave the country its founding myths.

kozy (goats). The most common slang expression for a woman's breasts, it literally means "goats." The word is another example of the Czech penchant for animalizing all aspects of human existence (see also → *vůl*). A popular joke goes: How many rabbits can you fit in a bra? Answer: Well, if two goats can get in there…

krajka (lace). One of the oldest folk traditions in the Czech lands—stretching back over four hundred years—is the making of bobbin lace. While its popularity has declined, lace is still displayed along with crystal (→ *sklo*) on many mantlepieces or hung on walls. It is often sold by old women on street corners.

Král Ječmínek (King Barley). Legendary figure. Purportedly the son of a king, Ječmínek was born in a barley field where his mother fled to escape her tyrannical husband. He is prophesied to save the agricultural region of → Haná and all of Moravia when annihilation threatens, and over the years has appeared to the peasants of Haná as a humble traveler bringing good fortune in his wake. Today, Ječmínek is the name of a beer.

Kramářova vila (Kramář's Villa). The Czech version of 10 Downing Street, *Kramářova vila* is the large manor associated with the country's prime minister. Built by the first Czech prime minister, Karel Kramář in

1915, the villa sits above the → Vltava at about the same elevation as the Prague Castle (→ *Hrad*), signaling that the prime minister and president are often at odds. After Kramář, the first prime minister to occupy the residence was Miloš Zeman in 1998, though he only used a small number of the villa's many rooms. The Ministry of Foreign Affairs is also referred to by its place of residence, *Černínská palác* (Černínský's Palace).

kramářská píseň (shopkeeper's ballad). A form of troubadour-type singing and storytelling popular from the sixteenth through the eighteenth century. Usually performed at a fair (→ *jarmark*), these ballads told long, rhyming stories about love found and lost, or sensational actual events like floods or fires; they were thus both entertaining and informative. In later eras, the ballads were widely parodied.

krátký zobák (short beak). A term used to describe the accent of people from → Ostrava and Silesia (→ *Slezsko*), who, influenced by neighboring Poland, shorten all of Czech's long vowels. This can lead to problems with spelling (→ *pravopis*) and occasionally even oral communication. Other regions with their own distinctive accents are → Haná, → Chodsko, and → Slovácko. Most of these have a folksy, old-fashioned appeal. Natives of Prague meanwhile speak in a high-pitched squeal.

Krteček (Little Mole). The title character of a popular series of books and cartoons. Created by Zdeněk Miler in the mid-fifties, Krteček's first adventure had him searching for a pair of pants, because they would give him pockets where he could store things. His winning innocence soon made the Little Mole one of the most beloved figures in the daily cartoons shown every evening (→ *večerníček*).

Krkonoše (Giant Mountains). These mountains, lying on the Polish border to the northeast of Prague, are probably the most popular domestic vacation destination in the country. In winter, hordes of Czechs show up for skiing at resorts like Špindlerův mlýn

(Špindler's Mill), while in the summer hiking and climbing the country's tallest mountain, → Sněžka (Mount Snowy), are equally popular. Legends about the region abound, the most popular referring to Krakonoš, usually portrayed as a white-haired, bearded old man smoking a pipe. Krakonoš's control of the severe weather in the region—which changes from brutal wind, snow, and hail to sunny and balmy in the midst of hours—allows him to help or hurt the denizens of the region according to his mood. A series of television cartoons (→ *večerníček*) about the young Anča and Kuba and their battles with Trautenberk (a relic of the Germans who once inhabited the region) are also set in the mountains and continue to be favorites.

kroj (folk costume). Virtually every Czech village (→ *vesnice*) or region once had its own folk costume. The distinctive designs and colors identified not only the hometown of the wearer, but also his or her occupation and marital status (married women wore head coverings, bachelors had long feathers in their hat). For women the *kroj* usually consisted of a white skirt and embroidered or woven vest over a white blouse. Men typically wore knee-length pants, high socks, and a white shirt with puffy sleeves. Villagers had largely ceased wearing *kroj* by the mid- to late nineteenth century, though it survives in isolated areas, particularly → Slovácko and → Chodsko. Today it is seen mainly at folklore festivals and village celebrations, and its wearers usually rent it from special shops.

Kryl, Karel (1944–1994). Folk singer whose songs symbolized opposition to the communist regime (→ *odboj*). Among Kryl's classic protest songs is "Little Brother, Close the Gate," written in reaction to the Soviet invasion. It begins with the lines, "Little brother, don't sob / Those aren't ghosts / Swallow your tears / Those are just soldiers who came in square steel caravans," and features the powerful refrain, "It's raining and outside dusk is settling / This night won't be a short one / The wolf has a taste for the lamb / Little brother, have you closed the gate?" Kryl emigrated from the country in 1969 and took up residence in Munich where he worked for Radio Free Europe (→ *Rádio Svobodná Evropa*). His commentaries were one of the highlights of the station's schedule, and thousands of Czechs taped his songs and loaned the static-filled recordings to friends. Kryl returned triumphantly in 1989, but quickly became disillusioned with the country's failure to come to terms with the old regime. His songs, however, have outlived both him and his time and continue to be sung around campfires (→ *tramping*).

KSČ (Komunistická strana Československa/ Communist Party of Czechoslovakia). The Communist Party of Czechoslovakia was founded in 1921 and, unlike other communist parties in the region, was allowed to compete legally in elections. Though the party was initially moderate, → Gottwald and his Karlín Boys (so named because they came from the Karlín quarter of Prague) conducted a purge in 1926 and made the party a loyal minion of the Soviet Union. After the war, the communists won a plurality of forty percent in free and fair elections and then took advantage of a government crisis to seize power (→ *Vítězný únor*). Membership in the party required a recommendation from a local government or enterprise council. Only those with the right *kádrový profil* (cadre profile)—i.e., a working class background and the correct political opinions—were given the green light (→ *kádrový spis*). Applicants then had to go through a two-year waiting period during which they had to prove—by participation in political activities—that they would make a good communist. Membership in the party brought benefits like a higher salary and special privileges, but it also required a large time commitment as members had to attend meetings and congresses. Communist party membership was often required for career advancement. Certain management positions were off-limits to all but party members and many joined for purely selfish reasons. Most up-and-comers

recall at least one invitation to "join us" in the party. At its height in the fifties, about a quarter of Czechs, mostly workers, belonged to the party. As mass mobilization died down and a quarter of members were expelled after the Soviet invasion (→ *srpnová invaze*, → *prověrková komise*), these numbers dropped to about ten percent. After the Velvet Revolution (→ *Sametová revoluce*), former members were not punished except in the court of public opinion, where membership can still damage (but not destroy) one's political prospects. In 1990, the party changed its name to the Communist Party of Bohemia and Moravia, but retained its Leninist ideology and consistently receives between ten and twenty percent of the popular vote. Members of the party were known by the slang terms *komouši* or *komanči*. See also → *rudá knížka*.

Ktož jsú Boží bojovníci (Ye Who Are God's Warriors). The title of a chorale sung by Hussite (→ *Husité*) soldiers to inspire them for battle. The song became so associated with their cause and their fierce ways that crusaders sent to put down their heresy reputedly fled after merely hearing it sung.

kůl v plotě (a stake in the fence). Miloš Jakeš, the last communist leader of Czechoslovakia, uttered this phrase to describe his position at a confusing and rambling speech to communist functionaries in the summer of 1989. Jakeš's inability to speak a grammatical sentence in Czech was an object of considerable mirth and proved to Czechs once and for all the incompetence of their leaders. The phrase *"kůl v plotě"* (meaning to be completely alone in the world) has entered popular consciousness as an indication of the bankruptcy of the old regime.

kupónová privatizace (voucher privatization). Method of privatizing state enterprises after the fall of communism. Through voucher privatization every citizen had the right to buy a set amount of vouchers (*kupóny*) for about thirty dollars, that they could then use to bid on shares in the state-owned enterprise of their choice. The plan was heralded by the neoliberal politicians who invented it as a unique Czech path to a market economy in contrast to the management buyouts and public auctions common in other postcommunist countries. Though the public was initially suspicious of the vouchers, heavy advertising by investment funds—especially the now infamous Harvard Fund—ensured mass participation. The genius of the plan was its appeal to Czech egalitarianism (→ *rovnostářství*), as all citizens were given an equal share in the country's economy. Due to corruption, however, many investors lost their money, and today voucher privatization has a negative tinge attached to it.

Květnové povstání (May Uprising). Term used to describe the rebellion of Czechs against their Nazi occupiers (→ *Protektorát*) in May 1945. The uprising, however, broke out only a week before the end of the war when the Germans' fate had already been sealed. Though many were killed during the action, Czechs can still joke, "What's the difference between the May Uprising and the movie about the May Uprising? The movie lasted an hour longer." Nevertheless, as with other wartime heroics (→ SNP), the communists mythologized the event as evidence of the essential goodness of the people. See also → *holubičí povaha*.

Květy (Flowers). The oldest Czech magazine in continuous circulation. It was founded in 1833 as one of the first outlets for original Czech prose and poetry, and as such played an important role in the revival of Czech culture (→ *Národní obrození*). Among its contributors were such greats of Czech literature as → Mácha, Tyl, and → Jirásek. Today it has mutated into one of dozens of interchangeable women's magazines featuring recipes and home decorating tips.

L

Lada, Josef (1887–1957). Graphic artist. If there is one artist who represents the way Czechs visualize their country, it is Josef Lada. He first gained fame with his broadbrush pen and ink illustrations for *The Good Soldier* → *Švejk*, which quickly established the definitive visual form of → Hašek's hero. His illustrations for dozens of books of fairy tales (→ *pohádka*) and nursery rhymes—some of which he even wrote like *Kocour Mikeš* (Mikeš the Cat)—likewise endeared him to child readers. As well loved are his paintings of Czech village life, the countryside, and Christmas celebrations. A typical Lada painting features thick black outlines, bright colors, simple smiling faces, and a myriad of details drawn from Czech traditions. Like Norman Rockwell, he portrayed a happy, idealized, eternally unchanging life—now reproduced endlessly in calendars and postcards—in which Czechs continue to find refuge and relief from an unkind world.

lágr (concentration camp). For Europeans who lived through World War II, it is this German word that was a synonym for concentration camp. Though there were no death camps in the Czech lands, the fortress of Terezín in northern Bohemia served as a transit camp for Czech Jews (→ *Žid*) who were later sent on to Auschwitz. Almost the entire Czech Jewish population perished in *lágry*, while large numbers of non-Jews were sent to German work camps. After the war, the communists set up their own camps in places like Příbram and → Jáchymov. Though westerners use the Russian acronym gulag (which itself incorporates the word *lágr*) to refer to the communist labor camps, Czechs continue to prefer the term *lágr*, signifying that little had changed as communism replaced fascism. Czechs did, however, coin their own acronym for a prisoner in one of these camps. The word *mukl* reputedly stands for *muž určen k likvidaci* (man designated for liquidation).

Landovský, Pavel (1936). Stage and film actor. Though born into a working-class family and never trained as an actor, Landovský proved to be a natural on stage and in front of the camera. His rough-mannered ways and lumbering frame made him into a star in the sixties and early seventies in films like *Soukromá vichřice* (Private Whirlwind) and productions of Chekhov in the *Činoherní klub* (Actors' Club). He has entered Czech consciousness as much for his acting as for his off-stage antics. A practical joker, inveterate skirt-chaser, and storyteller, Landovský's exploits were immortalized in books by Bohumil → Hrabal and Pavel Kohout. After the Soviet invasion, he joined Václav → Havel and others in opposing the new repressive regime and was continually harassed by the secret police. Landovský, however, took it in stride and would lead his pursuers on wild-goose chases through Prague. After signing → *Charta* 77, he left the country for a temporary acting engagement in Austria and was not allowed to return until 1989.

Lány. This small village in central Bohemia boasts the Czech president's summer/vacation home. It was first occupied by → Masaryk in 1918—he and his family are buried nearby—but has come to be used by later presidents as well. It was chosen for its good rail links to Prague and an excellent game park. Important state visitors are received in the residence, and speeches are given *z Lán* (from Lány). The president's main residence, however, is the Prague Castle (→ *Hrad*).

Laurin and Klement. The Czech equivalent of the Ford Model T. Václav Laurin and Václav Klement first joined together to build bicycles, but by 1905 they managed to produce the first Czech-made automobile and eventually founded a factory for manufacturing their cars, known as Laurin & Klements. They ultimately sold their business to the → Škoda Works, which, with their help, went on to produce the Škoda.

Laterna magika. At the 1958 World Expo in Brussels, Czech artists won world-wide acclaim with their unique blend of theater and film called *Laterna magika.* The brainchild of the director Alfréd Radok, this experimental style—with actors performing in tandem with projected images—found a home in the *Laterna magika* Theater in the center of Prague. It was here as well as at the *Činoherní klub* (Actors' Club) that the actors and dissidents (→ *disident*) who played a key role in the Velvet Revolution (→ *Sametová revoluce*) gathered to discuss strategy and issue demands in November 1989.

lázně (spa). The Czech lands are dotted with natural springs which have long been said to have healing properties. In the eighteenth and nineteenth centuries, spas were built around these springs in places like → Karlovy Vary (Carlsbad). Since the original clientele included royalty—Edward VII and Emperor → Franz Joseph were frequent visitors—spa towns quickly built up an appropriate class of hotels, restaurants, and gardens, often in a frilly *Belle Époque* style. A typical stay at a spa would last several weeks or months; the standard cure had patients bathing in the springs, drinking large amounts of the mineral water, and taking mud packs. Visitors could while away the rest of the day walking along finely manicured paths, and in the evening listen to music on colonnaded promenades, gamble in the casino, and attend elegant soirées. Czech spas attracted Europe's finest including such visitors as Goethe, Schiller, Beethoven, Freud, and Marx. Naturally, the communists nationalized the spas and opened them to the working class. Every citizen could thus receive a doctor's note for a free stay at a spa, something that thousands took advantage of despite the minimal health benefits. Today the spa towns have returned to their original wealthy, foreign clientele (though health insurance still covers some visits for ordinary Czechs), with Russians taking a particular shine to them. The best-known Czech spas—Karlovy Vary (Carlsbad), Mariánské lázně (Marienbad), and Františkovy lázně (Franzesbad)—are in western Bohemia, though every region of the country has at least one. Each spa specializes in a specific illness such as rheumatism, gastrointestinal problems, or tuberculosis. In the minds of Czechs, spas are associated with waferlike cookies (called *oplatky*), thin cups used for drinking the waters, a break from the daily grind, and even the possibility of romance or infidelity.

legionáři (legionnaires). Members of Czech army units that fought on the side of the allies against Austria-Hungary in World War I. The most famous units were formed from captured soldiers and deserters on the Eastern front who created the so-called Czech legions. At the legendary battles of Zborov and Bachmač in Russia, these legionnaires defeated German units and proved themselves a force to be reckoned with, a fact that helped to convince the allies that the Czechs deserved an independent state after the war. When Russia concluded a separate peace with the Axis, the Czech units—some 40,000 strong—were transferred to the Western front by way of Vladivostok. The Bolsheviks tried to recruit or disarm them, but, in their Siberian anabasis, the Czechs took control of the entire trans-Siberian railroad line to ease their exit. After the war, legionnaires were welcomed home as heroes, and many took leading positions in independent Czechoslovakia. The heroism of the legionnaires, however, had to compete with → Hašek's → Švejk as the image of the Czech soldier in the war. Under communism, all memory of the legionnaires was erased because of their successful battles against the supposedly invincible Russians and their fervent belief in freedom and democracy. Today, however, they are an object of patriotic pride.

letní noc (summer night). Outdoor parties held in villages on summer nights. They usually take place at a park, soccer field, or swimming pool, which is decorated with hanging colored lights. Music is provided by both brass bands (→ *dechovka*) and rock bands, often alternating in a format known as three and three (three songs for adults followed by three for young people). The whole village as well as young people from neighboring villages turn out for a night of dancing and drinking beer that does not end until morning. It is at these summer night celebrations that many Czechs find their first love (→ sex). See also → *zábava*.

letní zahrádka (summer beer garden). No summer is complete without a cold beer at a summer beer garden. Almost every pub (→ *hospoda*) has its own beer garden or at least places a table or two in its front or back yard.

lev (lion). A two-tailed lion is the Czech national symbol and appears on its coat of arms. It is said to come from the legendary King Bruncvík, a sort of Czech Ulysses, who befriended a lion during his adventures and brought him back to Prague. The domestic equivalent of the Academy Awards is the Czech Lion (→ Barrandov).

lhota (freehold). The most common name for Czech towns and villages. Over two hundred different municipalities have some form of the word *lhota* in their name. The reason is that the citizens who founded these towns were freed of the requirement to pay taxes in return for the service of expanding the country's economy. Other common town names include *brod* (ford), *újezd* (parish), and *ústí* (river mouth), which are modified by words like *starý* (old), *nový* (new), *horní* (upper), and *dolní* (lower). Small or insignificant towns are sometimes referred to humorously as *Horní Dolní* (Upper Lower).

Libuše. Legendary princess. Libuše was one of three daughters of King Krok, himself a descendent of the legendary Forefather → Čech. Each daughter possessed special powers: Kazi was a healer, Teta a priestess, and Libuše could foretell the future. After inheriting the crown from her father, Libuše was challenged by one of her subjects, who objected to a woman ruling over him. In response, Libuše chose a common ploughman named Přemysl as her husband, thus founding the Czech royal line of Premyslids (→ *Přemyslovci*). The decision might be considered an early indication of Czech egalitarianism (→ *rovnostářství*) and distrust of aristocracy (→ *šlechta*). Libuše is best known for her prophecy that on the seven hills of Prague (→ *Praha*) there would grow a city whose fame would one day reach the heavens. Libuše's marriage and prophecies became the subject of an opera by → Smetana, which opened the National Theater (→ *Národní divadlo*).

lid (the people). It was nineteenth century patriots (→ *Národní obrození*) who first associated the Czech nation with its ordinary people, but it was the communists who made "the people" into a political manifesto. They claimed to represent "the people" and everything they did was for "the people" or more frequently "the working people." The communist army was thus called the Czechoslovak People's Army, and the country was full of people's schools and people's libraries. One of the highest compliments that can still be paid to a person is that they are *lidový* (of the people, meaning folksy).

Lidice. Village near → Kladno leveled to the ground by the Nazis on June 10, 1942. Lidice was singled out for destruction in retaliation for the assassination of Reichsprotektor Reinhard Heydrich (→ *Heydrichiáda*). Every male in the town was executed, females were sent off to concentration camps (→ *lágr*), and children capable of re-education assigned to German families. In all, 340 of the village's 500 citizens were killed and the town itself razed. The ostensible reason for choosing Lidice was that residents had contact with the assassins, but in fact the Nazis simply wanted to set an example to remaining members of the Czech resistance (→ *odboj*). The warning was largely successful at home, though it proved a powerful rallying cry for the allies abroad, where several countries renamed towns after Lidice. After the war, Lidice was frequently invoked by a communist regime that styled itself the sworn enemy of fascism.

Lidová škola umění (People's School of Art). At the end of the school day, artistically or musically talented children attend these schools (renamed Basic Art Schools with the fall of communism) to learn a musical instrument, painting, or ballet. Their popularity is testimony to the important place of art in Czech culture (→ *umělec*).

Lidové milice (People's Militia). The loyal army reserves of the communist state. Their origins were in factory guards created after the war to prevent sabotage. These guards were controlled by the communist unions who used them both for propaganda purposes—distributing leaflets to workers—and to occupy factories during the coup (→ *Vítězný únor*). After the communists took power, the factory guards were re-christened as the *Lidové milice*, a sort of second army that was politically loyal—militiamen were almost exclusively party members—and could be called out in case of civil unrest. Made up of actual workers, the militia was presumed to be a reliable fighting force if the regular army refused to attack citizens. Indeed, it was re-ferred to as the *úderná pěst dělnické třídy* (the clenched fist of the working class). Members of the militia worked in ordinary jobs, but were given frequent leaves for military training and political indoctrination. The reward was better pay and considerable privileges. The *Lidové milice* was called out to break up demonstrations in 1968 (→ *srpnová invaze*) and again in 1988–1989. By November 1989, however, the old, overweight members saw that the time had passed for their hard-line views (→ *Sametová revoluce*).

Lidové noviny (People's News). The country's oldest daily newspaper. Founded in 1893 by the Moravian politician Adolf Stránský, *Lidové noviny* was originally published in the city of → Brno. Its most famous era was between the wars when editors and writers like Ferdinand Peroutka, Eduard Bass, and Karel → Čapek made the paper not only the country's most literate, but also its voice of liberalism and democracy in a time of political extremes. The communist government shut the paper down, but dissidents (→ *disident*) began putting out a → *samizdat* version in the late eighties. After the revolution, *Lidové noviny* again became a popular daily and resumed its democratic and intellectual ways as a strong supporter of Václav → Havel. The paper later became a platform for the neo-liberal reforms of Václav Klaus (→ *kupónová privatizace*).

lidovka (folk song). Traditional Czech folk songs, known colloquially as *lidovky*, are learned as early as nursery school and frequently sung around the campfire or in pubs. Their texts deal with family relationships ("*Ach synku, synku*"—Oh, Son, Son, → Masaryk's favorite song), love found or lost ("*Lásko, bože, lásko*"—Love, My God, Love), drinking ("*Vínečko bílé*"—Little White Wine), military service ("*Na tú svatú Kateřinu*"—On Saint Katherine's Day, the day that recruits entered the army), or the countryside. Several begin with the preposition *Okolo* (Around) followed by a place name (Hradec, Suč, or Třeboň). The melodies are typically → polkas, waltzes, or mazurkas and can be danced to. Many are guaranteed to bring a tear to the eye, and the best Czech classical music composers have borrowed them (→ Smetana, → Dvořák, Janáček). Another class of songs are those that can be attributed to real authors (rather than simply the people as in a true *lidovka*), but which have *zlidověla* (been folkicized). This includes patriotic songs like "*Čechy krásné, Čechy mé*" (Beautiful Bohemia, My Bohemia) or "*Ta naše písnička česká*" (Our Czech Song), as well as popular songs by the likes of Karel → Kryl and Honza → Nedvěd.

Limonádový Joe (Lemonade Joe). A musical parody of American westerns that was the most popular film of the sixties. It tells the story of Lemonade Joe, a teetotaling sheriff who brings the law to the corrupt town of Stetson City, saves the girl, and teaches residents to drink the soft drink (in Czech *limonáda* means soft drink, not just lemonade) Kola Loka instead of whiskey. The film's most famous line is the rhyming slogan, "*Chceš-li správným chlapem býti, musíš Kola Loku píti*" (If you want to be a tough guy, you have to drink Kola Loka). The film has become so fixed in

Most Watched Czech Films

These are the most watched Czech films as measured by number of tickets sold. They are grouped by decade because admissions dropped considerably after the fifties with the emergence of television. The only films to appear on both this list and the list of critics' top 50 choices are *Lemonade Joe, Loves of a Blonde, That Cat*, and *Kolya*. It is worth noting that with only a few exceptions, all of these films are comedies or fairytales.

English Title	Year	Director	Notes	Admissions
1950–1959				
The Proud Princess	1952	Zeman	Classic fairytale where manual labor teaches a princess humility	8,222,695
Once Upon a Time There Was a King	1954	Zeman	Fairytale version of King Lear	5,914,257
The Princess with the Golden Star	1959	Frič	A princess disguised in mouse fur finds her prince	5,033,874
The Strakonice Bagpiper	1955	Steklý	Filmed version of classic play about a village bagpiper (→ Švanda dudák)	4,567,494
Holiday with Angel	1952	Zeman	A ticket inspector enjoys collective recreation (→ revizor)	4,259,875
Smugglers of Death	1959	Kachyňa	Thriller about border guards (→ pohraniční stráž)	4,100,916
Playing with the Devil	1956	Mach	Fairytale in which a soldier rescues two girls from the devil	4,038,676
The Good Soldier → Švejk	1956	Steklý	The classic film version of → Hašek's novel	3,950,722
Angel in the Mountains	1955	Zeman	A ticket inspector on vacation again	3,788,716
The Show Is On	1954	O. Lipský	The state-owned circus comes to town	3,740,959

English Title	Year	Director	Notes	Admissions
1960–1969				
Lemonade Joe	1964	O. Lipský	Cult parody of American Westerns (→ *Limonádový Joe*)	4,556,352
If a Thousand Clarinets	1964	Roháč and Svitáček	Musical in which soldiers' guns turn into musical instruments (→ *Semafor*)	4,065,720
The Hop Pickers	1964	Rychman	Musical about young love on a summer work brigade (→ *Starci na chmelu*)	2,975,163
The Awfully Sad Princess	1968	Zeman	Musical fairytale in which two kings arrange for their children to be married	2,903,864
Men About Town	1969	Podskalský	Three manual laborers try to become sophisticated	2,836,686
The Witch Hunt	1969	Vávra	Historical film about seventeenth century witch trials	2,657,920
The Slinger	1960	Kachyňa	A little boy helps an army unit in WWII	2,295,078
Loves of a Blonde	1965	Forman	Bittersweet comedy of a factory town full of women	2,255,858
A Higher Principle	1960	Krejčík	A professor decides to oppose the Nazis after three students are executed	2,002,246
That Cat	1963	Jasný	A magician's cat turns people into the color of their personality	1,995,428
1970–1979				
Jachym, Put Him into the Machine	1974	O. Lipský	A shy auto mechanic is emboldened by a computer prediction	2,928,609
Three Nuts for Cinderella	1973	Vorlíček	The classic version of Cinderella	2,849,651
How to Drown Dr. Mráček	1974	Vorlíček	Crazy comedy set among the water sprites (→ *vodník*) of the Vltava	2,573,342
Apple Game	1976	Chytilová	Feminist comedy set in a hospital delivery room	2,237,240
The Girl on the Broomstick	1971	Vorlíček	A beautiful witch visits a high school	2,146,588
"Mareček, Please Pass Me a Pen"	1976	O. Lipský	Comedy about factory workers going to night school (→ *Hujer*)	2,062,306
You're a Widow, Sir	1970	Vorlíček	Crazy comedy full of brain transplants	1,862,463

English Title	Year	Director	Notes	Admissions
The Weddings of Sir Vok	1970	Steklý	Historical comedy about the wedding of an inveterate skirt-chaser	1,792,390
We'll Kick Up a Fuss Tomorrow, Darling…!	1976	Schulhoff	Comedy about small-town life	1,613,918
Let Him Face the Music	1978	Rychman	Musical comedy about composer whose talent emerges only when his life is in danger	1,504,044
1980–1989				
My Sweet Little Village	1985	Menzel	Gentle comedy about village life centered on a truckdriver and his mildly retarded assistant	4,428,556
Sun, Hay, and a Couple of Slaps	1989	Troška	Second installment in trilogy of lowbrow village comedies	4,058,095
Sun, Hay, Strawberries	1983	Troška	Lowbrow comedy about village life	3,352,398
Cutting it Short	1980	Menzel	Gentle comedy about life in pre-war brewery based on an autobiographical novel by → Hrabal	2,747,695
Big Money	1988	Olmer	Drama about blackmarket money changers in Prague (→ *vekslák*)	2,659,372
With You the World Is Wonderful	1982	Poledňáková	Three husbands take their kids on a ski vacation (→ *S tebou mě baví svět*)	2,587,136
Nurses	1983	Kachyňa	Drama about a young nurse forced to work in a small town	1,969,687
Every Girl Loves a Soldier	1987	Tuček	Light comedy about army life	1,876,197
Love from the Arcade	1984	Soukup	A teenage window washer gets caught up with criminals	1,754,147
How Poets Lose Their Illusions	1984	Klein	Second installment in series about the lives of med students	1,745,229
1990–1999				
The Tank Battalion	1991	Olmer	Nostalgic comedy about army life in the fifties	2,022,233
The Black Barons	1992	Sirový	Comic story of soldier/prisoners (→ *Černí baroni*)	1,470,531
Kolya	1996	J. Svěrák	A confirmed bachelor ends up with a Russian son; an Oscar winner	1,346,000
Cozy Dens	1999	Hřebejk	Nostalgic comedy about growing up in the sixties	1,059,182
The Elementary School	1991	J. Svěrák	Tragicomedy set at the end of WWII	1,040,135

English Title	Year	Director	Notes	Admissions
Discostory no. 2	1991	Soukup	Sequel to a popular teen comedy	985,113
Sun, Hay, Erotica	1991	Troška	Third sequel of a low-brow comedy	968,822
The End of Poets in Bohemia	1993	Klein	Fourth in series about med students	967,564
The Inheritance	1992	Chytilová	Comedy about a villager who hits the jackpot in restitution	810,862
She Picked Violets with Dynamite	1992	Růžička	Low-brow comedy about a family trying to get rich with a travel agency	736,221

Source: Compiled by the author from Václav Březina, ed., *Lexikon českého filmu* (Praha: Cinema, 1996).

popular memory that there is now a Kola Loka drink and a radio station in Prague named Lemonade Joe. The country's fascination with the American West—common in Europe thanks to Karl May's → Vinnetou novels—has even led to the construction of several Wild West theme parks (→ country).

lípa (linden or lime tree). National symbol of the Czech and other Slavic nations. The linden stands for freedom and independence and appears frequently in nationalist artwork (→ *Lucerna*) and state symbols.

Lipany. Battle that ended the Hussite Wars (→ Hus, → *husité*). Though the Hussite *polní vojsko* (field army) founded by Jan → Žižka had survived crusade after crusade and even the death of its founder, it finally met its end at Lipany, just east of Prague. The battle took place in 1434, when Czech Catholics united with moderate Hussites in Prague to attack the radical Taborites under their charismatic leader Prokop Holý. The fratricidal battle, pitting Czech against Czech, left 10,000 fighters dead and the *boží bojovníci* (God's Warriors) finally defeated. A panoramic painting and three-dimensional diorama of the battle by Luděk Marold is the object of countless school fieldtrips.

loutkové divadlo (puppet theater). One of the few folk traditions that has survived into modernity is puppet theater. Though originally a form of entertainment for adults and later a way of spreading Czech nationalism (→ Kopecký), puppet theater is now mainly performed for children. Many larger towns have a permanent puppet theater—the most popular is the → Spejbl and Hurvínek Theater—and a variety of troupes bring plays directly into schools. Their subjects are usually traditional fairy tales (→ *pohádka*) with princes and princesses and good triumphing over evil. Czechs also have a unique tradition of using puppets in film. It began with Jiří Trnka, who combined puppets with animation in a manner much admired among connoisseurs. Puppets come in a variety of forms, from marionettes to shadow puppets, and are a popular purchase for tourists in Prague. Children meanwhile often build their own puppet theaters at home. The popularity of puppet theater may be explained by the country's position as a puppet in the hands of great powers.

Lucerna (The Lantern). Written by Alois → Jirásek in 1905, this classic play tells the complicated story of the miller Libor who must defend his foster daughter and his linden tree (→ *lípa*) from nefarious forces. The play is chock-full of characters—including two water sprites (→ *vodník*)—making it a favorite of community theaters (→ *ochotnické divadlo*). It has both tragic and comic elements and even appeals to nationalist sensibilities when Libor resolves that he will not surrender the linden which has been in his family for ages. The play ends with the lady of the manor destroying the lantern, a symbol of her power, and Libor winning his freedom.

lufťák. Term used to refer to city dwellers who own a cottage (→ *chata*) or farmhouse (→ *chalupa*) in the countryside. It is derived from a verb meaning "to give an airing," which is exactly what the urbanites are doing. Permanent village (→ *vesnice*) residents often use it in a derogatory sense and have a decidedly lukewarm attitude to the many who use villages as a weekend and summer recreation area rather than a home and workplace.

lustrace (lustration). Deriving from an older term meaning ritual purification, *lustrace* is the name given to the post-communist practice of purging former communists from government service. After the Velvet Revolution, it was decided not to prosecute individuals who had collaborated with the old regime, but rather to ban them from high political posts. Indeed, so many were caught up in the regime's clutches that a real accounting would be too painful. The process was controversial because of procedural difficulties—it was originally impossible to lodge an appeal and some appear to have been unjustly accused of collaboration—but seemed preferable to either criminal trials or a general amnesty. This middle course is an indication of ambivalent attitudes towards the communist regime (→ *komunismus*).

M

Má vlast (My Country). Bedřich → Smetana's famous cycle of symphonic poems. Written in 1879, by which time he was deaf, these compositions paint an emotionally powerful and heartwarming picture of the Czech lands. They take the listener to six destinations across space and time—from the ancient castle of → Vyšehrad to the river → Vltava to the legendary rebel Šárka (→ *Dívčí válka*) to Bohemia's woods and fields (*luhy a háje*) to the Hussite (→ *husité*) fortress of Tábor, and finally to the sleeping knights of → Blaník. The Vltava section—which follows the river from its humble, meandering origins in the → Šumava Mountains to its broad majesty around Prague—is among the most beautiful and widely recognized pieces of Czech music. The cycle is played every year to open the Prague Spring music festival (→ *Pražské jaro*).

Mácha, Karel Hynek (1810–1836). The Czech exemplar of the great romantic poet. With his poem *Máj* (May) (→ *Byl pozdní večer*), Mácha virtually invented the Czech poetic idiom and brought the spirit of romanticism to the country. And like other romantic poets Mácha lived his creed. Attired in a gray cloak with red lining, he loved to prowl the countryside, visiting abandoned or ruined castles, graveyards, and execution grounds. One of his favorite spots for trekking in northern Bohemia—and later a popular tourist destination—is now known as *Máchův kraj* (Mácha's Region). To cement his position as the country's leading romantic, Mácha died fighting a fire at the tender age of twenty-six, just days before his wedding to his beloved Lori.

Maďarsko (Hungary). Though the two countries were once military rivals and then jockeyed for position in the Habsburg Monarchy, Hungary now mainly elicits a ho-hum from most Czechs, probably because it is so similar to their own country. Under communism, Czechs visited Hungary mainly for low-budget vacations at Lake Balaton or to gain a glimpse of Western culture—Hungary was far more open than Czechoslovakia and thus hosted Western rock bands and sold Western brand names. The reputedly difficult Hungarian language is sometimes parodied by Czechs.

máje (maypoles). A tall maypole decorated with wreaths, flowers, and banners is traditionally erected in village squares on the eve of May 1. In the past, young people not only danced under the pole, they also had to guard it from their rivals in neighboring villages, who would try to steal it during the night. At the same time, boys would place smaller maypoles (*májky*) in front of the homes of girls they were wooing. The tradition of maypoles survives today in many villages, especially in → Slovácko.

1. máj (May 1). International Workers' Day. As elsewhere in the world, the first of May celebrates workers and is an opportunity for trade unionists to march on the streets. Though the holiday actually commemorates the 1886 Haymarket riot in imperialist America, there was no greater celebration under communism than May 1. All workers were required to gather in the morning with red banners or flags and march past tribunes of communist dignitaries. Each factory had its own float (known as an *alegorický vůz* or allegorical vehicle), demonstrating its production techniques. During the parade, marchers frequently shouted, "Long Live May First" or "Long Live the Soviet Union," and the crowd would respond with a loud "Hurrah." Children marched in their Pioneer uniforms (→ *Pionýr*). Television stations meanwhile carried live broadcasts of similar parades from across the Soviet bloc. Like every holiday, festivities concluded with heavy drinking. May 1 remains a national holiday today, though Czechs have now adopted the European style of celebrating the working man with clashes on the streets between anarchists and the police.

majáles (spring student celebration). During the month of May, university students hold street parties with music and alcohol in celebration of the end of the school year. The students choose a king and queen—Allen Ginsberg was memorably elected king in 1968—who preside over the festivities.

Major Zeman. The hero of a popular TV cop show from the seventies. The series, lasting thirty episodes, followed Zeman's battles with criminals, subversives, and dissidents over the years 1945–1975. The show was notable for its aping of American models; it had a catchy opening sequence and dramatic endings. Many of the cases were based on actual events—from armed counter-revolutionaries in the fifties (→ Mašín) to smugglers (→ *pohraniční stráž*), murderers, spies, and even counterculture music groups (→ Plastic People). Indeed, the series was produced under the auspices of the Ministry of the Interior as homage to the work of the communist police force (→ StB, → VB). Though it shows its age—both ideologically and stylistically—many Czechs felt a campy thrill when it was rebroadcast in the late nineties.

mák (poppy seed). Poppy seeds are used to add flavor to a variety of foods. Most loved are twisted or rolled pastries that contain poppy seeds in between layers. The seeds are also ground up, mixed with sugar, and served with pasta.

malá domů (literally, little thing to the home). Under communism and even afterwards, it was common for workers to "borrow" goods from their workplace. A cook might take home a cut of meat, a construction worker building materials, and a bureaucrat office supplies. All of these items were known as *malá domů*. Because everyone worked for the state and goods were in such short supply, this stealing was not considered a crime or even moral failing. It was said that whoever did not steal from the state stole from his family.

maloměšťáctví (provinciality; literally "small-town mentality"). In contrast to the culture of most European countries, Czech national traditions arose more from the commoners than the aristocracy. After the Battle of White Mountain (→ *Bílá hora*), the Czech nobility was wiped out and the only people left to carry Czech culture were peasants. The result was a provincial culture that persists to this day. It is manifested, for example, in a high degree of egalitarianism (→ *rovnostářství*). With little fealty to either of the traditional bases for hierarchy—both the aristocracy (→ *šlechta*) and church (→ *katolická církev*) were foreign impositions—Czechs view each other as equals. They also tend to look askance at those who raise themselves up above others. Indeed, most consider envy (→ *závist*) to be the country's dominant personality trait, which made for a society highly receptive to the class warfare of the communists. The country's provincial roots also account for the idealization of village life (→ *vesnice*) as the essence of Czechness.

Malý Bobeš (Little Bobeš). Popular children's book. The title character of *Malý Bobeš* is a young boy growing up in a small village. When his father gets a job in the big city, the family is forced to move, and the sensitive Bobeš has to make new friends and adapt to a new environment. Though the book was written in the twenties, it remained required reading under communism because the family belonged to the lower rungs of the working class. Like the children's book heroes Mirek Dušín and Kája Mařík, Malý Bobeš has become a model of good behavior for generations of youngsters.

malý český člověk (the little Czech). A commonly used phrase to designate the typical, unassuming Czech, it carries both positive and negative connotations. On the negative side, the little Czech spreads malicious gossip about his neighbors, informs (→ *udavač*) on others to get ahead, envies (→ *závist*) any success of his peers, and rarely stands up for the persecuted. On the positive side, he is independent, hardworking, clever, and law-abiding. The little Czech is small not just as an individual, but also because he lives in a small country destined to have its fate decided by the more powerful. But at his or her best, the little Czech overcomes this disadvantage and, through persistence and talent (→ *zlaté ručičky*), shows the outside world that he or she (and by extension the Czech nation) is worthy of admiration and respect. It is this achievement, whether in reality (→ Karel IV, → Komenský, → Smetana) or fiction (→ Cimrman), that turns a little Czech into a great Czech.

mandelinka bramborová (Colorado beetle). In the early years of building communism, the regime tried to gain support by portraying the country as under threat from imperialist warmongers in the West. One of the largest propaganda campaigns focused on the Colorado beetle (or *americký brouk*, American beetle, as it was also known) that was supposedly unleashed on Czechoslovakia to destroy its crops. Postwar Czech agriculture was in fact hit by infestations of pests, and citizens were enlisted to remove them by hand. The cause of the problem, however, was not American spies or beetles, but the collectivization of agriculture (→ JZD) which destroyed the furrows between fields

where insect-eating birds roosted. The Colorado beetle nevertheless remained a potent symbol of the Cold War and the American threat (→ *Amerika*).

Mánes, Josef (1820–1871). Drawing inspiration from his travels in the countryside and his study of folk customs (→ *kroj*), Mánes was the first Czech painter since the baroque period to achieve worldwide renown. A devoted national awakener, he painted scenes of Czechs dressed in folk costumes, illustrated the Kingscourt Manuscripts (→ *Rukopis královédvorský*), and proposed costumes and emblems for the → *Sokol* patriotic movement. His most admired work is his twelve "idylls from the life of the Bohemian peasant," which were added to the Prague astronomical clock. Even Mánes's greatness did not put him in the first league of European art, testimony to the fact that Czechs are more a people of the ear than the eye.

mánička. Loosely translated as hippie, the word refers to a young man with long hair, who might also be a fan of rock music and wear blue jeans and T-shirts (→ Rifle). Communism's strict control of public morality meant that *máničky* were often the object of insults or discrimination.

Maria Theresa (1717–1780). Habsburg empress. Of the eighteen Habsburgs who sat on the Czech throne, Maria Theresa was the only woman. She inherited a backwards monarchy drained by war and after forty years of rule left it a modern, centralized empire. Despite her conservative opinions, she was an energetic, decisive ruler who allowed her enlightened advisors to reform the empire's taxation, transportation, and educational systems, all while giving birth to sixteen children. Though she never forgave the Czechs for opposing her coronation, she is probably the only one of their many foreign rulers who today enjoys widespread popularity. The phrase *za doby Marie Terezie* (during the time of Maria Theresa) is used to refer to something in the distant past.

mariáš. Popular Czech card game. In just about every Czech pub (→ *hospoda*) one can find a table of old men playing *mariáš*. The rules are somewhat similar to bridge as the three players win points by collecting tricks. One player makes a bid to win a given number of tricks; the other two players try to prevent him. *Mariáš* uses a German set of thirty-two cards: ace, king, overknave (*svršek*), underknave (*spodek*), and ten through seven in the four suits of acorns, hearts, leaves and bells. The name comes from the French for marriage, refering to marriage between the king and the overknave which is worth extra points. More complex than the game itself are the betting permutations, though the stakes are usually measured in *haléře*, the Czech equivalent of pennies (→ *koruna*).

Maryša. Probably the best-known and most frequently performed play in the Czech theatrical repertoire. Written by the brothers Alois and Vilém Mrštík in 1894, the play's eponymous heroine is a young girl forced by her father to marry an older widower she does not love. The climax of the play comes when her former beau returns from the army and is attacked by her husband. To save her lover, Maryša poisons her husband and is led off to the gallows. The appeal of the play lies in the melodrama, the traditional village (→ *vesnice*) setting, and the Moravian (→ *Morava*) dialect the characters speak.

Masaryk, Tomáš Garrigue (1850–1937). The first president of independent Czechoslovakia. If → Karel IV is the *otec vlasti* (father of the homeland) and → Palacký is the *otec národa* (father of the nation), then Masaryk is the nation's *tatíček* (little father). Born to a Czech-German mother and Slovak father in southern Moravia (→ *Morava*), Masaryk first made his name as a professor of sociology in Vienna where he took on taboo subjects like suicide and prostitution. He also figured prominently in Czech patriotic circles until his denunciation of forged historical manuscripts (→ *Rukopis královédvorský*) damaged his reputation. He again hurt

his standing, but developed a reputation for courage when he defended Leopold Hilsner, a Jew unjustly charged with ritual murder. His main contribution to the cause of the Czech nation, however, came in writings and speeches like → *Česká otázka* (The Czech Question) where he laid out a compelling interpretation of the Czech place in the world. In his rendering, the Czech contribution to the world and the reason they should have their own state was the humanistic and democratic vision of the Hussites (→ *husité*) and Union of Brethren (→ *Jednota bratrská*). Masaryk spent the First World War agitating for a Czechoslovak state in America, and having achieved his aim he became the obvious choice to be the country's first president. Reelected three times, he was the embodiment

---

Historical Figures Mentioned with Pride

This is a poll from the year 1990 asking Czechs which historical figures they mention with pride. Jan Masaryk was the son of President Masaryk and foreign minister. Štefánik was a Slovak pilot who helped to found Czechoslovakia. Dubček was the head of the Communist Party during the Prague Spring.

PERSON	PERCENTAGE
Tomáš G. → Masaryk	46.2
→ Charles IV (Karel IV)	13.2
Edvard → Beneš	11.9
Jan →Hus	10.0
J. A. → Komenský	8.6
Ludvík → Svoboda	8.5
Jan Masaryk	8.0
Jan → Žižka	4.2
Milan Rastislav Štefánik	4.0
Alexandr Dubček	3.1

Source: Ladislav Holý. *The Little Czech and the Great Czech Nation.* New York: Cambridge University Press, 1996, p. 135.

of the independent, democratic, and prosperous Czechoslovak state. While revisionist historians have characterized him as a manipulator and fixer, few doubt that he had the country's best interests at heart. Like many great statesman, he is known by his initials, T.G.M., the G coming from the surname of his American wife, Charlotte Garrigue. He is also referred to as the President–Liberator and is usually portrayed in old age with a bald pate, thick beard, and dressed in horse-riding attire. Though the communists avoided mention of him, he is now seen as the country's kind, all-knowing, and infallible father.

Mašín. Josef Mašín (1896–1942) and Josef Balabán (1894–1941), both former legionnaires (→ *legionáři*), joined with Václav Morávek (1904–1942) to form the legendary "Three Kings" who fought a guerilla campaign against the Nazis during World War II. They not only gathered intelligence for the allies, but also organized offensive actions, most famously an attempted assassination of Himmler in Berlin. All three were killed by the Germans—Balabán under torture, Mašín by execution, and Morávek in a shootout. After the war, Mašín's sons, Josef and Ctirad, remained true to their father's ideals by fighting a guerilla war against the communist regime. Despite an international manhunt, they ultimately blasted their way into West Berlin in 1953, and later settled in the United States. Needless to say, not only the brothers, but the Three Kings as well, were ignored and scorned under communism in favor of a myth that equated antifascist resistance with communism. The younger Mašíns are today viewed ambivalently with some considering them heroes for their attempted rebellion, and others villains because of the trail of dead bodies they left in their wake. The brothers have still never returned to the country because of bitter memories, the mixed feelings of the Czech public, and fear of prosecution.

maso bude vbrzku (meat will come soon). This phrase was party First Secretary Antonín Novotný's response to complaints about persistent shortages in basic goods in the early days of communism. It has entered popular memory because the word "*vbrzku*" (meaning soon) can be interpreted as "*v Brzku*" (meaning in the town of Brzko). Citizens thus joked to each other whether they knew where this meat-filled town of Brzko was. It turned out that shortages of most products remained until the very end of communism. The appearance of all sorts of consumer goods in unimaginable quantities has been probably the greatest change since the transition to democracy.

masopust (carnival; literally "meat fast"). The run-up to Lent traditionally began on the Thursday before Ash Wednesday with a pig roast (→ *zabíjačka*) to stock up for the coming feast. The next days were marked by gorging—especially of holiday pastries (*koblihy*)—and music and dancing in the local pub (→ *hospoda*). The holiday culminated on Tuesday with a masked parade around the village—popular costumes were of bears, Jews (→ *Žid*), horses, and Turks—and celebrations went on until midnight, the official start of Lent. These traditions were another of the casualties of the country's rapid modernization; virtually all that remains of them is the occasional masked ball (→ *ples*).

Masopust, Josef (1931). Soccer legend. Masopust made his name as the center half of → Dukla Praha during its glory years in the early sixties. Known as the country's greatest technical player, his trademark move was the Masopust slalom where he would dribble past three or four defenders before scoring. The high point of his career came in 1962 when he became the first Czech to win the Golden Ball as Europe's player of the year (the second was Pavel Nedvěd in 2003). That same year he also scored one of the most famous goals in Czech soccer history when he put the country ahead 1-0 in the World Cup Final against Brazil before the team succumbed to the champions. Masopust was recently voted the Czech football player of the century.

Czech Footballer of the Century

This poll was conducted by the magazine *Gól* (Goal) with a jury of 34 former players, 16 first-league coaches, and 15 journalists. *Gól* also conducted a fans' poll in which the final order was Bican first, Masopust second, and Plánička third.

Rank	Player	Team	Position	Votes
1	Josef → Masopust	→ Dukla	midfielder	591
2	Pepi → Bican	Rapid, Slavia	forward	524
3	Ivo Viktor	Dukla	goalkeeper	370
4	František Plánička	→ Slavia	goalkeeper	361
5	Pavel Nedvěd	Sparta, Lazio, Juventus	midfielder	251
6	Antonín → Panenka	Bohemians	midfielder	231
7	Ladislav Novák	Dukla	forward	145
8	Karol Dobiáš	Spartak Trnava	defender	127
9	Andrej Kvašňák	→ Sparta	midfielder	112
10	Zdeněk Nehoda	Dukla	midfielder	101

Source: *Mladá fronta Dnes*, 28 December 2000.

masová píseň (mass song). Rousing songs praising the communist regime. Most were composed during the Stalinist fifties and are indelibly associated with that era even though they were sung until the very end of communism. They featured inane lyrics about the beauties of socialism and the men who built it and carried titles like "*Sláva tankům*" (Hurrah for the Tanks), "*Za Gottwalda vpřed*" (Forward for → Gottwald), or "*Píseň o Fučíkovi*" (A Song about → Fučík). The songs were often performed by massive choruses—like the legendary *Armádní umělecký soubor* (Army Chorus)—and were a necessary component of any state holiday as well as school curricula. The best-known composer in the genre was Radim Drejsl whose most famous composition, "*Rozkvetlý svět*" (World in Blossom), features the lines "It's enough just to look around to see how much beauty surrounds us / Smoke from the factories and children in the sandbox." Upon return from his first trip to the Soviet Union in 1953, Drejsl was so disillusioned by what he saw that he took his own life.

Mattoni. Brand of mineral water. Drawn from the springs of → Karlovy Vary (Carlsbad), Mattoni is ordered by name in all coffeehouses (→ *kavárna*), restaurants, and bars (→ *hospoda*). Since tap water is not commonly served, mineral water is a necessary complement to many visits.

maturita (school-leaving exam). During May of their final year, students in college preparatory and specialized high schools (→ *gymnázium*) sit for school-leaving exams. Exam season begins when teachers hand out a set of approximately fifty questions in each major subject. Students have a week—the so-called *svatý týden* (holy week)—in which to prepare answers, the entire class of thirty usually pooling their knowledge. On the day of the exam, students, dressed in their Sunday best, enter their classroom individually and pick a question out of a hat. They are then grilled orally on this question by a committee composed of their homeroom teacher, a specialist on the subject in question, and a school inspector. Failure means that the student has to go to summer school and then retake the exam, or else repeat the entire year. Passing marks can sometimes be obtained through bribes or → *protekce*. During holy week, students about to sit the exam dress up in costumes and go out begging for donations to their graduation party. The party is an all-night drinking bout for students and teachers alike. The exams have given Czech students a common experience for almost a century and are the subject of numerous films and novels.

MDŽ (Mezinárodní den žen/International Women's Day). A holiday honoring women celebrated yearly under communism on March 8. Though acknowledged by the United Nations, International Women's Day was celebrated mainly in socialist-leaning countries, where it was supposed to replace Mother's Day. It originated, however, in the United States in 1909 and was first organized by the Socialist Party of America. In the communist celebration of MDŽ, women were given flowers and their contributions to the building of socialism honored in schools, factories, and offices. In reality, the holiday became just another excuse for Czech men to go out drinking. Today, it has largely disappeared and is gradually being replaced by Mother's Day. Another international holiday, MDD (*Mezinárodní den dětí*/International Children's Day), celebrated on June 1, however, has survived the revolution and continues to be marked by fun and games for the country's youngsters.

Menšík, Vladimír (1929–1988). Actor and entertainer. The prototype of what Czechs call a *bavič* or raconteur, Menšík could tell humorous anecdotes for hours without pausing or missing a beat (→ *tlachání*). One of his most popular stories was about a friend's glowing excrement (→ *hovno*) which leads him to suspect drugged wine and enlist the help of a doctor. Menšík was a frequent star in normalization (→ *normalizace*) film and television comedies and is still remembered for his yearly routines on the New Year's

Eve (→ *Silvestr*) variety shows that were always the most popular television events of the year. His brillo-like black hair, large flabby face, and gapped front teeth gave him a memorable look. The director Miloš Forman has called him one of the three great Czech comedians of all time (along with Vlasta → Burian and Jan → Werich).

Mikuláš a čert (Nicholas and the Devil). Nicholas (Mikuláš in Czech) was the gift-giving saint who was the inspiration for Santa Claus. Czechs, however, continue to celebrate the date in the Church calendar honoring him, December 6. On that day, parents hire groups of teenagers to dress up as Mikuláš (with his characteristic white beard and cardinal's miter), an angel, and a devil and visit their children at home. Mikuláš asks the children and their parents if they have been good all year; the children meanwhile often sing a song to put Mikuláš in a good mood. If they were good, they get a handful of sweets; if they were naughty, the devil scares them (by threatening to carry them away in his bag) and they get potatoes and coal. Most Czechs remember the devil's visit as one of the most traumatic moments of their youth.

Milá Sally (Dear Sally). A popular advice column that ran in the youth weekly *Mladý svět* (Young World) in the seventies and eighties. It was one of the few places where young people could hear relatively unvarnished opinions about sex and intimacy in a system that prided itself on a public culture devoid of sex and sexiness.

miss (beauty queen). Though frowned on by the communists, beauty paegants have returned with a vengeance since 1989. Known as *Miss* and the contestants as *missky*, the contest to choose Miss Czech Republic quickly became one of the year's most widely followed television events. For weeks preceding the finals, Czechs debate, with a harshly critical eye, the merits of the finalists. Though no *Miss* has yet gone on to become Miss Universe, winners remain recognized for years after they give up their crown, and some Czech beauties have gone on to become world-renowned supermodels. Naturally, these beauty contests have been dogged by the same scandals—i.e., nude photos and corruption—as those in other countries. Czech men take great pride in the beauty of their homegrown girls and are known to ask foreigners, with a nudge and a wink, how they like Czech women.

Mišík, Vladimír (1947). It was Mišík who brought real blues-influenced rock to the Czech lands. Along with his ETC band, he sang plaintive songs whose lyrics were often derived from poems by Václav Hrabě and Josef Kainar. Mišík was frequently banned in the eighties, but his fans still managed to listen to such heartfelt songs as "Love like the Evening Star" which put to shame the regime-approved top-forty music that dominated the airwaves (→ Gott).

místní rozhlas (local PA system). Most Czech villages (→ *vesnice*) are equipped with loudspeakers capable of broadcasting to all residents. This public address system is not just for emergencies; it is used almost daily. Common announcements are for local events like fairs, recycling days, community theater rehearsals, and the like. In isolated villages, where older residents are cut off from the world, the PA system may even play music (usually → *dechovka*) and broadcast the national news.

Mládek, Ivan (1942). The bald, banjo-playing Mládek is a popular figure among weekend campers (→ *tramping*). His clever lyrics to songs like "*Jožin z bažin*" (Jožin from the Swamp) and "*Medvědi nevědí*" (Bears Don't Know) are sung at gatherings across the republic. His cult grew so large under communism that the following joke was told about him: "President → Husák wakes after being frozen for a hundred years and in vain asks people on the street if they know him. Finally, he looks up his name in an encyclopedia and reads: Gustáv Husák—an insignificant poli-

tician in the era of Ivan Mládek." Mládek today hosts a popular variety show on television as he did under communism, and his songs live on not only around campfires, but also in the repertoires of several cover bands.

mladočeši (Young Czechs). Nationalist political party in the second half of the nineteenth century. The Young Czechs came into existence as an alternative to the first Czech political party in the Austrian Empire, the *staročeši* (Old Czechs). In contrast to the conservative and aristocratic Old Czechs, the Young Czechs were younger, more liberal businessmen who advocated more active opposition to the Austrians. They thus symbolized the move from a backward to a forward-looking sense of what the Czech nation could be. The Young Czechs became the stronger force after the 1891 elections, until they themselves were overwhelmed by the expansion of the franchise and the rise of the mass-based Social Democrats and Agrarians. Nevertheless, many of the founders of the independent Czechoslovak state, including the Prime Minister Karel Kramář (→ *Kramářova vila*) and T.G. → Masaryk, came from the ranks of the Young Czechs.

Mladý svět (Young World). Published by the Union of Socialist Youth (→ SSM), *Young World* magazine became a hit in the sixties by giving readers a more open take on social and cultural events than its stodgy competitors. Many of the country's best writers and journalists subsequently cut their teeth on the magazine's pages with—by prevailing standards—edgy reporting on new trends. Advertising with the rhyming slogan *Už jsi čet Mladý svět* (Have you read Young World), the magazine's popularity overwhelmed its limited circulation with the result that one had to pay a bribe to the magazine-seller to put a copy aside. See also → *Milá Sally*.

Mnichov (Munich). The German city of Munich is synonymous with the famous agreement of September 1938, in which Hitler, Chamberlain, Mussolini, and Daladier decided that Czechoslovakia should be dismembered and the majority German-inhabited Sudetenland (→ *sudetští Němci*) should become part of Germany. Neville Chamberlain's words on his return to Britain—"How horrible, fantastic, incredible it is that we should be digging trenches and trying on gas-masks here because of a quarrel in a far-away country between people of whom we know nothing"—demoralized the pro-Western Czechs who felt abandoned by their allies. Instead of defending the country, the well-trained and well-equipped army laid down its guns and allowed the Germans to control the borderland. Once they had given up their strongest military defense—their Maginot-like fortifications on the mountainous borders with Germany—it was just a matter of time before the Nazis took over the country completely, and in fact they marched in on March 15, 1939. The disappointment of Munich is said to have encouraged the Czechs to embrace the Soviet Union after the war and still arouses "what ifs" today.

"Modlitba pro Martu" (A Prayer for Marta). Song which became the anthem of opposition to the Soviet invasion (→ *srpnová invaze*). Originally written for a popular television series, the lyrics come from a text by the seventeenth-century Czech humanist Jan Amos → Komenský and include the line—cited by → Masaryk and → Havel in their first presidential addresses—"the lost government of your affairs returns to you, people." The song became associated with the popular singer Marta Kubišová, the best voice of her generation, who was banned from performing because of it (→ Golden Kids). She ended up shunned by her former friends and working in a low-level office job in the transportation authority. Hearing Kubišová sing *"Modlitba"* during the Velvet Revolution (→ *Sametová revoluce*) was a heartrending experience for many Czechs. Today Kubišová devotes her time to saving abandoned animals.

modrá knížka (blue booklet). A small blue card that pronounces its bearer unfit for mil-

itary service (→ *vojna*). These booklets were much in demand under communism when young men would fake insanity or injure themselves in order to get out of the mandatory two-year army term. Many paid bribes (→ *všimné*) to doctors to secure a blue book, though after the fall of communism would-be soldiers could choose civilian service instead.

montérky (overalls). Manual laborers (→ *dělník*) can be instantly recognized by their blue work overalls. The other distinctively dressed occupation is doctors all of whom wear white smocks and white pants.

Morava (Moravia). The eastern third of the Czech lands. Though the distinction between → *Čechy* (Bohemia, the western two-thirds of the country) and Moravia was once politically meaningful; today it is mainly a cultural relic. The differences between Czechs and Moravians include their accents and folk traditions. The rural areas of south Moravia are also the most religious areas of the country and thus a bastion for the Christian Democratic Party. While Moravians sometimes express a sense of pride in their region, the vast majority consider themselves Czechs above all. In the eyes of Bohemians, Moravians are more emotional and friendlier, their lands the home of wine and song. While many of the country's most important figures have come from Moravia—for example, → Masaryk, → Palacký, Freud, and Mahler—they inevitably achieved fame in Prague (→ *Praha*) or elsewhere.

Moravské pole (Moravian Field). Battle that ended the thirteenth-century reign of Otakar II. Through wise leadership, Přemysl (→ *Přemyslovci*) Otakar II built the Czech lands into one of Europe's largest empires, stretching almost to the Adriatic. Because he was so powerful, the nobility of the Holy Roman Empire were fearful of making him emperor and instead chose the insignificant Rudolf Habsburg. It was not long before the two met on the battlefield. The decisive moment came on 26 August 1278, when their armies clashed at Moravian Field near the Austrian village of Durnkrüt. The battle was closely fought until, legend has it, Otakar was betrayed by the Czech nobility as he had been two years earlier. Otakar lost his life and the Moravian half of his empire which fell to Rudolf, while the Bohemian half was taken over by the Brandenbergers (whose rule was immortalized in an opera by → Smetana). Like → *Bílá hora* and → Lipany, Moravian Field is another of the Czechs' great military defeats.

Mrazík (Grandfather Frost). A Russian Christmas film, combining elements of Cinderella and Sleeping Beauty, which was popular under communism and enjoys cult status today. Its complicated plot concerns the young and pretty Nastěnka who is treated badly by her stepmother and her ugly stepsister Marfuška (a name that has become synonymous in Czech for ugliness). Her budding relationship with handsome Ivan is interrupted by numerous crazy obstacles until they are rescued by Grandfather Frost (→ *Děda Mráz*). Today the film is simultaneously loved and made fun of for its characteristically Russian feel. *Mrazík* is currently being performed as a musical on ice, and the film's title song has been set to a dance track. Other memorable Russian imports include the children's cartoon *No pogodi* (Just You Wait) and countless films set during World War II.

Mucha, Alfons (1860–1939). Artist and illustrator. The Czech-born Mucha achieved fame in Paris with a poster of Sarah Bernhardt that gave birth to what was known as *Le style Mucha*. Influenced by art nouveau, it portrayed, in pastel colors, willowy female figures surrounded by floral decorative elements. Mucha's soul, however, belonged to the Czech nation; after making his fortune he returned to his homeland where he put his gifts in the service of the state, producing everything from stamps and banknotes to epic paintings of Slav history. His works, particularly the posters, continue to be favorites of both Czechs and visitors to the country.

N

nahota (nakedness). As a mostly atheist nation, Czechs are relatively unbothered by nudity. Women sunbathe topless, and it is not uncommon to see children up to five years old running around naked at the beach or pool. Similarly, men are not shy about greeting visitors or working on their car wearing only their boxer shorts.

náměstí (square). The typical Czech town is laid out around a main square which is fronted by two- or three-storey buildings with shops on the ground level and apartments above. The center of the square often features a plague column—erected in gratitude for surviving the black death—or public fountain. The names of squares often bear witness to the vicissitudes of Czech history—it is not uncommon for a single square to have been named for → Franz Joseph, → Palacký, the Red Army, and → Masaryk at different points in time. In all cases, though, the town square is the site of public celebrations as well as a place for running into friends and acquaintances.

Národní divadlo (National Theater). Built in the 1880s after a nationwide collection drive (→ *nazdar*), the construction of the National Theater was one of the culminating events of the National Revival (→ *Národní obrození*). It put in concrete form the growing weight of Czech cultural expression and gave new opportunities to the country's artists. The theater's foundation stones were brought from the most hallowed sites in the country: → Blaník, → Radhošť, → Říp, and → Vyšehrad.

That first building was destroyed in a fire, as memorable to the Czechs as the Chicago fire is to Americans. Another collection drive enabled it to be rebuilt and inaugurated with → Smetana's opera → *Libuše* about the woman who founded the country's first line of kings. The theater was so important to Czech cultural life at the time, that it inspired a literary movement known as the "Generation of the National Theater." To see a play at the National Theater is still an essential part of all organized trips from the provinces. Affectionately called the *Zlatá kaplička* (Golden Chapel) for its gold roof, the theater truly belongs to the country and appropriately bears the legend *Národ sobě* (The nation to itself).

Národní fronta (National Front). Political organization that coordinated the activities of all legal groups and parties under communism. The National Front was created after World War II to unite all the democratic parties in a grand coalition for the purpose of reconstructing the country. As the communists squeezed out all of their competitors, however, the Front became a mere cover for communist domination. Ultimately, all organizations that wished to exist legally had to join the National Front and accept the dictates of the Communist Party (→ KSČ). The all-encompassing nature of the National Front can be seen in its component parts, which included the Union of Invalids, the Czech Fishermen's Union, and even the Union of Czechoslovak Stamp Collectors. In politics, the National Front encompassed not just the Communist Party, but also the Czechoslovak Socialist Party and the People's Party, though the latter two retained virtually no independence. On election day, signs above polling places thus carried a red banner with the command "We Vote for Candidates of the National Front." All citizens were required to vote, even though they were presented with only a single list of candidates, and the National Front always won upwards of ninety-nine percent of the vote. The only possible protests were not showing up or crossing names off the list, but both were punishable offenses.

Národní muzeum (National Museum). Founded in 1818 by patriotic nobles to further the arts and sciences in the Czech lands, the museum was an important vehicle for the National Revival (→ *Národní obrození*). Its collections include everything that could possibly be associated with the Czech territory, from historic documents, maps, and coins, to native flora and fauna, to Czech arts and crafts. Moved to an imposing neo-Renaissance building at the top of Wenceslas Square (→ *Václavské náměstí*) in 1890, the museum played an important role in creating a sense of identity and pride for Czechs.

Národní obrození (National Revival). The National Revival was the reawakening of Czech culture in the first half of the nineteenth century. The background to the revival was Austrian repression after → *Bílá hora*, which had led to the virtual extinction of Czech high culture (→ *temno*). This began to change at the end of the eighteenth century. Inspired by the Enlightenment, a small group of priests, teachers, and nobility began to study and propagate Czech culture. According to legend, the group was so small that if a single roof had fallen, it would have destroyed the entire revivalist movement. These scholars, known as *buditelé* (awakeners), first concentrated on the language (→ *čeština*), which had almost ceased to function as a means of intellectual and artistic communication. Scholars like → Dobrovský and → Jungmann worked to systematize the grammar and enrich the vocabulary. The his-

torian → Palacký meanwhile gave the country a usable past. At the same time, the first original works of literature in modern Czech emerged from the pens of writers like → Erben, → Němcová, and Tyl. These developments all took place in the spirit of Romanticism, which saw the nation embodied in its language and literature, and the common people—with their folklore and fairy tales—as the carriers of the culture. The long-term achievement of the National Revival was to take a culture and language on the verge of extinction and transform it into one that could make a powerful contribution to Western civilization. Its members are thus considered the country's true founding fathers and mothers, and their traces can be found in all aspects of the Czech national image.

národní/zasloužilý umělec (national/merited artist). Communist-era titles awarded to artists for serving the cause of socialism. The award was accompanied by a pay raise and better working conditions. Though accepting the title may be seen as collaboration with the regime, few had the courage to refuse, and almost no one renounced the designation until 1989. Among the recipients of the National Artist title (the higher of the two designations) were the poets Vítězslav Nezval and Jaroslav Seifert, the actor and writer Jan → Werich, the animator Jiří Trnka, the actors Vladimír → Menšík and Miloš Kopecký, and the opera singer Peter Dvorský. Merited artists were even more numerous. Evidence of the titles can be seen in the credits to communist-era films, where names are followed by the abbreviations *nár.* or *zasl. umělec.*

národní výbor (national committee). Local government office under communism. Instead of town halls and county governments, the state administered local government through national committees, which existed at regional, district, and municipal levels. A whole variety of tasks—and under communism red tape was immense (→ *razítko*)—had to be taken care of at one or all of them. For this reason, it is *národní výbory* that remain a vivid memory of the era. As with all public functions, these committees were under the tight control of the Communist Party (→ KSČ), which used them to make its control over the population even tighter. In 1990, national committees were replaced by municipal authorities.

narozeniny (birthday). Czechs often invite their workmates out for a drink to celebrate their birthday. The person being celebrated, however, is expected to pick up the check for the whole group.

Naše země nezvkétá (Our country is not blossoming). In his memorable first New Year Address as president, Václav → Havel reminded his fellow citizens of the lies they had been told year in and year out by their communist leaders and promised that he would not lie to them. The truth that he had for them, encapsulated in this famous phrase, was that the country was not blossoming, but rather faced grave political, economic, and, most of all in his view, moral problems.

Naši furianti (Our Swaggerers). One of the most performed plays in the Czech theatrical repertoire. Written in 1887 by the long-standing artistic director of the National Theater (→ *Národní divadlo*), Ladislav Stroupežnický, the play is set in a small village and describes the battle among self-important village notables over the choice of a new night watchman. Because of its realistic and cynical take on small town life (→ *maloměšťáctví*), the play was originally panned by critics, but for the same reason it became a favorite of theatergoers.

nazdar. A popular greeting that originated when patriots collected donations for the construction of the National Theater (→ *Národní divadlo*) with the words *Na zdar Národního divadla* (To the success of the National Theater). Today it simply means hello or in the phrase "*No, nazdar*" expresses mildly unpleasant surprise like "gosh!" or "gracious me!" Among young people it is shortened to *zdar* or *zdarec*.

na zdraví (to your health). Common toast. When clinking glasses, Czechs will make sure to look each other directly in the eyes and touch their drink to the table before taking a sip. At celebrations honoring a specific person, the crowd will shout out the Serbo-Croatian "*živijo*" (long live) four times in succession. Another common toast, perhaps harking back to peasant days, is "*Ať jsme tlustí*" (Here's to being fat). *Na zdraví* is also used to mean "gesundheit."

Nedvěd, Honza (1946). Folk and country singer. The bald, overweight, and near-sighted Nedvěd was an unlikely candidate to become a hero to young rebels, yet his romantic folk songs have become anthems to the → *tramping* movement. He entered the limelight in the early seventies as the folk scene emerged. He performed first with a group of fellow tramps who called themselves Brontosauři (The Brontosauruses), later with the Spirituál Kvintet (The Spiritual Quintet), and finally as a solo artist. Among his campfire hits are songs like "*Hráz*" (Dam), "*Na kameni kámen*" (A Stone Left Unturned), "*Stánky*" (Kiosks), "*Tulácký ráno*" (A Tramp's Morning), and "*Valčíček*" (Little Waltz). Though criticized for sentimentality and kitsch, his gift for catchy melodies brought the folk and tramp scene to the masses for the first time. His crossover success was so great that he became the only domestic act who could fill the stadium on → Strahov.

Němcová, Božena (1820–1862). Author and patriot. Němcová is part of the Czech pantheon not only for her novel → *Babička* (Granny), but also for her work in collecting folk and fairy tales (→ *pohádka*) in the rural countryside and propagating the National Revival (→ *Národní obrození*). Considered one of the most beautiful women of her time, she was linked romantically to several of her fellow patriots. She was, however, far more courageous than most of them. During the period of Bach's Absolutism (→ *Bachův absolutismus*), she was one of the few to associate with the dissident writer Karel → Havlíček

Borovský, and even laid a crown of thorns on his head at his funeral. Němcová's unparalleled devotion to the Czech cause earned her a place as one of the country's most beloved founding mothers.

Němec (German). Since the National Revival (→ *Národní obrození*), Czechs have seen their history as a constant battle between themselves and the Germans. It was not merely that the country was (and is) an island in a sea of Germans; ever since the twelfth century when Czech kings invited German colonists to settle the underpopulated land and promote urban development, the two groups lived side up side. Many towns in the Czech lands—like → Karlovy Vary (Carlsbad), Liberec (Reichenberg), Svitavy (Zwittau), and Cheb (Eger)—thus came to be dominated by Germans. The same was true in other Slavic lands, leading all of them to refer to Germans by the word for deaf (*němý*) since they could not communicate in the local language. Czechs distinguish between their former Austrian (→ *Rakousko*) rulers—whom they see as kindlier—and Germans proper whom they portray as cold, efficient, and cruel. Relations finally came to a head after World War II, when Czechs forcibly expelled the entire German population from the Sudetenland (→ *sudetští Němci*, → *odsun*). Like all its national rivalries—the Russians and Slovaks are the others—this one matters primarily to one side.

Nemocnice na kraji města (Hospital on the Edge of Town). The most popular and widely considered the best Czech television show of all time. Lasting for twenty episodes between 1978 and 1981, it portrays life at a small town hospital. Its charm comes from a set of unforgettable characters—all created by the indefatigable screenwriter Jaroslav → Dietl—who have since become Czech archetypes. They include the strict but fair Dr. Sova, the grumpy but lovable Dr. Štrosmajer, the skirt-chasing Dr. Blažej, and the incompetent Dr. Cvach. The series was so popular that streets and pubs emptied during its broadcast. Tears still well up in the eyes of Czechs when they remember Štrosmajer's death in the last episode. The series was good enough to play on West German television and still entertains today. New episodes were filmed in 2004.

Nepomucký, Jan. A legendary figure based on a fourteenth-century priest. The original Jan of Pomuk (1345–1393) was the general curate to the archbishop of Prague, and was tortured and thrown to his death from Charles Bridge in an obscure quarrel between King Wenceslas IV and the archbishop. In the sixteenth century, there appeared, alongside the original Jan of Pomuk, the legend of Jan Nepomucký, said to be martyred because he would not reveal the confession of the queen. During the Counter-Reformation, the Jesuits (→ *jezuité*) played up the legend in an effort to replace Jan → Hus in popular memory. Canonized in 1729, Nepomucký was warmly accepted by the laity both in the Czech lands and throughout Europe. Even though he was later disavowed by nationalists as too closely tied with Habsburg oppression, and even stripped of his sainthood by the Vatican, his statue on Charles Bridge, purportedly at the spot where he was thrown to his death, is still touched to bring good luck.

neschopenka (sick note). Taking time off from work for sickness requires a special doctor's note known as a *neschopenka* (the word *neschopný* means incapacitated). Demand for notes is high, as Czechs visit the doctor upwards of ten times a year and are likely to take seven to ten days off for a bout of the common cold. To prevent abuse, special inspectors ring the doorbells of those with a *neschopenka* to make sure they are genuinely at home recuperating. Nevertheless, there used to be a considerable black market in sick notes with doctors collecting bribes from those who wished to avoid work.

nohejbal (football tennis). A popular sport invented by Czechs that is an eclectic mix of soccer, tennis, and volleyball. It is played by two-man teams on a volleyball court with the net set at tennis height. From there on, it resembles volleyball except that players can strike the ball with any part of their body except the hands and arms, and the ball is allowed to bounce once after each touch. Points are usually closed out by a spike with the leg swinging down from shoulder level. *Nohejbal* is played by young and old at all summer recreation areas. The name translates badly (*noha* means foot), and so outside the country it is referred to as football tennis. It is the one sport in which the Czechs are perpetual world champions.

normalizace (normalization). The communist leadership's name for the process of restoring order after the Soviet invasion (→ *srpnová invaze*). During the Prague Spring (→ *Pražské jaro*), citizens had learned to speak their mind about political matters and challenge authority. The Soviets thus installed a new communist leadership, led by Gustáv → Husák, that would clamp down on any remnants of liberalization and, in their terms, "normalize" society.

For Husák and company, this meant throwing tens of thousands of intellectuals and artists out of their jobs and relegating them to menial labor as stokers, window-washers, or night-watchmen (→ *prověrková komise*). Others were allowed to keep their jobs, but at the cost of publicly pledging gratitude to the Russians for the invasion. Most Czechs survived normalization by keeping their heads down: they retreated to their weekend cottages (→ *chata*) or plugged into a new consumerist culture. The regime ultimately liquidated all but token resistance and lasted almost unchanged until its dramatic and sudden fall in 1989 (→ *Sametová revoluce*).

Nová vlna (New Wave). A generation of avant-garde filmmakers that emerged in the mid-to late sixties. Taking inspiration from the French *nouvelle vague*, directors like Miloš Forman, Jiří Menzel, and Věra Chytilová rebelled against the prevailing canons of socialist realism and its requirement that films be politically engaged, and portray heroic par-

Critics' Choices for Film of the Century

This list was the result of a survey sent to 100 leading Czech and Slovak film critics in 1999 (54 responded). Each was asked to pick the ten best Czech and Slovak films and rank them from one to ten (the best film received 10 points, the next best 9 and so on). The scores were added up and the films ranked according to the total number of points received. Noteworthy is that the majority of the films, especially in the top ten, come from a short period in the sixties, the Czech New Wave (→ *Nová vlna*). Slovak directors are marked with an asterisk.

	CZECH TITLE	ENGLISH TITLE	DIRECTOR	YEAR	POINTS
1	Markéta Lazarová	Markéta Lazarová	František Vláčil	1967	325
2	Obchod na korze	The Shop on Main Street	Ján Kadár* and Elmar Klos	1965	252
3	Všichni dobří rodáci	All the Good Countrymen	Vojtěch Jasný	1968	222
4	Hoří, má panenko	Firemen's Ball	Miloš Forman	1967	163
5	Intimní osvětlení	Intimate Lighting	Ivan Passer	1965	134
6	Daleká cesta	The Long Journey	Alfréd Radok	1949	122
7	Démanty noci	Diamonds of the Night	Jan Němec	1964	121
8	Ostře sledované vlaky	Closely Watched Trains	Jiří Menzel	1966	121
9	Spalovač mrtvol	The Cremator of Corpses	Juraj Herz	1968	79

	Czech Title	English Title	Director	Year	Points
10	Případ pro začínajícího kata	The Case for the New Hangman	Pavel Juráček	1969	71
11	Ucho	The Ear	Karel Kachyňa	1970	68
12	Sedmikrásky	Daisies	Věra Chytilová	1967	57
13	Lásky jedné plavovlásky	Loves of a Blonde	Miloš Forman	1965	53
14	O slavnosti a hostech	Report on the Party and the Guests	Jan Němec	1965	53
15	Vynález zkázy	Invention for Destruction	Karel Zeman	1958	52
16	Zbehovia a pútnici	Deserters and Pilgrims	Juraj Jakubisko*	1968	51
17	→ Černý Petr	Peter and Paula	Miloš Forman	1963	48
18	Vtáčkovia, siroty a blázni	Birdies, Orphans, and Fools	Juraj Jakubisko*	1969	47
19	Obrazy starého světa	Pictures of the Old World	Dušan Hanák	1972	39
20	Rozmarné léto	Capricious Summer	Jiří Menzel	1967	36
21	Skřivánci na niti	Larks on a String	Jiří Menzel	1969	32
22	Tisícročná včela	The Millennial Bee	Juraj Jakubisko*	1983	30
23	322	322	Dušan Hanák*	1969	28
24	Kočár do Vídně	The Coach to Vienna	Karel Kachyňa	1966	27
25	Návrat ztraceného syna	The Return of the Prodigal Son	Evald Schorm	1966	25
26	→ Staré pověsti české	Old Czech Legends	Jiří Trnka	1952	25
27	Adelheid	Adelheid	František Vláčil	1969	24
28	Slnko v sieti	The Sun in a Net	Štefan Uher*	1962	24
29	Obecná škola	The Elementary School	Jan Svěrák	1991	21
30	Žert	The Joke	Jaromil Jireš	1968	20
31	Extase	Ecstasy	Gustav Machatý	1933	19
32	Panelstory aneb Jak se rodí sídliště	Panelstory or How a Housing Development Is Born	Věra Chytilová	1979	19
33	Romance pro křídlovku	Romance for the Flugelhorn	Otakar Vávra	1966	19
34	Údolí včel	Valley of the Bees	František Vláčil	1967	18
35	Smuteční slavnost	Funeral Rites	Zdenek Sirový	1969	17
36	→ Limonádový Joe	Lemonade Joe	Oldřich Lipský	1964	15
37	Postava k podpírání	Josef Kilian	Pavel Juráček and Jan Schmidt	1963	15
38	Kristián	Kristián	Martin Frič	1939	14

	Czech Title	English Title	Director	Year	Points
39	Holubice	The White Dove	František Vláčil	1960	13
40	Kolja	Kolya	Jan Svěrák	1996	13
41	Až přijde kocour	That Cat	Vojtěch Jasný	1963	11
42	Kráva	The Cow	Karel Kachyňa	1993	11
43	Ja milujem, ty miluješ	I Love, You Love	Dušan Hanák*	1980	10
44	Pytlákova schovanka	The Poacher's Foster Daughter	Martin Frič	1949	10
45	Šeptej	Whisper	David Ondříček	1996	10
46	Anton Špelec, ostrostřelec	Anton Špelec, Sharp-shooter	Martin Frič	1932	9
47	Ovoce stromů rajských jíme	We Eat the Fruit of the Trees of Paradise	Věra Chytilová	1969	9
48	Praha—neklidné srdce Evropy	Prague—Restless Heart of Europe	Věra Chytilová	1984	9
49	Sladké hry minulého léta	Sweet Games of Last Summer	Juraj Herz	1969	9
50	Touha	Desire	Vojtěch Jasný	1958	9

Source: Personal communication from Jiří Králík, director of the Summer Film School in Uherské Hradiště.

tisans and workers fighting against villainous fascists and capitalists. The filmmakers of the New Wave instead turned to the small stories of ordinary people and their everyday existential dilemmas. Thus, Forman's *Loves of a Blonde* portrayed a young girl trapped in a town with a shortage of men, and Menzel's *Closely Watched Trains* followed a sexually inexperienced railroad signalman. For all their art-house qualities—many of them were stylistically innovative—the films were a breath of fresh air for the broader public and achieved considerable popularity, not to mention world renown. The New Wave was cut off in its flower by the Soviet invasion (→ *srpnová invaze*), and its leading protagonists either emigrated, were silenced, or made deals with the regime in order to continue working (some directed a socialist realist film as an apology). Many of the best films ended up tucked away in vaults (→ *trezor*) until the fall of communism in 1989. Today the New Wave films are more admired than watched by ordinary Czechs, who prefer lighter fare like → *S tebou mě baví svět*.

Nový, Oldřich (1899–1983). Film and theater actor. Nový was the paragon of elegance and grace during the First Republic (→ *První republika*) and into the forties. Known as the Czech Chevalier, he portrayed suave, sophisticated bankers, entrepreneurs, and lovers in dozens of romantic comedies. His most famous role was in the comedy *Kristián*, where he played a poor, married man who once a month dresses up and flirts with beautiful high-society women. Though one smitten woman tracks him down to his ordinary job in a travel agency, he remains faithful to his wife who in the end quits her domestic ways and makes herself glamorous. In a recent poll, the film's line, "Close your eyes, I'm leaving," his way of saying farewell to his conquests, was named the best line in a Czech film. As the film representative of the bourgeois First Republic, Nový found himself out of favor after the communist takeover and was, to the shock of audiences used to seeing him in a tuxedo, even forced to don worker's overalls in one film.

O

občanský průkaz (identification card). Czech citizens are required to carry a state-issued identification card at all times. Formerly a passport-like booklet and now a laminated card, the *občanský průkaz*, known for short as an *občanka*, summarizes such basic information as date of birth, marital status, and nationality (Czech, Slovak, Roma). Under communism, the card also contained information about the bearer's work history, criminal offenses, and social class. It used to be common for policemen (→ VB) to stop people on the street and demand their *občanka*. Failure to produce it led to a fine or a trip to the police station. Though such harassment has subsided, the *občanka* must still be shown when conducting official business, visiting a doctor, or borrowing billiard equipment.

ochotnické divadlo (amateur theater). In the latter half of the nineteenth and first half of the twentieth century, virtually every village in the Czech lands had its own amateur theater. Usually under the direction of the local teacher, these troupes put on classics of the Czech repertoire like Josef Kajetán Tyl's *Strakonický dudák* (→ *Švanda dudák*), Alois Jirásek's → *Lucerna*, and Václav Kliment Klicpera's *Hadrián z Římsů* (Hadrian from Římsy). The plays usually featured broad humor and nationalist themes. Though still in existence in some villages, amateur theaters were largely pushed out by television and films in the postwar era. Their historical significance is in creating fellow feeling and a sense of pride in being Czech after centu-

ries of oppression. They were also instrumental in the revival of the Czech language (→ *čeština*).

odboj (resistance). It is a testament to the tragedies of Czech history that people number their country's various rebellions against dictatorial and foreign rule in the twentieth century as first, second, and third. The first *odboj* was against their Austrian rulers during World War I. Though the vast majority of Czechs at the time did not agitate for independence, a few brave souls risked prison and death by opposing the regime. A group known as the *Maffie* represented a home-grown though not overly effective fifth column. The second resistance was against Nazi rule (→ *Protektorát*) and despite general public compliance, figures like the Three Kings (→ *Mašín*) or the communist Julius → Fučík tried to sabotage the German war effort. The culmination of the second *odboj* was the short Prague Uprising (→ *Květnové povstání*), and the longer Slovak National Uprising (→ SNP). The third resistance was against the domestic oppression of communist rule. With the exception of the Mašín brothers, this *odboj* did not truly take off until the seventies and eighties, when dissidents organized in the → *Charta* 77 movement. Even then not quite two thousand citizens took part in seemingly innocuous acts like signing petitions, putting on plays, and teaching courses in private apartments. Together the weakness of the three resistance movements testifies to the Czech penchant for passivity and collaboration (→ *holubičí povaha*). More generous observers would call it rationality in the face of certain destruction or a preference for → Švejkian subversiveness.

odsun (transfer). Term used to refer to the forcible expulsion of the German (→ *Němec*) population from Czechoslovakia after World War II. Since the German colonization of the twelfth century, Czechs and Germans had lived side by side on the territories of Bohemia and Moravia. Though relations between them were never idyllic, it was only the Nazi occupation (→ *Protektorát*) and the perception that German Czechs (→ *sudetští Němci*) had betrayed their country, which rendered continued coexistence impossible. Indeed, immediately after the cessation of hostilities, a *divoký odsun* (wild transfer) erupted and violently forced over six hundred thousand Germans out of their homes and across the border. Negotiations at Potsdam approved the transfer of Germans out of all Eastern Europe, and the new Czechoslovak government completed a more orderly expulsion of 2.2 million more Germans, leaving only a few tens of thousands behind. The *odsun* emptied most of the country's borderlands, and Czechs along with gypsies (→ *cikán*) took over formerly German houses. Though largely suppressed during communism, memories of the expulsion were revived after 1989, when Germans expelled from the Sudetenland—who had mainly settled in Bavaria—began demanding restitution of their property and revocation of anti-German laws passed after the war (→ *Benešovy dekrety*). The vast majority of Czechs, however, are adamant about not recognizing German claims and continue to regard the *odsun* as unfortunate but eminently justified.

okurková sezóna (cucumber season). Journalists refer to the summer months as cucumber season because most politicians are on vacation at their cottages (→ *chata*). Theaters close for the holidays as well with the result that newspapers in July and August are generally devoid of any interesting news.

Olomouc. City in eastern Moravia (→ *Morava*). Once the capital of Moravia, Olomouc is still home to the region's archbishopric, though it is mainly known for its baroque architecture and as a college town. The second oldest university in the country was founded here in the sixteenth century by Jesuits (→ *jezuité*) and now teaches under the name of → Palacký University. The city is also home to the odorous cheese → *tvarůžky*.

Olympic. Popular rock group. Founded in 1963 as one of the country's first rock and roll bands, Olympic was initially home to a changing cast of many of the country's best rockers. Working first as a backup band in the → Semafor Theater, Olympic became an artistic force under the leadership of vocalist and guitarist Petr Janda in the late sixties. The group's bread and butter was early Beatles-style love songs and middle-of-the-road classic rock. Their signature tune is "*Dej mi víc své lásky*" (Give Me More of Your Love) with the catchy refrain "My dear, give me more / my dear, give me more / my dear, give me more of your love / there's almost nothing I want / there's almost nothing I want / I only want to caress your hair." Their list of popular singles, all of which are campfire favorites, includes "*Želva*" (Turtle), "*Jasná zpráva*" (Clear News), "*Osmý den*" (Eighth Day), and "*Okno mé lásky*" (Window of My Love). Like aging rock pioneers in the West, Olympic continues to play forty years after its founding, and the balding Janda still attracts admirers. A new musical in Prague traces the group's history.

omáčka (sauce). When Czechs refer to their favorite meals, they usually identify them by their sauces, which are widely considered the heart of Czech cuisine. While meat and dumplings (→ *knedlík*) are the substantive part of most meals, it is the *rajská* (tomato), → *svíčková* (cream), *koprová* (dill), *houbová* (mushroom), or *křenová* (horseradish) sauces which give them their identity. From the graces of their mothers' sauce come most Czechs' favorite gastronomic memory.

Oslíčku, otřes se (Shake, Donkey). This fairy tale donkey, like the mythical leprechaun, gives out gold coins or precious gems whenever it shakes its tail. When a Czech is asked for money, he might reply, "Who do you think I am? The shake donkey?"

Ostrava. City in the northeast of the country known as "the steel heart of the republic." An industrial powerhouse, Ostrava is home to coal mines and steel plants (the largest being Nová Huť) and their attendant militant workers. Even today it remains the left-wing bastion it was under communism and before. It is as well known though for its atrocious living conditions. The soot-filled air leads people to refer to the city as black Ostrava. The city's architecture, designed in accord with communist aesthetics, consists of miles of identical concrete buildings (→ *panelák*, → *sorela*). Though such conditions made Ostrava (along with Ústí nad Labem and Most) a town looked down upon and avoided at all costs, workers were lured there with promises of good wages and accessible housing. Today the city is an economic mess with twenty percent unemployment, though it boasts a surprisingly vibrant night life (especially, the famed Stodolní Street) and music scene. Fans of Ostrava's soccer team (→ *fotbal*) Baník are known as the most passionate and violent in the country.

osudové osmičky (fateful eights). The belief, largely a product of the eventful twentieth century, that fateful events befall the Czechs in years ending in eight. Independent Czechoslovakia was founded in October 1918 and came to an end with the Munich (→ *Mnichov*) agreement and the Nazi takeover of the borderlands in 1938. The year 1948 (→ *Vítězný únor*) saw the seizure of power by the communists who kept their tight grip on power until the liberalization of the Prague Spring (→ *Pražské jaro*) and then the Russian invasion in 1968 (→ *srpnová invaze*). Expectations for 1988, however, were not fulfilled until a year later (→ *Sametová revoluce*). More detailed searches of history reveal such additional fateful years as 1278

(→ *Moravské pole*), 1618 (→ *Třicetiletá válka*), and 1848. Belief in the fateful eights reflects the Czechs' faith that their country's history contains a secret meaning, which has guided them past (or into) one obstacle after another (→ *smysl českých dějin*).

Otesánek (Stump Boy). A popular but chilling fairy tale (→ *pohádka*) in which a barren couple adopt a tree stump as their son. The stump, however, comes to life and eats everything in the house, including his parents, until an energetic grandmother kills him with a hoe. While its message of being careful what you wish for belongs more to the days of peasants, it is still enjoyed by children today.

Ottův slovník naučný (Otto's Encyclopedia). The one and only great Czech encyclopedia was published by the Prague bookseller Jan Otto between 1888 and 1908. Its twenty-seven volumes cover the range of human knowledge at the time and were prepared by the best and brightest minds the country had to offer. Czech history has stood in the way of a successor. The short First Republic was not given time for another great encyclopedia, and the constant rewriting of history under communism—important figures fell in and out of favor, first erased from history, then rehabilitated, only to be erased again—meant that any comprehensive encyclopedia would soon become politically uncomfortable. Such was the fate of the sixty-five volume Great Soviet Encyclopedia which often disappeared from libraries for revision. New encyclopedias are currently being written, but for the time being *Otto's Encyclopedia* has again cornered the market with a print and CD–ROM re-edition.

-ová. All Czech women's surnames end in -*ová*. The suffix is actually the possessive (like the apostrophe "s" in English) and originally indicated that the woman belonged to her father or husband. Thus, Martina Navrátilová's father is named Navrátil. The only exceptions to the rule are adjectival names (for example, Šťastný—Happy) which end in a *ý* for men and *á* for women, and names ending in a long *ů* (for example, Martinů, Janů) which are the same for both sexes. Even foreign women get the *–ová* added to their name, so in Czech magazines one reads about Meryl Streepová or Margaret Thatcherová. Some women protest against the tradition, but they are few and far between. The word "feminism" still carries heavy negative connotations in the country. Though Czech women are more likely to work and support a family than their American counterparts, they tend to associate feminism with extreme manifestations of political correctness such as outlawing compliments on a woman's looks.

P

Palach, Jan (1948–1969). Student who became a symbol of opposition to the Soviet invasion (→ *srpnová invaze*) by immolating himself on Wenceslas Square (→ *Václavské náměstí*) in January 1969. His funeral became one of the last expressions of opposition to the escalating repression (→ *normalizace*), and the twentieth anniversary of his death in 1989 was again marked by protests.

palačinky (crepes). This common dessert consists of thin, sometimes greasy, crepes made from flour, water, and eggs and rolled up with jam or cottage cheese. The crepes are as often made at home as ordered in restaurants or from street stands.

Palacký, František (1798–1876). Historian known as the *otec národa* (father of the nation). It is a testament to their uncertainty about their place in history that Czechs consider a historian their founding father. Palacký's magnum opus, *Dějiny národa českého v Čechách a v Moravě* (The History of the Czech Nation in Bohemia and Moravia), was a five-volume tome based on primary sources in eleven languages that traced Czech history from its origins through the Hussite revolts and ended in 1526 when the first Habsburg sat on the Czech throne. In his vision, Czech history was a constant battle between Slavs and Germans (→ *Němec*). Palacký thus organizes his work not by dynasties, but according to whether Czechs or Germans had the upper hand in the Czech lands. His history begins with the ancient democratic Czech tribes, moves on to the German colonization and feudalism, reaches its climax with the Czech Hussites, and ends with the triumph of foreign rulers. The aim of all Palacký's work was to defend the existence of the Czech nation, and chronicle its contributions to Europe (a task that many Czechs continue to this day). Though he originally defended the Austrian state—he memorably remarked that if it did not exist, it would have to be created—as a bulwark against Russia and Germany, his devotion to the Czechs was total and in the end his position hardened, as in his famous remark → "*Byli jsme před Rakouskem, budeme i po něm*" (We were here before Austria, we will be here after it). Palacký himself died just a month after completing the history that helped to establish a modern Czech identity.

pálení čarodějnic (Burning of the Witches). Folk ritual to ward off witches. Medieval lore had it that witches gathered on the night of April 30 to worship the devil. To protect themselves and their livestock, peasants thus built funeral pyres where they burnt effigies of witches. In the seventeenth century, witch hysteria erupted in northern Moravia, where the inquisitor Boblig had dozens of accused witches put to death. Even today some villages celebrate the Burning of the Witches, though often with an ironic twist such as the election of a → Miss Witch. See also → *ježibaba*.

pan (mister/sir). The Czech word for mister accompanies all titles. Thus, in addressing a doctor or professor, Czechs will say *pane dok-*

tore (Mr. Doctor) or *pane profesore* (Mr. Professor). The female equivalent is *paní*. Those with higher degrees stack numerous abbreviations before and after their name. It is not uncommon to see a doc. MUDr. Jan Novák, CSc, Dr.h.c. This all reflects the heavy weight of formality and respect for formal attainments.

pan Brouček (Mr. Brouček). The main character in several books by the patriotic writer Svatopluk → Čech, which satirize the narrow-minded petty bourgeoisie of the late nineteenth century. In a series of excursions, Mr. Brouček, whose name translates as Beetle, travels to extraordinary locations like the moon or the Hussite rebellion in the fifteenth century, but in every case demonstrates his own egocentrism and small-mindedness. He represents the average Czech who has an opinion on everything, but himself does nothing.

panelák (prefabricated apartment building). Every Czech city and many small towns are surrounded by a ring of identical-looking white concrete apartment buildings. Named after the prefabricated panels that made construction of them so easy, they are home to millions of Czechs and hated by most of them. First built in the fifties and dominating construction in the sixties, seventies, and eighties, they combined a functionalist, unornamented aesthetic with cheap technology. The *panelák* proliferated throughout the Soviet bloc and was meant not only to house the growing working class, but also to integrate home and work. Factories were located close by, and the developments were usually accompanied by a school, polyclinic (→ *poliklinika*), supermarket, and cultural center. Despite these potential advantages, shoddy construction, excessive heating, and the sheer monotony of dozens of identical buildings (in one Soviet film a drunken man ends up in a far-off city, but manages to go "home" to a flat identical to his own) made a *panelák* apartment an unpopular solution to the country's housing shortage. In-

deed, they are often referred to as *králíkárny* (rabbit hutches). They have, however, avoided being turned into ghettoes: they housed (and continue to house) doctors and lawyers next to factory workers and waiters. Politicians today use residence in a *panelák* as proof that they are still of the people (→ *lid*). A looming problem for the country is what to do with the rapidly deteriorating buildings that still house a third of the population.

Panenka, Tonda (1948). Football (→ *fotbal*) midfielder. Few have brought as much pleasure to Czechs as the footballer Antonín Panenka when he sent the winning goal into the net at the 1976 European Championship. His kick in the penalty shootout was headed straight down the pike—some believed he mis-hit the ball, but Panenka claims that it was intentional—and outwitted the West German goalkeeper who dove to the right. The winning team was feted throughout the country, though Slovaks claim that the victory was really theirs as the team had a majority of Slovak players. Panenka himself was a star for Prague's fourth team, Bohemians (→ Sparta/Slavia), who were the rebels of the league; they wore green uniforms (no communist red) and had a kangaroo mascot (symbolic of Australia). Today the mustachioed Panenka uses his fame to sell used cars.

Pankrác. A Prague quarter that has become synonymous with the jail located there. Since the 1880s, most arrestees in Prague have spent at least some time in Pankrác before coming to trial. It was here that the communist martyr Julius → Fučík wrote his memoirs while imprisoned by the Nazis. It was in Pankrác as well that the communists put on their major show trials (→ *politické procesy*) of enemies like Rudolf → Slánský and Milada → Horáková in the fifties. Later, dissidents (→ *disident*) like Václav → Havel came to know the jail's cells. Under communism, conditions in all prisons were abysmal, especially for those designated enemies of the state. Long interrogations, beatings, and meager rations were common; ordinary criminals had free rein to tyrannize political prisoners. In the fifties, when thousands were jailed for innocuous offenses like shirking at work, telling jokes, or attending church, a popular anecdote featured a conversation between two prisoners: "How long are you in for?" asks one. "Ten years," replies the other. "What did you do?" "Nothing." "That's impossible. The sentence for nothing is only five years." After a stay at Pankrác, convicts move on to long-term prisons like Bory near Plzeň, Mírov outside of → Ostrava, Leopoldov in Slovakia, and, in the past, Špilberk in → Brno. It is one of the tragedies of Czech history that many of the country's greatest heroes, including Karel → Havlíček Borovský and the founding father Karel Kramář, spent a considerable part of their lives in one of these prisons.

pantofle (slippers). Upon entering a Czech home, one traditionally removes one's shoes and dons a pair of slippers laid out by the door. Shoes are stored in a *botník* (shoe closet) or may simply be left in the hallway. The same applies in schools where students are required to have their own slippers. Like the habit of changing into a set of home clothes (→ *tepláky*) after work, this custom is meant to keep one's possessions (including the apartment) clean and long-lasting. A henpecked man is said to be *pod pantoflem* (under the slipper).

papaláš (fat cat). Slang term for highly-placed communist functionaries. *Papaláši* were almost exclusively older men who had worked their way up the hierarchy through years of loyal service in the party. They were immediately recognizable as they were chauffeured around in large black Tatra 613s—the Czech equivalent of a limousine—and were greeted everywhere by groups of Pioneers (→ *Pionýr*) and citizens dressed in folk costumes (→ *kroj*). *Papaláši* enjoyed numerous privileges not available to ordinary citizens: they were able to travel abroad (→ *výjezdní doložka*), their children were automatically accepted at university, and they were able

to shop in → *Tuzex* stores. They thus fulfilled Milovan Djilas's prophecy that even in a classless society there would be class distinctions.

paralen. Popular pain reliever. Just as Americans reach for Tylenol, so *paralen* has become the Czech synonym for cold and pain relief. The round, white pills, whose active ingredient paracetamolum is similar to acetaminophen, are a staple of every family's first-aid kit and a necessity on any trip to the great outdoors. The medicine has even survived the transition to the capitalism and the new wave of foreign drugs.

Pardubice. City east of Prague (→ *Praha*). Besides its art nouveau architecture, Pardubice is known for its gingerbread (*perník*), its annual steeplechase, and its rivalry with the neighboring city of Hradec Králové.

pěstitelské práce (cultivation work). Also known as *práce v dílně a na pozemku* (work in the workshop and field), this was a graded exercise for elementary school students in which the entire class spent several hours every week taking care of the school garden and grounds, for example, by planting flowers or vegetables.

pětiletka (five-year plan). Under the planned economy of communism, all economic activity had to be organized in advance. Numerical targets were set for all branches of production on an annual basis, while five-year plans encapsulated long-term goals. The logic of the plan was to motivate workers and managers in the absence of price and wage incentives. Planning was also supposed to show the superiority of socialism to the irrational chaos of capitalism: after all, was it not better to know how many tons of steel would be available at the end of the year than to leave it up to chance? Stories about record grain harvests or steel production—factories would regularly exceed targets by 108 or 120 percent—were thus the bread and butter of a regime constantly comparing itself to the

West. In fact, however, plans were rarely realized and all statistics were exaggerated. Nevertheless, citizens did feel increased pressure at the close of every plan.

pětka (the five). Name for the group of five political parties that governed the country after independence. The *pětka* was made up of the Agrarians, the People's Party, the National Democrats, the National Socialists, and the Social Democrats. In the years 1920 to 1926, virtually all important governmental decisions were made at private meetings of the leaders of these five parties instead of through normal parliamentary channels. This arrangement was heavily criticized as antidemocratic—especially by communists, Slovaks, and Germans who were all left out—even though the five parties professed to be committed to democracy. The *pětka* was disbanded in 1926, though it continued in expanded versions (with six or eight parties) until Munich (→ *Mnichov*). Along with the Trade Finance Bank (→ *Živnostenská banka*), the *pětka* remained a warhorse of communist propaganda against the bourgeois First Republic (→ *První republika*).

Petra. Brand of cigarettes. Though most communist products have been pushed out by Western competitors, cigarettes have held their own. The most popular brand—then and now—goes by the woman's name Petra, its most attractive quality being its low price. The communist-era brands Start and Sparta have similarly retained their popularity. This is no triumph for Czech nationalism, though, since Philip Morris has bought up all three brands. Other popular brands under communism were the bargain basement Mars and Clea (known as Klejky). As for smoking itself, until recently there was hardly a place in the country where smoking was banned—except for the few restaurants that outlawed it during lunch hour. Even more revealing, a common gratuity left for doctors is a carton of cigarettes (or a bottle of liquor) (→ *poliklinika*). The popularity of smoking stemmed from the fact that there

was so little to live for under communism; outlets like cigarettes, alcohol and → sex thus grew in importance. Even under democracy, many Czech public figures, including Václav → Havel and the Prime Minister Miloš Zeman, are chain smokers.

Petřín. Name given to the grassy hill that rises over Prague (→ *Praha*). For residents of the city, it is their one place for a romantic stroll; it offers a scenic and quiet respite from the hustle and bustle of the city. A miniature replica of the Eiffel Tower near the top of the hill is called the *Eiffelovka*.

PF. While Americans send Christmas cards to family and friends, Czechs are more partial to New Year's Cards, known as PFs. The cards feature an artistic design—often a pen and ink drawing, etching, or photograph—and the year along with the initials PF (from the French *pour féliciter*). Some of the more beautiful PFs are on sale as works of art in second-hand bookshops.

Pionýr (Pioneer). The communist equivalent of the Boy Scouts. The Pioneers originated in the Soviet Union and were exported to all its satellites. Its aim was to indoctrinate young people into socialist values. All children were required to become members, attend regular meetings, and wear the regulation red kerchiefs. Children began as *jiskry* (sparks) between the ages of six and eight (something like Cub Scouts or Brownies) and then moved up to the Pioneers. After turning fifteen, young people could join the more serious Union of Socialist Youth (→ SSM). Like the Boy Scouts, the Pioneers used the motto "Always prepared," but their preparedness was "to build and defend a socialist homeland." Other socialist elements can be found in their bylaws: "to be devoted to the Czechoslovak Communist Party" and "a friend of the Soviet Union and defender of progress and peace throughout the world." Pioneers were always on hand at major holidays, elections, or welcoming ceremonies for foreign dignitaries. Weekly meetings of the Pioneers, however, were less ideological. Though occasionally involving public service work—for example, cleaning up trails in the forest or collecting paper for recycling—they more often simply provided opportunities to play sports or go camping. Today most young people prefer scouting (known as → *Junák*), but the Pioneers still retain a loyal following.

pivo (beer). If there is anything that gives Czechs their self-image, it is beer. Hops (→ *chmel*) was cultivated in the country as far back as the ninth century, and Saint Wenceslas (→ Svatý Václav) even persuaded the pope to revoke a ban on beer brewing. The first golden age of Czech beer was in the Renaissance when a popular rhyme went "*Unus papa Romae, una cerevesia Raconae*" (One pope in Rome, one beer in Rakovník). A folk song likewise claims "*Kde se pivo vaří, tam se dobře daří*" (Where beer is brewed, there the living is good). In the eighteenth century, the great Czech brewer, František Ondřej Poupě, invented new scientific techniques for beer production and wrote the first brew-ing handbook. More home-spun advice says that to keep beer at the proper temperature it should sit on the seventh step down to the cellar. Beer brewed in → České Budějovice, known to Czechs as Budvar and Germans as Budweiser, meanwhile became "the beer of kings" (not the king of beers as its American imitator claims). Like Cologne and perfume, the town of → Plzeň (Pilsen) and a particular style of beer are intimately linked; bottom-fermented beer, now known around the world as Pilsner, was invented there in 1842. Czechs remain devoted beer drinkers and boast the highest per capita consumption in the world; a bottle a day is consumed for every man, woman, and child. Beer is drunk on just about every social occasion—workers can be seen drinking beer at kiosks as early as six in the morning and even the country's presidents often pose with a glass in hand—and it complements every Czech meal. The writer Jaroslav → Hašek proclaimed that any government that raised the price of beer would fall within a year. It actually took four years after the price rise in 1985. Today the price

Most Popular Czech Beers (→ *pivo*)

Though the number of breweries has been decreasing since the revolution, there are at least fifty still in operation. The large number is likely due to Czechs' refusal to drink anything but domestic brands. The effect of the competition is to keep beer prices extremely low. Among the brands listed below, the best known are Budvar, Gambrinus, Kozel, Krušovice, Plzeňský Prazdroj, Radegast, and Staropramen. Among other interesting facts, the former president Václav → Havel once worked in the brewery in Trutnov, while the writer Bohumil → Hrabal memorialized his youth at the brewery in Nymburk in the novel *Cutting It Short*.

Brand	City	Founded
Bernard	Humpolec	1552
Bohemia Regent	Třeboň	1379
Braník	Prague (→ *Praha*)	1898
Březňák	Velké Březno	1753
Budvar	→ České Budějovice	1895
Černohorský (Black Mountain)	Černá Hora	1530
Chmelař (Hop Grower)	Žatec	1801
Chodovar	Chodová Planá	1573
Dačický	Kutná Hora	1573

Brand	City	Founded
Doktor	Svitavy	1256
Eggenberg	Český Krumlov	1560
Ferdinand	Benešov	1897
Gambrinus	→ Plzeň	1869
Herold	Březnice	1506
Holba (Pint)	Hanušovice	1874
Hostan	Znojmo	1720
Janáček	Uherský Brod	1894
Ječmínek	Prostějov	1897
Ježek (Hedgehog)	Jihlava	1860
Kalich (Chalice)	Litoměřice	1720
Klášter (Monastery)	Hradiště nad Jizerou	1570
Konrád	Vratislavice	1872
Korbel (Tankard)	Malý Rohovec	1848
Kozel (Goat)	Velké Popovice	1874
Krakonoš	Trutnov	1582
Krušovice	Krušovice	1581
Litovel	Litovel	1893
Lobkowicz	Vysoký Chlumec	1466
Louny	Louny	1892
Měšťan (Burgher, Town-Dweller)	Praha	1898
Nektar	Strakonice	1649
Novopacké	Nová Paka	1872
Opat (Abbot)	Broumov	1348
Ostravar	Ostrava	1897
Ostrožan	Uherský Ostroh	1592
Pepinova	Nymburk	1895
Pernštejn	→ Pardubice	1871
Platan (Plane Tree)	Protivín	1598
Plzeňský Prazdroj (Pilsner Urquell, Original Source)	Plzeň	1842
Podkováň (Horseshoe)	Dolní Cetno	1434
Podlužan	Břeclav	1522
Poličan	Polička	1517
Poutník (Pilgrim)	Pelhřimov	1551
Primátor (Mayor)	Náchod	1872
Radegast (→ Radhošť)	Šošovice	1970
Rebel	Havlíčkův Brod	1333

Brand	City	Founded
Rychtář (Magistrate)	Hlinsko	1913
Samson	České Budějovice	1795
Starobrno (Old Brno)	→ Brno	1872
Staropramen (Old Source)	Prague - Smíchov	1869
Svijanské	Svijany	1564
Vsačan	Vsetín	1848
Vyškovské	Vyškov	1680
Zlatopramen (Golden Source)	Ústí nad Labem	1867
Zlatovar (Golden Brew)	Opava	1825
Zubr (Bizon)	Přerov	1872

Source: *www.radio.cz/en/html/breweries.html* and *www.svetpiva.cz*

remains lower than nearly anywhere in the world due to intense competition among the country's countless small breweries. Among the popular favorites are Plzeňský prazdroj (Pilsner Urquell—*prazdroj* means original source), Gambrinus, Radegast, Velkopopovický kozel, Budvar, and Staropramen. Most labels sell both a more alcoholic (known as 12°) and less alcoholic (10°) version, though the numbers do not refer to the percentage of alcohol, but rather to the amount of malt extract. Light beer, however, is unknown.

pizza. One of the few foreign foods to be adopted wholeheartedly by Czechs. It is, however, typically served with a dollop of ketchup on top. Chinese food, where it exists, is often accompanied by French fries rather than rice.

Plastic People of the Universe. Rock band. In the seventies, the Plastic People tried to put a Czech twist on American alt-rockers like the Velvet Underground and began playing small gigs at pubs and cottages (→ *chata*). They might have disappeared into history had the communist authorities not decided to arrest them in 1976 for playing indecent music. The arrest inspired Václav → Havel to put together the dissident movement → *Charta* 77, which called on the regime to respect its constitutional guarantee of free expression. The group was chosen precise-

ly because it was apolitical; the case involved only the right of self-expression. The Plastic People gained worldwide fame as a result of the movement, but their music remains a minority taste among Czechs who prefer top forty and disco music.

ples (ball). The formal ball is another social custom—like coffeehouses or opera—imported from Vienna (→ *Vídeň*). Its roots are in Empress → Maria Theresa's decision to relax the ban on the waltz and the opening of aristocratic pastimes to the masses in the wake of the French Revolution. Formal balls reached their peak in the late nineteenth and early twentieth century when virtually every professional and voluntary association—lawyers, police-officers, bakers, hunters, and students—held its own ball, most during ball season, which begins after New Year and ends at Lent (→ *masopust*). Even today most Czechs attend at least one ball every year. Dress for balls is by Czech standards formal—a suit rather than a tuxedo—and the featured music is usually a brass band (→ *dechovka*). Dancing lessons are still popular among secondary school students as preparation for ball season.

Plzeň (Pilsen). A city in the western part of the country that is best known as the birthplace of Pilsner beer (→ *pivo*) and the home of the Pilsner Urquell brand. It was one of the few cities liberated by Americans during World War II. The rest of the country had to suffer under Soviet occupation.

Podkarpatská Rus (Subcarpathian Ruthenia). A small region currently in the western Ukraine, but forming an eastern tail to Czechoslovakia (→ *Československo*) between the wars. Though it has few cultural or linguistic ties with the Czechs or Slovaks, it was awarded to the newly formed country in 1918 at the expense of war-losers Austria and Hungary. Despite its small size and short affiliation with the Czechs, Ruthenia remains an object of considerable fascination. In contrast to the heavily industrialized Czech lands, it stands for unspoiled nature and traditional village lifestyles. Its inhabitants, known as Ruthenians, included romantic highwaymen like Nikola → Šuhaj and bearded orthodox Jews, and its architecture features picturesque wooden churches. Though the Soviet Union annexed the region in 1945, Czechs continue to hold a soft spot in their hearts for Ruthenians and devour literature and films devoted to their lives.

podpultovka (under the counter item). Inefficiency and the lack of real prices under communism meant that virtually all goods, except perhaps bottled sauerkraut, were in short supply. The more sought-out products—new electronics, better clothing styles, sensational books—were kept under the counter (hence the name) by the sales clerk and dispensed only to friends or those willing to pay a bribe. One might thus give a magazine seller twenty crowns (→ *koruna*) and ask him to set aside the next issue of the magazine *Mladý svět* (Young World). Among the biggest beneficiaries of the system were butchers, who lived like kings from the bribes they received for better cuts of meat. At Christmas time, many of these *podpultovky*, especially tropical fruits, suddenly became available above the counter as a special gift from the regime.

pohoda (comfort). As the journalist Benjamin Kuras notes, every Czech's ideal is to achieve comfort. The aim here is not fame or fortune, but an absence of work and stress. Comfort means a job that does not require much effort and has an early quitting time. It is having one's own apartment and a cottage on the side. It is having pocket change to go out for beer every evening and take a trip to the beach in the summer. All this is enough to live a comfortable life. Of course, the single-minded pursuit of comfort may be the largest obstacle to social and economic progress in the country. The word is used commonly in conversation to mean that things are okay or cool.

pohádka (fairy tale). When Czech national awakeners (→ *Národní obrození*) wanted to restore the national culture after centuries of neglect, they had to turn to ordinary villagers and their oral tales. Early patriots like Karel Jaromír → Erben and Božena → Němcová thus crisscrossed the countryside collecting fairy tales and published them in editions which sell out to this day. The fairy tales told not only of princes and princesses—e.g. → *Pyšná princezna* (The Proud Princess) or *Zlatovláska* (Princess Golden-Hair)—but also of ordinary people like → *hloupý Honza* (stupid Jack). They were originally intended for an adult audience, and even now, when their primary audience is children, they retain an adult level of violence. In the Czech version of Little Red Riding Hood, for example, the little girl is eaten by the wolf and is saved only when a doctor cuts open the wolf's belly (shown in graphic detail in children's theaters). Even worse is the ever-popular → *Otesánek* (Stump Boy), where a barren couple adopts a tree stump that eats them out of house and home. A Czech innovation is the filmed fairy tale. Beginning in the fifties, Czech directors started making feature-length films of classic fairy tales with live actors. They soon became some of the most popular films in the country and are rebroadcast in marathon sessions at Christmas (→ *Vánoce*). The obsession with fairy tales may help to explain many Czechs' belief in a harmonious resolution to all conflicts, and their faith that magical outside forces will rescue them from danger.

128

pohraniční stráž (border guard). After the communist takeover (→ *Vítězný únor*), the western borders of Czechoslovakia were closed and barbed wire laid across the boundaries. Villages near the border were evacuated to make enforcement easier. The *pohraniční stráž* meanwhile was given the job of preventing citizens from fleeing the country. Their orders were to shoot on sight (they killed over 170 citizens), and their "bravery" was lionized in communist propaganda. They even adopted the Dog's Head symbol of the country's medieval border guards (→ Chodsko). Closed borders were necessary both to stem mass emigration and to prevent citizens from seeing the greener pastures on the other side, though the communists usually justified them as a means of keeping foreign spies from infiltrating the country. Those who wished to leave the country illegally usually chose the swamps and forests of → Šumava as the best escape route or fled through a socialist country with more liberal border controls like Yugoslavia or Hungary. The cutting of the barbed wire between Czechoslovakia and its neighbors was one of the symbolic moments of the fall of communism.

pohřeb (funeral). Traditional funerals begin with a musical procession and end with the playing of the deceased's favorite song, usually a traditional folk melody (→ *lidovka*). More recently cremation has become preferred to burials, evidence of Czechs' lack of religiosity. Flowers for the deceased are always sent in even numbers, so even-numbered bouquets should never be given to friends or lovers. Most Czechs are conscientious about visiting the graves of friends and relatives whenever there is a national holiday.

polévka (soup). Every sit-down meal must start with soup, which is considered the hearty and filling portion of the meal; a popular saying has it that soup is the *grunt* (foundation) and meat is the *špunt* (cork or stopper). Traditionally ladled out from a large tureen, the best-loved soups are beef broth, tripe, and cabbage.

poliklinika (polyclinic). Healthcare facility that includes general practitioners and a wide range of specialists. Under communism, all citizens were assigned to a polyclinic near their home and, in the case of illness, had to be treated by whichever doctor was available. Typically, patients arrived at the clinic by six or seven in the morning to wait for a doctor whose office hours ended at noon. All care was free, but service was poor because doctors received low, fixed salaries. This made bribes—usually cigarettes, alcohol, or money—necessary to move up the waiting list for rationed care or to guarantee higher quality service. Visits to the doctor were and still are frequent, as a doctor's note (→ *neschopenka*) is necessary to miss work. One of the perks of the old system was relatively easy access to spa cures (→ *lázně*). Since 1989, the general standard of care has risen with the importation of new technology and the freedom to choose one's doctor.

politické procesy (show trials). As soon as the communists took power in 1948 (→ *Vítězný únor*), they began to punish their enemies. Thus began a series of political trials that lasted for the better part of six years and led to 234,000 convictions and 178 executions (plus the deaths of another 244 inmates shot while "attempting to escape"). Each set of trials went after a particular group: army generals, members of opposition political parties (→ Horáková), the Catholic Church (→ *katolická církev*), the peasant "Green International," and Catholic writers, to name some of the more prominent. Ultimately, the party began searching for enemies in its own ranks and jailed such stalwart communists as Rudolf → Slánský and Gustáv → Husák as traitors or bourgeois nationalists. Virtually all of these convictions were based on forged evidence and forced confessions. Their aim was not only to scare the population into supporting the new regime, but also to give the regime an excuse for its manifest failures. Some of the victims of the trials were rehabilitated in the sixties, but most had to wait until the fall of communism.

Polívka, Bolek (1949). Popular comedian. The roots of Polívka's comedy are both in the European clown tradition—where he uses his long, lanky frame to great affect—and in the theater of the absurd. Much of his appeal comes from his folksy ways (→ *lid*)—he perfectly embodies the talky, vulgar, joke-telling Czech everyman. In his most popular film, *Dědictví* (The Inheritance), he plays a country bumpkin who gets rich from property restitution (→ *restituce*). Polívka remains one of the few stars who has resisted the lure of Prague; he focuses his career on the country's second city, → Brno, as well as on his farm where he reigns as King of → *Valašsko*.

polka. The Czech national dance. Said to have originated in the 1830s in the Czech lands, the polka caught on quickly— → Smetana included it in his Bartered Bride (→ *Prodaná nevěsta*) as a symbol of Czechness—and became a fixture at all popular entertainments (→ *zábava*) and balls (→ *ples*). Its name comes not from Poland, but from the word *půlka* (half), a reference to the fast 2/4 beat, though it was Polish immigrants who helped to spread it around the world. The most famous Czech polka is → "*Škoda lásky*" also known as the "Beer Barrel Polka."

Polsko (Poland). Czechs see their northern neighbor as a backward, poorer, and far more religious version of themselves. Many cross the border with Poland to buy cheap food or consumer goods—Poles have an image as wheeler-dealers—which they carry home in large bags known as *polské kabely* (Polish bags).

pomlázka (Easter whip). In traditional Easter (→ *Velikonoce*) celebrations, boys construct braided whips from willow branches, which they use to gently lash female acquaintances. They are then rewarded with a decorated egg or a colored ribbon tied to the end of the whip. The custom seems to have originated as a fertility rite or an offering to ensure a good harvest. In its contemporary version, boys buy the *pomlázka* on the street or make them at school and are rewarded with

chocolate or shots of → *slivovice* depending on their age. In some regions of the country, girls are doused with water to drive away evil spirits. See also → *Hody hody doprovody*.

pomocná stráž veřejné bezpečnosti (auxiliary public security patrol). Under communism, retired citizens often served as so-called "auxiliary patrols" of the police (→ VB). They took it upon themselves to enforce public morality by informing the police of any suspicious behavior in their neighborhood and were known for abusing their powers. Children got used to having their bicycle tires deflated by zealous auxiliary patrolmen cracking down on reckless riding.

Porta. Folk and country music festival. Porta was founded in 1967 to give a public stage to the emerging → *country* and folk scenes. It functioned as a contest with artists competing first at local and then at the national level. The concerts at Porta attracted thousands of young fans, many of whom associated the music with the freedom of America (→ *Amerika*). Indeed, support for a genre praising the open road and individuality was, like → *tramping*, a sort of protest against the stifling atmosphere of the communist dictatorship. As evidence of the regime's concern over the political implications of the music, several seminal country groups were forced to change their English names after the coming of normalization (→ *normalizace*). Thus, Rangers became Plavci (Swimmers) and Greenhorns turned into Zelenáči (Green Ones). Major figures involved with Porta were Honza → Nedvěd, Michal Tučný, Jaromír Nohavica, and Karel Plíhal.

poslušně hlásím (respectfully report). The traditional formulation for addressing superior officers in the Austro-Hungarian army (→ Švejk). It was later replaced by "*dovolte mi promluvit*" (allow me to speak).

posvícení (village fair, feast). Villages typically celebrate *posvícení* on a Sunday in the autumn. Though the day is often connected with the town's patron saint or the consecration of the local church, there are no real religious roots to the celebration. It is simply a time for good food (the harvest has just ended), music, dancing, and drinking. The fun-loving Czechs were once such enthusiasts of these entertainments that the Emperor Josef II had to decree that each village could only celebrate *posvícení* once a year.

poúnorový (post-February). Like other Eastern European nations, the Czechs have a penchant for naming historical events and periods by the month when they occurred or began. Thus, the communist putsch in February 1948 is known as Victorious February (→ *Vítězný únor*) and the entire communist era is known as the post-February era. Meanwhile, the men of January, the reformist politicians who came to power in January 1968, were the architects of the Prague Spring (→ *Pražské jaro*). Their work was shattered by the Soviet invasion in August (→ *srpnová invaze*) and followed by the dismal post-August era. Today Czechs finally live in the freedom and security of the post-November era (communism fell in November 1989, → *Sametová revoluce*) and try to avoid looking at pre-November events (that is, communism). Since the month of March is also in use to designate the period after Munich (→ *Mnichov*) and the men of October helped to achieve independence (→ *28. říjen*), Czechs are nearly at the end of months to label their country's traumas.

pouť (pilgrimage/fair). While for modern-day Czechs, the word *pouť* conjures up images of merry-go-rounds and sweets, it originally referred to religious pilgrimages to such holy sites as Hostýn, → Říp, Svatá Hora (Holy Mountain), and Svatý Kopeček (Holy Mound). Catholics would make the long journey to these holy places by following trails marked with wayside crosses (→ *boží muka*). Since not all could travel these distances, every village instituted its own *pouť* on the anniversary of the local saint or the founding of the church. Though of religious significance

and marked by special church services, they are now part entertainment and part commerce. Rides and games are set up on the village square, and merchants in small wooden stalls sell such treats as decorated gingerbread hearts (→ *jarmark*). In the evening, there is music and dancing. At home, fair days are marked by a large meal and the baking of *pouťové* → *koláče* (fair cakes).

povinná četba (required reading). Phrase that refers to the classics of Czech literature, which are a required part of the school curriculum and appear on school-leaving exams (→ *maturita*). It includes such classics as → Němcová's → *Babička*, → Jirásek's → *Temno*, → Erben's *Kytice*, and → Hašek's → *Švejk*. Under communism, the oeuvre of left-wing writers like → Bezruč was added to reading lists. While most Czechs know these works by title and reputation, few have read more than a chapter or two. Many survive their exams in Czech literature with the help of cribs that contain short summaries of all of these works.

Pozdrav pánbůh (God bless you). A traditional greeting that is still sometimes used by old people or in rural areas. One properly responds with "*Až na věky*" (May it be for ages). A more common form of this address is the shortened form *Těbůh* (God to you).

práce šlechtí (work ennobles). Oft-cited proverb. Industriousness and hard work are traditional components of the Czech self-image. Pulling one's weight was seen as the only way to ensure the nation's survival against more powerful neighbors. For a time this work ethic seemed to pay off as the country became a world-class industrial power in the nineteenth and twentieth centuries. Following the example of the Emperor → Franz Joseph, the working day traditionally begins at the unreasonably early hour of 6 a.m.. Though the nobility of work was a central pillar of Marxist ideology (→ *čest práci*), the communist regime nearly destroyed these traditions by eliminating all work incentives

What Czechs Most Esteem in Themselves

These are the results of a poll asking Czechs what characteristics they most esteem in themselves.

CHARACTER-ISTIC		PERCENT-AGE
Pracovitost	Industriousness	26
Pohostinnost	Hospitality	11
Manuální zručnost	Handiness	9
Vynalézavost	Inventiveness	7
Vzdělanost	Educatedness	6
Smysl pro humor	Sense of Humor	5
Flexibilita	Flexibility	4
Soudržnost	Solidarity	4
Odpovědnost	Responsibility	3
Vlastenectví	Patriotism	3
Skromnost	Modesty	2
Tolerantnost	Tolerance	2
Jiná odpověď	Other Answer	6
Nic	Nothing	3
Neví	Don't Know	9

Source: Poll reported in *Mladá fronta Dnes*, 17 April 2003.

and elevating politics over talent. The effect of the system was better encapsulated in sayings like "What you can do today, you can do tomorrow" and "Whoever works hard, shortens his life." Since the fall of communism, Czechs have, with much grumbling, again become used to longer work hours.

pracovní sobota (working Saturday). As all citizens of communist Czechoslovakia were employees of the state, it was the state which set their working hours. During the fifties and sixties this meant a six-day workweek and even occasional working Sundays, which were supposedly necessary to fulfill the five-year plans (→ *pětiletka*), build socialism, and overtake the West. In 1968, the five-day workweek was introduced, but intermittent working Saturdays continued, first on odd-numbered weeks and then more sporadically, whenever the plan needed a shot in the arm. But these work habits need not arouse pity. As a popular saying went, "We pretend to work, and they pretend to pay us." Similarly, a film of the late seventies called *Friday Isn't a Holiday* paid tribute to the habit of workers leaving early on Friday to work on their cottages (→ *chata*) or stand in line at department stores.

Praha (Prague). Prague's history is customarily dated from the first Czech dynasty, the Premyslids (→ *Přemyslovci*), who made it their capital. → Libuše, the first queen of the Czech people, said of the city that its fame would one day reach the stars, and since then Prague has been called the "Mother of Cities." These first rulers lived in the castle → Vyšehrad, though the ruling family soon moved to the Prague Castle (→ *Hrad*) on the other side of the → Vltava. The city received a Gothic makeover as well as the construction of many of its monuments under → Karel IV, but was completely reconstructed in the baroque style (→ *české baroko*) that made it famous during the Habsburg-led Counter-Reformation in the seventeenth century (→ *Bílá hora*). It was then that Prague became the *stověžaté* (hundred-towered) town that it is today. Prague's beauty lies in the preservation of this Gothic-baroque core with all its twisting alleys and stone buildings; the Czechs' penchant for surrendering to invading armies (→ *holubičí povaha*) meant that the city avoided pitched battles and wartime destruction. The city center was only marred by the communists, who decided to build a freeway through the center of town so that tanks could easily put down demonstrations. Prague's size—more than a tenth of the population lives there—has made it the unrivaled center of the country. It is home to virtually all influential cultural, economic, and political institutions. This position, however, draws complaints of Pragocentrism from both Slovakia and the Czech hinterlands, which ultimately lose all their talented sons and daughters to the bright lights of Prague. Indeed, cars with Prague license plates—those starting with an A—are often honked at in the provinces. Never-

---

World Heritage Sites in the Czech Republic

The World Heritage Convention was adopted by UNESCO in 1972 to protect the world's cultural and natural heritage. Each year sites from around the globe are nominated for inclusion on a list of World Heritage sites. The following are the Czech sites that have been accepted by UNESCO and the date of their acceptance. The complete list can be found at www.unesco.org/heritage.htm. The brief descriptions are taken from the website.

Historic Center of Prague (→ *Praha*) (1992)

Built between the 11th and 18th centuries, the Old Town, the Lesser Town and the New Town—with their magnificent monuments, such as Hradčany Castle, St. Vitus Cathedral, Charles Bridge, and numerous churches and palaces, built mostly in the 14th century under the Holy Roman Emperor Charles IV—speak of the great architectural and cultural influence enjoyed by this city since the Middle Ages.

Historic Center of Český Krumlov (1992)

Situated on the banks of the → Vltava River, the town was built around a 13th-century castle with Gothic, Renaissance, and baroque elements. It is an outstanding example of a small Central European medieval town whose architectural heritage has remained intact thanks to its peaceful evolution over more than five centuries.

Historic Center of Telč (1992)

The houses in Telč, which stand on a hilltop, were originally built of wood. After a fire in the late 14th century, the town was rebuilt in stone, surrounded by walls and further strengthened by a network of artificial ponds. The town's Gothic castle was reconstructed in High Gothic style in the late 15th century.

Pilgrimage Church of St. John of Nepomuk (→ Nepomucký, Jan) at Zelená Hora (1994)

This pilgrimage church, built in honor of St. John of Nepomuk, stands at Zelená Hora, not far from Žďár nad Sázavou in Moravia. Constructed at the beginning of the 18th century on a star-shaped plan, it is the most unusual work by the great architect Jan Blažej Santini–Aichel (→ *české baroko*), whose highly original style falls between Neo-Gothic and baroque.

Kutná Hora: Historical Town Center with the Church of Saint Barbara and the Cathedral of Our Lady at Sedlec (1995)

Kutná Hora developed as a result of the exploitation of the silver mines. In the 14th century it became a royal city endowed with monuments that symbolized its prosperity. The Church of St. Barbara, a jewel of the late Gothic period, and the Cathedral of Our Lady at Sedlec, which was restored in line with the baroque taste of the early 18th century, were to influence the architecture of Central Europe. These masterpieces today form part of a well-preserved medieval urban fabric with some particularly fine private dwellings.

Lednice-Valtice Cultural Landscape (1996)

Between the 17th and 20th centuries, the ruling dukes of Liechtenstein transformed their domains in southern Moravia into a striking landscape. It married baroque architecture (mainly the work of Johann Bernhard Fischer von Erlach) and the classical and Neo-Gothic style of the castles of Lednice and Valtice with a countryside fashioned according to English romantic principles of landscape architecture. At 200 sq. km., it is one of the largest artificial landscapes in Europe.

Holašovice Historical Village Reservation (1998)

Holašovice is an exceptionally complete and well-preserved example of a traditional Central European village. It has a large number of outstanding 18th- and 19th-century vernacular buildings in a style known as "South Bohemian folk baroque," and preserves a ground plan dating from the Middle Ages.

Gardens and Castle at Kroměříž (1998)

Kroměříž stands on the site of an earlier ford across the Morava River, at the foot of the Chřiby mountain range which dominates the central part of Moravia. The gardens and castle of Kroměříž are an exceptionally complete and well-preserved example of a European baroque princely residence and its gardens.

Litomyšl Castle (1999)

Litomyšl Castle was originally a Renaissance arcade-castle of the type first developed in Italy and then adopted and greatly developed in Central Europe in the 16th century. Its design and decoration are particularly fine, including the later high-baroque features added in the 18th century. It preserves intact the range of ancillary buildings associated with an aristocratic residence of this type.

Holy Trinity Column in → Olomouc (2000)

This memorial column, erected in the early years of the 18th century, is the most outstanding example of a type of monument specific to Central Europe. In the characteristic regional style known as "Olomouc baroque" and rising to a height of 35 m, it is decorated with many fine religious sculptures, the work of the distinguished Moravian artist Ondřej Zahner.

Tugendhat Villa in → Brno (2001)

The Tugendhat Villa in Brno, designed by the architect Mies van der Rohe, is an outstanding example of the international style, the modern movement in architecture which developed in Europe in the 1920s. Its particular value lies in the application of innovative spatial and aesthetic concepts that aim to satisfy new lifestyle needs by taking advantage of the opportunities afforded by modern industrial production.

The Jewish Quarter and St. Procopius Basilica of Třebíč (2003)

The ensemble of the Jewish Quarter, the old Jewish cemetery, and the Basilica of St. Procopius in Třebíč are reminders of the coexistence of Jewish and Christian cultures from the Middle Ages to the 20th century. The Jewish Quarter bears outstanding testimony to the different aspects of the life of this community. St. Procopius Basilica, built as part of the Benedictine monastery in the early 13th century, is a remarkable example of the influence of Western European architectural heritage in this region.

theless, Czechs eagerly sign up for company-sponsored trips to the capital, where they stroll around the old town, shop in the department store Kotva (→ Prior), and take in a play at the National Theater (→ *Národní divadlo*). Besides the historic core, Prague also includes ritzy neighborhoods like Vinohrady, working class ones like → Žižkov and Karlín, as well as the inevitable prefabricated concrete blocks (→ *panelák*) on the outskirts.

pranostika (weather-lore). Despite a moderate, continental climate, the Czech lands boast countless rhymes about the weather. Thus, we hear that "A cold January means a green April," "A white February strengthens the fields," "When July warms, winter at Christmas glitters," and most popularly, "March—we crawl behind the stove, April—we're still there." Others are connected with various saints' days (→ *jmeniny*), so, for example, Saint Martin (November 11) is said to arrive on a white horse. Czech remains one of the few languages not to have adopted international names for the months of the year. All of the months thus have poetic associations: January is *leden* (*led* means ice), February *únor*, March *březen* (for the birch tree), April *duben* (for the oak), May *květen* (from the word for flower), June *červen* (from the word red), July *červenec* (even redder), August *srpen* (named for the sickle), September *září* (glowing), October *říjen* (rutting season), November *listopad* (meaning leaf fall), and December *prosinec* (grey or white).

Pravda vítězí (Truth triumphs). A phrase associated with → Svatý Václav that has become a motto for the Czech nation. As the journalist Benjamin Kuras writes, it expresses a typically Czech view of the world: "It is comforting. It soothes a Czech to know that whatever disaster he might be going through, truth will triumph. He knows that truth is not triumphing right now but that it will triumph eventually. Some day. It just has to... And when it doesn't, it's nobody's fault. Its time just hasn't come yet. But it is soothing to know it will." The slogan has been cited

prominently by Jan → Hus and Tomáš → Masaryk. Václav → Havel even came up with his own enlarged version: "Truth and Love Will Triumph over Lies and Hate." It appears both on the statue of Hus on Old Town Square and also on the Prague Castle (→ *Hrad*).

pravopis (spelling, literally "correct writing"). For a nation which professes to have a complex language (→ *čeština*), Czechs are extraordinarily sensitive about grammar. Bad spelling or punctuation is taken to be a sign of low intelligence. The special bane of Czech writers are → *vyjmenovaná slova* (exception words) and foreign words. The sensitivity may have to do with the fact that Czech intellectuals only began using the language in the mid-nineteenth century and associate the fate of the culture with the language (→ *Národní obrození*). Worries about *pravopis* today focus on the deleterious effects of new electronic technologies. Some believe that because text messages and e-mails are written without accent marks, people will forget how to use them. As evidence of Czechs' interest in grammar, the Czech Language Institute at the Academy of Sciences runs a telephone advice line for grammar and spelling that receives upwards of ten thousand calls a year.

Pražské jaro (Prague Spring). The brief period of liberalization in Czechoslovakia in the spring of 1968. The roots of the Prague Spring were in the economic problems of the sixties and the increasing boldness of writers and students in criticizing the regime. In January 1968, the First Secretary of the Party, Antonín Novotný, was removed from office and replaced by the more liberal Alexander Dubček, who initiated his famous "Socialism with a human face" (→ *Socialismus s lidskou tváří*). The hesitancy of Dubček and the "Men of January" to crack down on dissent led to a loosening of censorship and a more open media. By April, the Central Committee (→ ÚV KSČ) adopted an Action Program calling for more democratization (though not democracy). But public opinion ran ahead of government action. In June, the writer Ludvík Vaculík issued a manifesto calling for a speeding up and deepening of reforms. His *2000 Words* attracted signatures from the leading lights of the artistic, scientific, and athletic communities. All this time, the party had been receiving increasingly stern warnings from the Soviet Union to keep to the socialist line. On August 20-21, the Soviets' patience finally ran out, and Warsaw Pact forces entered the country (→ *srpnová invaze*), kidnapped the reformist communist leaders, and "normalized" (→ *normalizace*) politics. In world-historical terms, the crushing of the Prague Spring put a definitive end to any illusion that communism could be reformed, a change that ultimately led to the fall of the Soviet bloc. The events still arouse mixed feelings. For many, it was a glowing, beautiful moment that could have led to real freedom; others criticize its leaders as naïve, misguided communists who played with fire and got burned. Prague Spring also refers to the music festival started in 1946 to celebrate the end of the war. It has been held continuously since then, attracting some of the stars of the classical music world, including Rostropovich, Bernstein, von Karajan, and Kubelík. The festival always starts on May 12 (the day of Smetana's death) with → Smetana's patriotic → *Má vlast* (My Country) and concludes with Beethoven's *Ode to Joy*.

Přemyslovci (Premyslids). The first and only Czech royal lineage. The line allegedly came into existence when a dissatisfied subject challenged the right of the people's female ruler → Libuše to decide cases involving men. Libuše was forced to take a husband who would assume ruling duties and in an act worthy of Czech egalitarianism (→ *rovnostářství*), chose a common ploughman named Přemysl rather than any of her more distinguished suitors. Přemysl proved a wise ruler, though his poor treatment of women led to the War of the Maidens (→ *Dívčí válka*). His offspring governed the country from the ninth century until the start of the fourteenth century. Among the best-known Premyslids are Saint Wenceslas (→ Svatý Václav) and Otakar II

(→ *Moravské pole*). The lineage was raised to the status of kings in 1212 with the coronation of Otakar I and died out with the murder of Wenceslas III in 1306, succumbing to the hereditary disease of royalty: failure to produce a male heir. From then until 1918 the Czechs were ruled by non-Czech royal families.

Prior. Communist-era department store. Though the selection was limited by Western standards, Prior brought the first taste of consumer society to residents of major Czech cities. While most major cities had a Prior, all Czechs had to travel to Prague (→ *Praha*) to visit the one-of-a-kind department stores Kotva (Anchor) and Bílá labuť (White Swan). All three of these stores, however, have been eclipsed in the postcommunist period by Western-owned big box retailers. These new consumer choices have led Czechs to put aside their traditional weekend pastimes of cottaging (→ *chata*) and hiking (→ *Klub českých turistů*) in favor of shopping.

Prodaná nevěsta (The Bartered Bride). Opera written by Bedřich → Smetana. Beloved for its village setting, earthy humor, and catchy melodies, *The Bartered Bride* is a constant feature in opera companies' repertoires. It opens with that prototypical image of Czechness: villagers dancing the → polka and singing on the main square (→ *náměstí*). It tells the story of Mařenka, a peasant girl, who is being forced by her parents to marry the son of the wealthy landowner Mícha instead of her true love, Jeník. All is happily resolved when Jeník reveals that he is Mícha's long-lost son from a previous marriage and can thus marry Mařenka. The opera continues to be loved for its danceable polkas and portrayal of beer-drinking, fun-loving Czechs.

prodavačka (sales clerk). Czech sales clerks can be counted on to ignore customers, provide no help with finding products, and look permanently put upon. These poor service habits were a product of the communist regime, where the profit incentive did not exist and workers were considered the betters of their bosses. Since the fall of communism, these habits are slowly changing, especially in foreign-owned firms like McDonald's.

protekce (pull). A word that designates such practices as favoritism, nepotism, string pulling, and even what would be now called networking. Though endemic under communism, its roots are much older. A classic film of the thirties stars Vlasta → Burian as a hospital patient who is mistakenly identified as a VIP and treated accordingly. After the communist coup, however, chronic shortages in everything made *protekce* a fact of daily life. It was widespread in education, healthcare (→ *poliklinika*), and housing (→ *dekrety na byty*), where inside connections needed to be paid off to get a place at university, high-quality medicines, and even a new apartment. Children of influential parents who receive advantages as a matter of course are known as *protekční děti* (protected children). The tradition continues even after the end of communism. As one car mechanic put it, "*Protekce* ended, but old buddies remained."

Protektorát (Protectorate). After the Nazi takeover of Bohemia and Moravia in 1938 and 1939 (→ *Mnichov*), the German-inhabited borderlands (→ *sudetští Němci*) were incorporated directly into the German Reich, while the rest of the country was turned into the Protectorate of Bohemia and Moravia and presided over by a Nazi-appointed Reichsprotektor. Despite heavy-handed rule—many were assigned to work camps—and constant shortages, most Czechs found ways to get along with their occupiers. With the exception of the assassination of Reichsprotektor Reinhard Heydrich (→ *Heydrichiáda*), there was little partisan activity in the country (→ *odboj*, → *holubičí povaha*). As in all territories directly occupied by the Nazis, the government oversaw the almost complete destruction of the country's substantial Jewish population. For Czechs, however, more memorable was the destruction of the entire adult population of the village of → Lidice as retaliation for the assassination of Heydrich.

prověrková komise (screening commission). These commissions were established after the Russian invasion (→ *srpnová invaze*) to cleanse the Communist Party of internal enemies. All members of the party as well as those holding positions of authority were required to stand before a screening commission and declare that they agreed with the entrance of the Warsaw Pact armies. Those who refused were expelled from the party or dismissed from their jobs. The ultimate result of these purges was that thousands of the country's most qualified administrators, professionals, and academics were reduced to manual labor and their places taken by unskilled opportunists.

První republika (First Republic). In the eyes of most Czechs, the First Republic—lasting from October 1918 (→ *28. říjen*) to the Munich capitulation in 1938 (→ *Mnichov*)—stands for hard work, prosperity, and freedom. Czechoslovakia at the time was one of the world's major industrial powers and the only country in Central and Eastern Europe to remain continuously democratic. These achievements were seen as proof of the claim of National Revivalists (→ *Národní obrození*) that the Czechs deserved their own independent state. As much as its political and economic successes, fond memories are held of its cultural achievements and its bourgeois pastimes. Many covet images of well-dressed middle class citizens whiling away time in luxurious coffee houses, attending elegant soirées, and traveling abroad on vacation. Symbols of the First Republic include President → Masaryk, the writer → Čapek, and the industrialist → Baťa. The communists did all they could to discredit this golden age; they portrayed it as a time of poverty, exploitation, and oligarchical rule by a handful of powerful politicians (the → *pětka*) and large firms (→ *Živnostenská banka*). These prejudices all disappeared with the fall of communism. Present-day Czechs of virtually all political stripes turn to the First Republic for inspiration and symbolic capital. Besides the First Republic, the only other numerical designation in widespread use is the Second Republic which lasted for only a few months between Munich and the Nazi occupation. Today Czechs live in either the Fourth, Eighth or even First Republic, depending on whether one counts the several communist constitutions and the breakup of Czechoslovakia as regime changes.

ptydepe. The name of an artificial bureaucratic language invented by Václav → Havel in his play *Vyrozumění* (The Memorandum). In the play, the introduction of this incomprehensible language for intra-office communication allows a bureaucrat to push out his boss and take over the firm. It thus served as a thinly disguised allegory of the way that the ruling communists manipulated the Czech language to keep themselves in power. Words came to mean their opposite—democracy meant rule by a select group of workers; sloganeering replaced real thought—one could say that "Stalin is the people," and a bureaucratic jargon permeated all communication. A letter to the Central Committee could thus go like this, "We send you sincere comradely greetings from the deliberations of the Third Congress of the Czech Hunter's Union. We can report to you that we fulfilled the decisive tasks of socialist hunting which we set down in accord with the conclusions of the Fourteenth and Fifteenth Congresses of the Communist Party of Czechoslovakia."

Pucholt, Vladimír (1942). Film and theatrical actor. As much as any one person, Vladimír Pucholt symbolized the liberalization of the sixties. He starred in several classic films of the Czech New Wave (→ *Nová vlna*) as a naïve, but brash (like the decade itself) young adult, and could make humor out of the rep-

etition of a single word (most famously *ahoj* in Miloš Forman's film → *Černý Petr*). He left the republic at the height of his career without money or prospects, but eventually fulfilled his childhood dream by studying to be a pediatrician, an occupation he practices to this day in Canada.

Punťa (Spot). The most common name for a dog, it is derived from the word *puntík* (spot). Other common names include Alík, Azor, Brok, Rex, Ťapka (Paw), Betyna, and Ketyna. Always popular, dog-owning has enjoyed a boom in the last decade with German shepherds and daschunds the most popular breeds. Though owners rarely clean up after their dogs, they are required to buy tickets for them on public transportation (→ *tramvaj*). Cats are often called Micka, Mourek, Macek, and Minda.

Pyšná princezna (The Proud Princess). The most watched Czech film of all time. *The Proud Princess* is based on a fairy tale by Božena → Němcová and tells the story of the headstrong princess Krasomila who refuses all suitors until King Miroslav, disguised as a humble gardener, tames her spirit and wins her heart. In its 1952 filmed version, the story takes on communist elements: a good empire triumphs over an evil one and willingness to do manual labor is the sign of the new aristocracy. The film inaugurated a Czech tradition of filmed fairy tales (→ *pohádka*) with live actors. These films are produced almost annually and include such classics as *Byl jednou jeden král* (There Once Was a King), *Šíleně smutná princezna* (The Awfully Sad Princess), and *Tři oříšky pro Popelku* (Three Nuts for Cinderella). They are shown continuously during the Christmas holidays (→ *Vánoce*).

R

ř. Letter in the Czech alphabet. Czech (→ čeština) is written with the Roman alphabet (unlike some Slavic languages that use Cyrillic), though several letters have an upside-down caret over them which palatalizes their sound. Thus, č is pronounced as ch, š as sh, and ž as zh. Known as a háček (little hook), the diacritic above the letters is the handiwork of the Church reformer Jan → Hus. The most distinctive of these letters is the ř, a combination of a trilled r and a ž, which gives foreign speakers of the language fits. The sound causes difficulties for the Czechs themselves: it is typically the last sound a child masters, and some never master it at all. Nevertheless, it occurs in a large number of common words like říci (to say) and names like → Dvořák.

Radhošť. A mountain in the Wallachia (→ Valašsko) region of eastern Moravia (→ Morava). It was here that an ancient pagan people who predate the Czechs worshipped a god of the harvest and fertility named Radegast and celebrated the summer solstice. The place was later consecrated a Christian holy site and was associated with the Slavic missionaries → Cyril and Methodius. By the nineteenth century, it had become a symbol of Czech and more so Moravian (→ Morava) nationalism. An important nationalist gathering was held on the mountain in 1862, and a stone quarried there provided one of four foundation stones of the National Theater (→ Národní divadlo). The mountain and its history have been featured in numerous artistic works—widely known is a statue of Ra-degast with a lion's head and horned helmet. A popular beer bears the name Radegast.

Rádio Jerevan (Radio Yerevan). Although it actually existed as a radio station in the Soviet Republic of Armenia, Radio Yerevan was better known as the fictional source of a series of political jokes popular throughout Eastern Europe. These jokes take the form of a question addressed to Radio Yerevan, followed by the station's humorous answer. For example, Q: Is it true that the Soviet poet Mayakovsky committed suicide? A: Yes, we even recorded his last words: Don't shoot, comrades. Q: Can we introduce communism into Switzerland? A: Yes, but it would be a shame. Folklorists say that the jokes refer to Yerevan because of a long Eastern European tradition of Armenian jokes (often told in fake Armenian accents). The butt of most native Czech jokes, however, are stupid policemen (→ VB). Humor of course flourished under communism because of the lack of other outlets for dissatisfaction and the general misery of life. All agree that jokes have noticeably deteriorated since the revolution.

Radio Luxembourg. This powerful radio station broadcasting pop hits from the Grand Duchy often made it through the radio jamming of the Soviet bloc. It thus gave many Czechs their first introduction to Western pop culture.

Rádio Svobodná Evropa (Radio Free Europe). A radio station founded by the U.S. government in 1950 to broadcast objective news about domestic affairs to the subjugated countries in Eastern Europe. Its first broadcasts were aimed at Czechoslovakia, and the head of the Czechoslovak service was the famed liberal journalist and friend of → Čapek and → Masaryk, Ferdinand Peroutka. Despite frequent jamming by the communists, Czechs were often able to tune in to the Munich-based broadcasts, though they could be punished for doing so. One of the most popular programs was hosted by Karel → Kryl, a folk singer whose music was banned after his emigration in 1969. Radio Free Europe is also associated with the Czech spy, Pavel Minařík, who infiltrated the station in the seventies and claimed partial credit for the bomb attack which destroyed part of its building in 1981. In 1993, at Václav → Havel's invitation, the headquarters of the station were transferred to the former Federal Assembly in Prague, which stood empty after the breakup of Czechoslovakia (→ *Sametový rozvod*).

rádiovka (beret). Berets are popular headgear for middle-aged and older men. The Czech name comes from a small antenna-like projection on the top.

Řád práce (Order of Labor). This medal was awarded by the communist regime for "extraordinary results in the economic field." It was given not only to individual workers, but also to entire factories or collective farms for exceeding the plan (→ *pětiletka*) and other heroic achievements at work. Other common awards from the time were the Decoration for Outstanding Work and the Decoration for Merit in the Construction of Socialism.

Rakousko (Austria). It is hard to capture Czech feelings about their former rulers. Though Czech patriots always portrayed them as oppressors, who had extinguished Czech freedom and humanism in the sixteenth and seventeenth centuries, most recognized that life was not so bad under the liberalizing monarchy, and few actively sought the end of the empire. By the nineteenth century, the Czech lands were one of the richest parts of Austria-Hungary, and though their political rights were still limited, most Czechs could do more or less as they pleased. Czechs lived for so many years under Austrian rule—from 1526 to 1918—that they could not help pick up similar habits, from cuisine (coffeeshops, pastries, and Wiener schnitzel) to music (operettas) to government (endless bureaucracy and red tape). After the First World War the shrunken Austrian state no longer posed a threat to the Czechs, and most people turned their attention to the more threatening Germany and Russia. Today one still finds a few Czechs waxing nostalgic for the old securities of the empire, but the majority still bristles at Austrian intervention in their affairs.

razítko (rubber stamp). No Czech document is official until it is covered in stamps. Indeed, Czech bureaucrats use the power of their rubber stamps to lord it over ordinary citizens who must frequently travel from one government office to another gathering stamps. This enormous bureaucracy was an inheritance of the Austro-Hungarian Empire and only expanded under the central planning of communism. Contrary to expectations, the transition to capitalism and democracy has led to a further increase in the number of civil servants (though they might be better called civil masters).

recitace (recitation). Recitations are a standard part of the Czech educational experience. At least once a month, students are required to learn a poem by heart and recite it in front of the class. They are graded not just on memorization, but also on intonation and gestures. Under communism, statewide recitation contests were popular (sort of like spelling bees in America). A competition called Wolker's Prostějov (named for a famous poet and his hometown) featured Czech poetry, and another, Pushkin's Memorial, was devoted to Russian classics.

Reed, Dean (1938–1986). An American teen singing idol from the fifties who found fame and fortune in the Soviet bloc. His sympathies for the downtrodden were first aroused on a tour to South America, where he settled for a time and became a pop star. After being deported from Argentina for his leftwing politics, he moved to Western Europe and starred in several spaghetti westerns before ending up behind the Iron Curtain. Known there as a "fighter for peace," he lived in East Berlin and toured the countries of the Warsaw Pact, singing both political folksongs and pop music to adoring masses. His fame was such that Eastern Europeans assume he is well-known even in the U.S. He died under mysterious circumstances; some claim he was murdered by the Stasi.

Remek, Vladimír (1948). The first and only Czech astronaut. On 2 March 1978, → Libuše's prophecy that the Czechs would build a nation that touches the stars was fulfilled. It was then that the cosmonaut Vladimír Remek became the first Czech (and the citizen of only the third nation after the Soviet Union and the U.S.) to orbit the earth. Flying with a Russian partner on Sojuz 28, Remek stayed aloft for a week before returning home to a hero's welcome. His flight, taking place on the thirtieth anniversary of the communist putsch, was portrayed as testimony to the Soviet Union's role as model and friend to Czechoslovakia. Remek was chosen both so the Soviet Union could regain some sympathy after the debacle of the invasion (→ *srpnová invaze*), and because as the son of a Slovak father and Czech mother he truly represented the Czechoslovak nation (→ *Československo*).

restaurace (restaurant). Dining out in restaurants is still relevantly uncommon among Czechs. While many have lunch in a small pub (→ *hospoda*), ordering one of the low-priced daily specials, there is little inclination to seek out new and interesting places to eat. With the exception of pizzerias, most restaurants serve the same traditional meals (→ *jidlo*), perhaps with one or two foreign specialties (for example, the newly popular chicken kung-pao).

restituce (restitution). Since the fall of communism, those whose land or property was confiscated by the old regime have sought restitution (→ *znárodnění*, → JZD). The government has obliged under certain circumstances for victims of communist nationalization, but has avoided trying to untangle the complicated property changes undertaken by the Nazis and democratic Czech governments. Particularly controversial are attempts by former aristocrats (→ *šlechta*) and the Church (→ *katolická církev*) to regain large tracts of land.

revizor (ticket inspector). The bane of streetcar (→ *tramvaj*), bus, and subway riders. As opposed to American public transport, where you are required to purchase a ticket as you board, public transport in the Czech Republic uses the honor system: you buy your ticket before boarding and insert it in a machine to be stamped after you board. Occasionally, however, inspectors check tickets and fine ticketless riders who are known as *černí pasažéři* (black passengers). Avoiding the *revizor* is considered a minor art form and has its own set of rules. It is believed—mistakenly—that *revizoři* are all young to middle-aged men, that they never carry a bag, and that they always board from the back of the bus or streetcar (the better to surprise ticketless passengers). Two of the most popular films of the fifties were about a Prague ticket inspector named Anděl (Angel).

Rifle. A synonym for jeans throughout Eastern Europe. In the 1950s, the Italian Fratini brothers, Giulio and Fiorenzi, decided to challenge the American monopoly on the manufacture of blue jeans and started a factory to make their own under the label Rifle. They had their greatest success exporting the jeans to Eastern Europe. By 1986, they had sold three million pairs in Russia and had conquered the Czech market to such an extent that Czechs began to use the word *Rifle* (pronounced ree-fleh) in place of *džíny* (jeans). Though more stylish and prized than Rifle, Levis were available only in → Tuzex shops and commanded top dollar on the black market. Besides being the uniform of the young, jeans are associated with the dissident (→ *disident*) movement and figures such as Václav → Havel. Jeans are also sometimes referred to as *texasky*.

28. říjen (October 28). Czechoslovak (and now Czech) independence day. On 28 October 1918, Czechoslovakia (→ *Československo*) declared its independence from the Austro-Hungarian Empire and thus presented the international community with a brand-new state. The groundwork for independence had been laid by the future presidents, T. G. → Masaryk and Edvard → Beneš, and the Slovak pilot Milan Rastislav Štefánik, all of whom tirelessly campaigned abroad during the war for a new state joining Czechs and Slovaks. Working on the domestic front, the founding fathers of the new state—often called the "Men of October" (→ *poúnorový*)—were the politicians Kramář, Rašín, Soukup, Stříbrný, and Švehla. In a repeated Czech theme, independence itself was achieved peacefully as the Monarchy crumbled from within. The day was soon celebrated as a national holiday, though the communists added nationalization of enterprises and the federalization of the state to the anniversaries of October 28, in order to erase memories of the bourgeois First Republic (→ *První republika*). Even after the breakup of Czechoslovakia (→ *Sametový rozvod*), the Czechoslovak version of the Fourth of July continues to be honored, though celebrations are relatively muted.

Říp. It was on this mountain—actually closer to a hill—north of Prague that the forefather of all Czechs, himself named → Čech, is said to have founded the Czech nation. Legend has it that after a long journey, he surveyed the surrounding land from the top of Říp and spoke the magic words, "This is the promised land, rich in game and fowl, overflowing with sweet honey." His brother Lech meanwhile carried on to the north to found the Polish nation; a third brother, Rus, stayed

Restaurant Menu

This is an actual restaurant menu from 1974. Notice the emphasis on pork and the lack of any vegetarian options except fried cheese. It should also be noted that eating out has never been a popular pastime.

WEIGHT		PRICE
	Cold Appetizers	
210/130	Steak tartar, toast	11.10
100g	Javor cheese, 20 g. butter	4.60
100/70g	Smoked bacon, horse-radish	4.70
50g	Cod liver with garnish	4.70
	Smoked Meats	
100g	Parisian salami, mustard	4.20
100g	Headcheese with onions and vinegar	3.60
	Soups	
	Beef broth with marrow dumplings	1.10
	Beef broth with batter drops	1.00
	Beef broth with noodles	1.20
		0.70
	Hot appetizers	
100g	Fried cheese, boiled potatoes, tartar sauce	8.50
50g	Fried egg on toast	2.60
	Ready Meals	
100g	Viennese goulash, bread dumplings	6.10
100g	Beef with garlic, boiled potatoes	6.10
100g	Znojmo beef, rice	7.30
100g	English roast beef, boiled potatoes, tartar sauce	10.80

142

100g	Spring of pork with mushrooms, bread dumplings	7.80
100g	Spring of pork village-style, sauerkraut, bread dumplings	8.50
100g	Szeged goulash, bread dumplings	5.60
100g	Pot roast with stewed vegetable salad, boiled potatoes	7.50
50g	Pork risotto, cabbage salad	4.80

Meals Made to Order

100g	Beefsteak with egg, boiled potatoes, pickle	13.20
100g	Viennese pot roast, boiled potatoes, tartar sauce	12.00
100g	Grilled roast, boiled potatoes, tartar sauce	11.50
100g	Pork kebabs, boiled potatoes, tartar sauce	10.90
100g	Wiener schnitzel, potato salad with eggs	9.90
150g	Fried fish filet, boiled potatoes with butter, cabbage salad	9.40

150g	Grilled fish filet, boiled potatoes with butter, cabbage salad	8.50
	Dessert: Rolled crepe with jam	1.80
	Beer snacks: Bread with grated blue cheese	2.60
	Finger sandwich with sardines	2.60

Side dishes

200g	Boiled potatoes	2.20
200g	Potatoes with butter	2.90
100g	Sauerkraut	1.60
160g	Bread dumplings	1.30
150g	Boiled rice	0.90
50g	Toast	0.80
100 g	Potato salad with eggs	1.70
50 gr	Tartar sauce	1.60
50 gr	Stewed plums	0.80
50 gr	Pickle	0.70
	Cabbage salad	0.70
50 gr	Bread	0.20

behind in Russia. Despite Říp's unimpressive stature—it rises only 230 meters above the surrounding fields—Czech patriots proudly make the pilgrimage to the Chapel of St. Jiří, which stands at its summit. According to legend, Jan → Hus's sermons from Říp could be heard throughout the country. In fact, Říp's proportions are appropriate to the Czechs' self-image as a small, peace-loving people. Today the mountain is a necessary stopping point on all political campaigns and a common destination for school fieldtrips.

řízek (filet). Like the Austrians (→ *Rakousko*), Czechs have a soft spot for Wiener schnitzel, or as it is called in Czech *smažený vepřový řízek* (fried pork filet). Usually served with boiled potatoes, it is on the menu of all restaurants and is a staple of Sunday afternoon dinners. It is often prepared and wrapped in plastic for long bus and train trips.

robot. The one genuine Czech contribution to the languages of the world (the word "pistol" may or may not be another). It was invented by the writer Karel → Čapek at the suggestion of his brother Josef in the play *R.U.R.* (Rossum's Universal Robots), where robots all but take over the world. The term's origins are in the Czech word *robota*, which referred to the days that a serf was bound to work his master's fields. Even today Czechs talk of *robota* to refer to the unpleasant daily grind.

rohlík (bread roll). Eaten at all times of the day—with butter in the morning, with cheese and deli meats for lunch, and with yogurt for a light dinner—the *rohlík* is the country's all-purpose food. Towns often produce their own distinctive style of *rohlík*, though the general crescent type is immediately recognizable. Like beer it is often used as a gauge for price rises—while a *rohlík* once cost only 10 *haléře* (cents) now it takes an entire crown (→ *koruna*, about three cents) to buy one. A popular fast food is *párek v rohlíku* (frankfurter in a roll), which differs from an American hot dog in that the hot dog, lubricated with mustard, is placed in a hole made down the length of the roll by a special apparatus. This allows it to be eaten one-handed.

ROH (Revoluční odborové hnutí/Revolutionary Trade-union Movement). The one and only trade union under communism. Though it was supposed to support the interests of workers—in the jargon of the regime to serve as a transmission belt between the party-state and its citizens—ROH was mainly a large bureaucracy that disbursed benefits to its members. It was in charge of the social security system and owned a vast network of cultural and recreational facilities for the use of unionists, i.e., virtually all citizens. Just about every Czech thus remembers an ROH-sponsored trip to the theater, countryside, or even foreign country. After the revolution, it was quickly and quietly transformed into a democratic union, known as the Czech-Moravian Confederation of Trade Unions.

rovnostářství (egalitarianism). Communist ideology proclaiming the equality of all workers fell on fertile ground among Czechs. Most Czechs intuitively feel that they are the equals of their neighbors and deserve equal rewards for their labors. This leads of course to envy (→ *závist*) and a general perception that riches, fame, and success are undeserved and must be the result of corruption, connections (→ *protekce*), or twists of fate. The communists could embarrass people simply by publishing their salaries. The roots of this egalitarianism

are in Habsburg rule when the native aristocracy was destroyed and ordinary Czechs were blocked from any hope of advancement. The result is a fundamental sense of Czechness as everyone being stuck in the same boat. Only the advent of capitalism has finally started to break down the age-old feeling of social equality, though even today the rich and famous are reluctant to reveal the extent of their wealth.

rudá knížka (little red book). Membership booklet for the Communist Party. Looking something like a passport, the *rudá knížka* was issued to all members of the Communist Party (→ KSČ). It was mainly used during meetings and congresses when members voted, always unanimously, by raising their booklets in the air. After the Soviet invasion (→ *srpnová invaze*), some party members symbolically turned in or destroyed their *rudé knížky*.

Rudé právo (Red Right). The official newspaper of the Communist Party of Czechoslovakia (→ KSČ). Part showcase for the achievements of socialism—it documented record grain harvests and workers exceeding the plan (→ *pětiletka*)—part exposé of the evils of Western imperialism, the paper's aims were almost entirely propagandistic. Reporting described most events with stock phrases like "a long, unflagging ovation," "unanimously approved and carried," and "they participated in a long and heartfelt discussion." Only well-informed readers could discern policy changes from the paper, noticing, for example, that a particular commissar's name had not appeared for days or was relegated from page 1 to page 2. Even the sports pages were careful: a headline could not proclaim that the Czechoslovak hockey team "defeated" much less pummeled the Soviet Union, only that the final score was 6:1. Though the paper was required reading (or at least a required prop) for members of the party and managers of enterprises (its motto was "the largest and the most read"), most citizens turned to other papers and to foreign broadcasts for re-

Newspapers and Magazines

This is a list of the best-known newspapers and magazines over the last half century. Under communism, newspapers and magazines were published by quasi-independent organizations—trade unions, ministries, political parties—but all were subject to the same censorship.

Czech name	English name	Founded	Notes
100+1 zahraniční zajímavosti	100+1	1964–	A digest of interesting articles from foreign magazines
Blesk	Lightning	1992–	Tabloid complete with page-three girls that is the country's best-selling newspaper
Čtyřlístek	Four-Leaf Clover	1969–	Fun and games for children with the cat Myšpulín, the dog Fifinka, the pig Bobík, and the rabbit Pinďa
→ Dikobraz	Porcupine	1945–1995	Communist-era magazine with political satire and general humor
Hálo noviny	Hello News	1991–	Newspaper published by the post-1989 Communist Party
Hospodářské noviny	Economic News	1957–	Czech version of the *Financial Times*
→ Květy	Flowers	1834–	Country's oldest magazine
Lidová demokracie	People's Democracy	1945–1994	Newspaper published by the People's Party, originally an independent party, later included in the communist-run National Front; slightly more independent news than → *Rudé právo*
→ Lidové noviny	People's News	1893–1945, 1988–	Liberal daily originally published in Brno; banned by communists and revived by dissidents in samizdat; since the revolution the leading voice of dissident and then free market views
Literární noviny	Literary Magazine	1952–1968, 1990–	News and opinion for intellectuals
Mateřídouška	Thyme	1945–	Children's magazine founded by the poet František Hrubín
Mladá fronta (since 1990 Mf Dnes)	Young Front	1945–	Once a communist newspaper published by → SSM, today the country's best-selling daily and known as *Dnes* (Today)
Mladý svět	Young World	1959–	Magazine for young adults originally published by SSM
Obrana lidu	Defense of the People	1947–1993	Newspaper of the Ministry of Defense
Ohníček	Little Flame	1951–2001	Children's magazine
Práce	Labor	1945–1997	Communist daily published by the Central Council of Trade Unions

Czech name	English name	Founded	Notes
Reflex	Reflex	1990–	Current events from a slightly alternative angle
Respekt	Respect	1990–	Intellectual news analysis
Rovnost	Equality	1885–	Moravian (→ *Morava*) regional newspaper
→ Rudé právo (after 1995 Právo)	Red Right	1920–	For decades the official organ of the Communist Party, today an independent left-wing daily
Sport	Sport	1993–	Sports daily
Stadion	Stadium	1953–1993	Sports weekly
Svobodné slovo (1997–2000 Slovo)	Free Word	1945–2000	Daily newspaper, published under communism by the Czechoslovak Socialist Party
Tvář	Face	1964–1969, 1990–	Originally an influential literary magazine for artists and writers of the Prague Spring (→ *Pražské jaro*); banned after the Soviet invasion
Týden	Week	1990–	News weekly modeled on *Time* and *Newsweek*
Vlasta	Vlasta	1947–	Popular women's magazine
Zemědělské noviny	Agricultural News	1945–	Newspaper focusing on rural and agricultural issues

al news (→ *Rádio Svobodná Evropa*). After the revolution, the paper dropped the word "red" from its name and continued as an independent left-wing daily.

Rudolf II (1552–1612). Habsburg emperor. The melancholy Rudolf is remembered by Czechs both because he chose Prague (→ *Praha*) for his imperial residence and for his eccentric ways. A particular passion of his was alchemy and at one point he supported two hundred alchemists, including the infamous John Dee and Edward Kelley. He was also a patron of the sciences—both Johannes Kepler and Tycho Brahe found refuge at his court—and an avid collector of all manner of trinkets. His rule thus gave rise to the image of Prague as a city of magic and mystery.

Rukopis královédvorský (Kingscourt Manuscript). Forged manuscript put forward as the oldest in the Czech language. In 1817,

the writer and national awakener Václav Hanka announced to the world that in the tower of a church in Dvůr Králové (King's Court), he had found an ancient Czech manuscript that he ultimately dated to the thirteenth century. Known as the Královédvorský Manuscript, its text described the successful battles of Czechs against foreigner invaders. A year later a similar manuscript was discovered in Zelená Hora (Green Mountain) and pushed the date of Czech literature back to the tenth century, making it among the most venerable in Europe. The manuscripts were greeted with euphoria, translated into foreign languages, and served as inspiration for poets, artists, and musicians—including → Smetana. Yet as soon as they were discovered, doubts were raised about their genuineness. By the 1880s, the so-called Manuscript Battles broke out, with important scholars, among them → Masaryk, proving definitively that the manuscripts were forgeries, probably written by Hanka himself. The debunkers were for a time considered traitors to the nation and even today occasional voices can be heard in defense of the authenticity of the manuscripts. Literary critics meanwhile praise their poetry while doubting their genuineness. The most telling aspect of the whole incident is the desire of Czechs to prove to the rest of the world the worth of their nation.

rum. The hard alcohol of choice among the less well-off. Czech rum is usually the cheapest liquor served in pubs and thus a popular choice among drinkers. In the winter it is served piping hot as *grog*. Accession to the European Union, however, spelled the end of the name rum. Since Czech rum is made from sugar beets rather than the more authentic sugar cane, the Czech version now must be sold under the label *tuzemák* (the word *tuzemský* means domestic). Similar fears that the EU would ban the odorous cheese → *tvarůžky* or forbid pig roasts (→ *zabíjačka*) did not come to pass. Another popular liquor is Fernet, the Czech version of Jägermeister. Mixed with tonic, it becomes a *bavorák* (Bavarian). Until recently other cocktails—screwdrivers, Manhattans, etc.—tended to be unknown or frowned upon. Hard alcohol is almost always taken in shots (known as *panáky*).

Rumcajs. The hero of an animated children's TV show (→ *večerníček*). Rumcajs is a shoemaker in the town of Jičín whose livelihood is taken away by the intemperate local lord. Helped by his wife Manka and his son Cipísek, he turns to life as a robber and acts as a sort of Robin Hood, defending ordinary people who suffer under the local aristocracy (→ *šlechta*). His home town today hosts an annual festival in September called Jičín—Fairytale City.

Rusalka (The Water Nymph). One of the most popular Czech operas. Composed by Antonín → Dvořák, it tells the story of a water nymph (→ *vodník*) named Rusalka who falls in love with a prince and trades her voice for a chance to be human and win his heart.

The fickle prince, however, proves unfaithful, and both he and Rusalka are cursed forever. The aria where Rusalka beseeches the moon to tell her where her lover has gone is among the most beautiful and heartrending in Czech music. Rusalka's popularity rests not only on its melodies, but also on its romantic and fairytale (→ *pohádka*) plot.

Rusko (Russia). At the time of the National Revival (→ *Národní obrození*), many Czech patriots—including Josef → Jungmann and František → Palacký—put their faith in Russia and the Tsar as the guarantor of the Czech nation's future existence. Indeed, the idea of pan-Slavism—the belief in the spiritual if not political unity of all Slav nations—got its start among Czech thinkers concerned over the country's position as an island of Slavs in a sea of Germans. The tradition of looking to the Russian savior continued in the interwar period, when many of the country's major artists and thinkers saw a model in the Soviet Union. Of course, when these enthusiasts visited the country of their dreams, they usually returned disabused of all illusions. This admiration received a boast with World War II: many Czechs believed that the Western allies had betrayed them at Munich (→ *Mnichov*) and viewed the Russians as their liberators. This required overlooking how Soviet soldiers raped, stole—they had a particular penchant for watches—and generally acted like barbarians, many not understanding the concept of indoor plumbing. Nevertheless, when the communists took power, the slogan, "the Soviet Union, our model," was put into practice in every aspect of Czech life. It took the invasion of August 1968 to destroy once and for all any admiration or respect for the Russians (→ *srpnová invaze*), though Czechs were and remain far less anti-Russian than their Polish neighbors (→ *Polsko*). Today Russia evokes little interest or fear and mainly serves as an important hockey (→ *hokej*) rival.

ruština (Russian language). Over the forty years of communist rule, all students were required to study Russian throughout elementary and high school. Russian classes were universally hated, and most students tried to get by with minimal effort. Though Czech and Russian are both Slavic languages, they are not mutually intelligible and the differences are substantial. Because many words share the same roots, Czechs often try out their own translation schemes. The Czech *h*, for example, often becomes a *g* in Russian and so enterprising learners believe that a word like *hajzl* (bathroom) will be *gajzl* in Russian. Despite their high exposure to the language, the only Russian words to stick in Czech minds, if only temporarily, are *kolkhoz* (a synonym for → JZD) and → *chozrasčot*. A few still remember the children's songs that they sang in school. Since the revolution, many of the country's Russian teachers have reconstituted themselves as English teachers.

Ruzyně. Quarter of Prague that is home to and synonym for its main airport. Until recently, Ruzyně was a quiet backwater, as few Czechs were permitted to travel abroad (→ *výjezdní doložka*). The end of communism, however, has led to a boom in travel to exotic destinations, and the airport is now small but bustling. Some also associate Ruzyně with the prison that used to be located there (see also → Pankrác).

rybník (fish pond). Though not originally a land of many lakes, Czech and German noblemen began to have fish ponds built for their private enjoyment in the sixteenth century. They hired pond constructors like Štepánek Netolický and Jakub Krčín, who achieved fame for turning the flat lands of south Bohemia into the country's lake district. Their handiwork includes both large and deep ponds like Rožmberk and Svět, and small shallow ones that are ideal for raising fish. Harvesting of carp (→ *kapr*), trout, and eel continues to provide livelihoods even today. During the fall, fishermen drag large nets across the ponds, and much of the catch becomes Christmas (→ *Vánoce*) dinner. In summer, the ponds host camps and other recreational activities, while in winter they serve as outdoor hockey (→ *hokej*) rinks and may account partially for the country's success in that sport.

rýžový nákyp (rice souffle). A popular lunch dish for children. It consists of rice mixed with milk and sugar and is topped off with fruit. Rice souffle is one of a number of sweet-tasting main dishes that are favorites in school cafeterias. Others are sweet buns with custard (*buchtičky s krémem*), mashed semolina sprinkled with cocoa powder (*krupicová kaše*), and fruit-filled dumplings (*ovocné* → *knedlíky*). Children look forward to the appearance of these dishes on the school lunch menu, and adults in turn retain happy memories of them.

S

sádlo (lard). A squat glass jar full of lard is a fixture in all kitchen pantries. It is used in cooking or, for a quick snack, spread on a slice of bread and topped with scallions.

Sametová revoluce (Velvet Revolution). The fall of the communist regime. Though by November 1989, the Polish, Hungarian, and East German communist regimes had given up their monopoly on power, Czechoslovakia remained in the grip of hard-core communists, who resisted reforms tooth and nail. The regime's fall began innocuously on November 17, with a government-approved parade of students in commemoration of the fiftieth anniversary of the closing of universities by the Nazis. The marchers, however, began to denounce the regime, and the police (→ VB) moved to cut them off at *Národní třída* (National Boulevard) and brutally disbanded the march. Rumors that a student had been killed provoked student groups to call a strike, and the country's actors (→ *divadlo*) joined them. By November 20, six-figure crowds demonstrated in Prague calling for an investigation of the attack and a change in the country's politics. Most remember the following days and weeks as ones of general euphoria with speeches, concerts, and the public appearance of figures like Alexander Dubček, Marta Kubišová (→ Golden Kids, → *Modlitba*), and Karel → Kryl for the first time in two decades. In a memorable scene, citizens jangled keys above their heads to symbolize that the time

Current Calendar		
This calendar lists national holidays in the year 2003.		
MONTH	DAY	HOLIDAY
January	1	New Year's Day, Origin of the Independent Czech Republic Day
Moveable Holiday		Easter Monday (→ *Velikonoce*)
May	1	Labor Day (→ *1. máj*)
May	8	Liberation from Fascism Day (→ *Den osvobození*)
July	5	Holiday of Saints → Cyril and Methodius
July	6	Anniversary of the Burning of Master Jan → Hus
September	28	Saint Wenceslas Day (→ *Svatý Václav*)
October	28	Origin of the Independent Czechoslovak State Day (→ *28. říjen*)
November	17	Battle for Freedom and Democracy Day (→ *Sametová revoluce*)
December	24–26	Christmas (Christmas Eve, Christmas Day, St. Stephen's Day) (→ *Vánoce*)

had come for the communists. Realizing that it lacked both domestic and international support, the regime crumbled. By November 26, the government agreed to meet with the opposition led by Václav → Havel at a round-table. After a general strike, the communists agreed to end the legally guaranteed "leading role" of the communist party. By December, opposition leaders held ministerial posts, and on December 29 Havel was elected president. As Timothy Garton Ash put it, "What took 10 years in Poland, took 10 months in Hungary, 10 weeks in East Germany and ultimately 10 days in Czechoslovakia." The name "Velvet Revolution" comes from the smoothness of the regime change, which proceeded without violence or law-breaking (and perhaps secondarily from Havel's passion for the rock group The Velvet Underground). Though the euphoria gave way soon after, November 17 has become a little-celebrated national holiday known as the Battle for Freedom and Democracy Day. ·

Sametový rozvod (Velvet Divorce). The break-up of the Czech and Slovak Republics on 31 December 1992. After the fall of communism (→ *Sametová revoluce*) in 1989, one of the first issues on the agenda of the new democracy was the structure of the state. While Slovaks (→ *Slovensko*) preferred a loose federation or confederation, Czechs wanted a unitary state. More specific controversies included the "hyphen war"—whether there should be a hyphen in between the Czech and Slovak parts of the country's name—and the nature of economic reforms. Despite extensive negotiations, no solution commanded majority support in both parts of the country. After elections in 1992 brought Slovak nationalists to power in their half of the federation, it was only a matter of time before the country split in two. The divorce remains controversial as a majority of both Czech and Slovak citizens desired to remain in a single state. While some blame Slovak nationalists for the breakup, others accuse Czech economic reformers of wishing to dispense with the more backward Slovak economy. Since the

Sametový rozvod—so-called because like the Velvet Revolution it proceeded so bloodlessly—relations between the two countries have been amicable, though Slovakia had to suffer an undemocratic spell as a result of its new nationalist leaders.

samizdat (self-published literature). A Russian word for books reproduced illegally under communism. With all publishing houses under state control and rigorous censorship in force, the only way to publish independent or anti-communist work was through clandestine self-publishing. Though enterprising self-publishers could occasionally get a hold of a printing press or mimeograph, books were most frequently reproduced by typewriter. Copyists would type, for example, Solzhenitsyn's *One Day in the Life of Ivan Denisovitch*, on as many carbons as they could stuff into the typewriter and distribute them to friends who would then pass the smudged, dog-eared copies on to other acquaintances. While much *samizdat* was the product of individual initiative, the writer Ludvík Vaculík organized his own *samizdat* publishing house called *Edice Petlice* (Padlock Editions). *Samizdat* operated in a legal gray area. Unlike the Catholic Church, the communists never produced a list of banned books. Citizens, however, could not plead ignorance if caught with a copy of, say, Orwell. Authorities would argue that they should have recognized the anti-communist message and turned it into the police. The penalty for producing or possessing *samizdat* could be demotion at work, difficulty traveling abroad, or even prison.

sedláci u Chlumce (peasants at Chlumec). In 1775, Czech and German peasants demanding the end of serfdom (→ robot) rebelled against their feudal masters. At the town of Chlumec, forty thousand of the Empress's soldiers put down the rebellion and pushed many of the peasants into a nearby pond. The phrase *dopadnout jako sedláci u Chlumce* (to end up like the peasants at Chlumec) has thus come to mean "end up badly."

Semafor. Musical theater founded by Jiří Suchý and Jiří Šlitr in the late fifties. The name is an acronym for Seven Small Forms (song, dance, music, mime, poetry, skits, and dialogues), which were combined in a cabaret revue whose wit and openness set the cultural tone for the sixties. Its main legacy today is its music. The cleverness of the lyrics (written by Suchý) and the catchy melodies (composed by Šlitr) made songs like "*Zuzana*" (Susanna), "*Ta láska nebeská*" (That Heavenly Love), or "*Pramínek vlasů*" (A Lock of Hair) into folk tunes which are sung wherever Czechs gather. Virtually every pop act of the next twenty years got its start in the theater, including singers like Eva Pilarová, Waldemar Matuška, and Hana Hegerová. It was such a launching pad for stars that Miloš Forman made a film of one of its auditions (entitled *Konkurz*) to which thousands of aspiring actresses and singers showed up. Šlitr's accidental death (some believe it was a suicide) and Suchý's opposition to the Soviet invasion put a dent in the theater in the seventies and eighties, but Suchý's prolific output has kept it alive into the new century.

semtex. A plastic explosive manufactured in the village of Semtín (hence its name). Semtex has become a favorite of terrorists around the world because it is light, flexible, odorless, and, most importantly, packs a powerful punch. Invented by Stanislav Brebera for industrial use in 1952, it was soon exported to allied countries and gained worldwide renown when it was found on the plane that went down over Lockerbie. One of the ironies of Czech history is that they are talented producers of world class weapons they do not use themselves. It was the Czech armaments industry, the world's sixth largest between the wars, that helped to create the great German fighting machine in the thirties and forties. The Israelis too benefited from Czech weapons in their battle for independence, though when the communists took over, arms were exported exclusively to allies of the Soviet Union. Semtex today is also the name of a popular energy drink.

sex. While the communists enforced a puritanical public morality—one film director was famously told that one female breast could be shown in a film, but not two—citizens found refuge from political repression in promiscuous lifestyles. Lack of religious belief and heavy industrialization likewise contributed to a very matter-of-fact attitude towards sex. Czechs begin to have sex at a young age—their first sexual experiences often happen at cottages (→ *chata*) and village entertainments (→ *zábava*). Infidelity is likewise considered an inevitable fact of life.

Silvestr (New Year's Eve). Like their German neighbors, Czechs call New Year's Eve Silvestr after the saint honored on December 31 (→ *jmeniny*). The holiday is celebrated with heavy drinking and popping of champagne corks, though Czechs are as likely to locate themselves at a cottage (→ *chata*) in the woods as on Old Town Square in Prague for fireworks. Typical refreshments, as at any celebration, are open-faced sandwiches (→ *chlebíčky*) often topped with a garlic spread. At midnight it is tradition to sing the national anthem (→ "*Kde domov můj*"). The evening has also become home to a television extravaganza that is the most anticipated show of the year and features virtually all the country's celebrities singing and telling jokes. See also → *Jak na Nový rok*.

"Skákal pes" (The Jumping Dog). One of the first songs that children learn. It tells the story of a dog who loves to scamper over fields. When his master asks him why he is always so merry, the dog replies, "I'd tell you, but I don't know myself," and scampers away again. Several of the best-known Czech children's songs have English parallels. "*Prší, prší, jen se leje*" translates as "It's Raining, It's Pouring," while "*Kolo, kolo mlýnský*" (The Mill Wheel) ends—like "Ring-around-the-Rosie"—with the singers falling to the ground. Rounding out the canon of children's songs is "*Ovčáci čtveráci*" (The Rascal Shepherds) and "*Pec nám spadla*" (Our Stove Fell In).

sklo (glass, crystal). A traditional specialty of Czech industry is its glassblowing. Since the seventeenth century, Czech glaziers have been world leaders in glass painting, cutting, and engraving. Many Czechs stock their shelves with crystal vases, platters, and wine glasses that are more for show than actual use. Glass is thus a common holiday gift. Among the famous producers of Czech crystal are Moser, Egermann, and Jablonex.

Škoda. Automobile manufacturer. In 1925 the first Czech car manufacturers, Laurin and Klement, fused their company with the Škoda Machine Works (founded by Emil Škoda in 1869) and began producing a car called the Škoda. Along with other large firms, Škoda was nationalized after the war and granted a virtual monopoly in car manufacturing. Mass car ownership came to the country in the sixties with the introduction of the Škoda 120, produced in runs of over a million. The 120 was distinguished not only by its boxy design, but also by its rear motor (a design feature shared at the time only with Porsche and Mexican manufacturers). Despite mass production, waiting lists for cars remained, as the low price attracted more potential buyers than there were cars.

Though Czechs had the opportunity of buying other makes from their socialist neighbors (including the East German Wartburg and Trabant, the Russian Lada, Moskvic, and Zil, the Polski Fiat, and the Romanian Dacia), most remained loyal to the home product. Unlike other communist-era carmakers, Škoda was able to reinvent itself after communism, a tribute to Czech technology and an investment from Volkswagen, and produce a car that is sold not only at home but also around the world.

"Škoda lásky" (Unrequited Love). Voted the most popular song of all time in a millennium poll, "*Škoda lásky*" is better known in English as the "Beer Barrel Polka" and in German as "*Rosamunde.*" Written by the Czech → polka king Jaromír Vejvoda in the thirties, its Czech lyrics are not a hymn to beer drinking, but to the memory of a lost love. The song's refrain says, in a woman's voice, "The sorrow of the love which I gave you / Today I would cry out those eyes of mine / My youth fled just like a dream / All that's left in my heart is a memory." Its popularity among Allied soldiers during World War II meant that Vejvoda found himself out of favor after 1948.

People's Choice for Song of the Century

These are the results of a people's choice poll for Czech song of the century. The public voted for the best song of each decade and the winners then advanced into a final round.

	SONG	ENGLISH TITLE	YEAR	LYRICS/MUSIC	SUNG BY	NOTES
1	→ Škoda lásky	Beer Barrel Polka	1929	Zeman/ Vejvoda	-	The original Beer Barrel Polka
2	Medvídek	Teddy Bear	1999	Kodym/ O. Petr	Lucie	Hit by the most popular rock group of the nineties; its video was banned for encouraging drug use
3	Holubí dům	Home of Doves	1973	Svěrák/ Uhlíř	Schelinger	Sentimental rock ballad; its singer died mysteriously in a fall from Bratislava's main bridge

	Song	English Title	Year	Lyrics/Music	Sung by	Notes
4	Zvonky štěstí	Bells of Happiness	1984	Rytíř/ Zmožek	→ Gott/ Rolincová	Bubble-gum pop duet between aging star and 12-year-old girl
5	Holky z naší školky	Girls from our Kindergarten Class	1982	Žák/Vágner	Hložek/ Kotvald	Jokey pop song with refrain featuring girls' names
6	→ Modlitba pro Martu	A Prayer for Marta	1969	Rada/Brabec	Kubišová	Classic protest against the Soviet invasion
7	Píseň pro Kristýnku	A Song for Kristynka	1954	V. Dvořák/ Z. Petr	Salač	Sweet love song
8	Jsi můj pán	You're My Master	1996	Borovec/ Svoboda	→ Bílá	Ballad from the Czech musical *Dracula*
9	Ta naše písnička česká	That Czech Song of Ours	1932	→ Hašler	-	Classic patriotic and sentimental tune
10	Ach, ta láska nebeská	Oh, That Heavenly Love	1962	Suchý/Šlitr	Pilarová/ Matuška	Romantic duet from the → Semafor theater

škola (school). Grade school is a disciplined affair which packs children full of facts and rules. The school day begins with children either walking or taking public transport to school. Upon arrival, they put away their shoes and don slippers (→ *pantofle*). When the teacher comes into the classroom, students immediately stand up and do not sit down until the teacher greets them with "*Dobrý den, posaďte se*" (Good morning. Take a seat). Under communism, teachers were required to stick closely to the textbook (a habit they have maintained even today), so much that learning takes place with students reading aloud or reciting poems they have memorized (→ *recitace*). Dictations (→ *diktát*) are another common exercise, their goal being to reinforce spelling (→ *pravopis*). Quizzes take place frequently, a random student being called up to the front of the class to answer oral questions from the teacher. Grades (→ *vysvědčení*) are delivered immediately and out loud (→ *žákovská knížka*). A single class of approximately thirty students remains together for all eight years of elementary school (for grades one through four, they usually have the same teacher). Each class has to take care of its own bulletin board (*nástěnka*) where it posts important announcements and anniversaries (in the past mainly of a political character). One of the highlights of the school year is *škola v přírodě* (nature school) when the entire class spends a week in the woods. Students finish school with a strong set of fundamentals and a large supply of memorized facts and dates, which leads them to score well on international tests. On the other hand, they are actively discouraged from creative or independent thinking. See also → *gymnázium*.

SKP (Sdružený klub pracujících/Club of Working People). A cultural events hall found in many towns and villages during communism. The SKP played host to a variety of functions including theatrical and musical performances, special interest clubs, and even meetings of the Communist Party (→ *KSČ*). Interestingly, the SKP often occupied the former → *Sokol* building and was sometimes referred to as such.

Slánský, Rudolf (1901–1952). First secretary of the Communist Party found guilty of treason and executed. Slánský was one of the architects of the communist putsch (→ *Vítězný únor*) and its reign of terror in the late forties and early fifties. Despite being the second most powerful man in country, he was arrested in 1951 and falsely charged with heading an "anti-statist conspiratorial center" of Zionism and Titoism. After months of interrogations and torture, he admitted his guilt at a public show trial (→ *politické procesy*) and accepted as just the death sentence handed down on him. In fact, Slánský was chosen for exemplary punishment both because he was Jewish (→ *Žid*) and because the party hoped to show the public that others should be blamed for economic difficulties. For Czechs, the trial was one of the first signs that no one was safe from the new dictatorship (→ *totalita*).

Slavín (Pantheon). The final resting place of great Czech artists. Built from 1889 to 1893 on the grounds of → Vyšehrad, the Slavín cemetery was meant, following the French Pantheon, to house the bones of individuals who contributed to the "education, progress, and welfare of the Czech nation." The first to be buried here was the poet Julius Zeyer, who had coincidentally once written the lines, "The dust of its great sons / The motherland returns to the land / Their deeds rejoicing / Call to mankind for the ages." Among other graves are those of Ema → Destinová, Alfons → Mucha, Božena → Němcová, and Jan Neruda. Karel Hynek → Mácha's remains were dramatically transported to *Slavín* from his grave in Litoměřice when the Germans took over the Sudetenland in 1938 (→ *Mnichov*). Since 1989, the cemetery has seen symbolic burials or reburials for Vlasta → Burian, Milada → Horáková (whose body had been destroyed), and Ferdinand Peroutka, but diehard communists like Zdeněk Nejedlý have not been removed. Not all great Czechs are buried in *Slavín* though. Some remain in their hometowns or in family graves. Others were not interred in the cemetery for rea-

sons of religious faith. Most interestingly, while *Slavín* is home to writers, singers, actors, scientists, and athletes, politicians have been explicitly excluded. Their contributions to Czechness are considered too divisive for a monument to national unity (→ *apolitická politika*). The cemetery's motto is the poetic "*Ač zemřeli, ještě mluví*" (Though they have perished, still they speak).

šlechta (nobility). As European countries go, Czechs are fairly cool towards inherited privilege. The one native Czech royal family was the Premyslids (→ *Přemyslovci*) who died out in 1306 when they failed to produce a male heir. As a result, the Czech crown passed on to foreign lines—the Luxembourgs, Jagellonians, and ultimately the Habsburgs—though an indigenous lower nobility survived and frequently asserted its power against the monarch. Only at the Battle of White Mountain (→ *Bílá hora*), where the Czech estates took a last ditch stand against their marginalization, were they finally brought under total control of the Habsburg rulers. The country's native nobility was then exiled, killed, or Germanized. Important Czech noble families included the Rožmberks, Šternberks, and Pernštejns, though all spoke German more than Czech and few members retained sympathy for the Czech cause. At the creation of independent Czechoslovakia (→ *28. říjen*), → Masaryk banned titles of nobility—the aristocracy was stripped of its privileges and not allowed to use the German noble prefix *von* (as in von Stroheim) or its Czech equivalent *z* and *ze* (as in ze Lvovic)—a step greeted generally with enthusiasm. What Masaryk started, the communists completed by nationalizing the country's castles and manors (→ *hrady a zámky*). Since 1989, descendents of the country's former aristocrats—among them the Lobkowicz, Schwarzenberk, and Kinský families—have returned to the country either to participate in public life or restitute their former estates. The Czech public, however, remains highly suspicious of nobility and worries about them snatching up the country's land (→ *rovnostářství*).

Slezsko (Silesia). The smallest of the three historical regions comprising today's Czech Republic. The others are Moravia (→ *Morava*) and Bohemia (→ *Čechy*). Most of Silesia lies in Poland, but a small portion of it makes up the northeast corner of the country. The region is known for its heavy industrial core which brought with it support for the communists, pollution, housing projects (→ *paneláky*), and more recently high unemployment. Czech Silesians also have a characteristic way of speaking that shortens all of Czech's long vowels (→ *krátký zobák*). The largest city in Silesia is → Ostrava, but the historic center is Opava.

slivovice (plum brandy). Though mainly a beer-drinking people, Czechs still have a soft spot for the fiery taste of *slivovice*. Made from plums or other fruit, its taste resembles that of bitter almonds and its alcohol content is high. Though it is illegal to manufacture *slivovice* at home, countless Czechs have their own backyard stills. The process starts with gathering plums, pears, or apples and storing them in a covered barrel. After several weeks, the resulting mush is boiled and the distillate captured. Some prefer to leave bottles buried in the ground to strengthen the taste. It is downed in one shot (*na ex*) whenever welcoming new friends or at any celebration. It is also a handy remedy for illness or the winter freeze.

Slovácko. A region in the southwest of the country on the border with Slovakia, a fact reflected in the local accent. Slovácko is best-known for its traditional culture: distinctive national costumes (→ *kroj*) are still occasionally worn, folk traditions like the Ride of the Kings (→ *Jízda králů*) still celebrated yearly. Some of the most popular Czech folk songs (→ *lidovka*) like "*Když sem šel z Hradišťa*" (When I Left Hradišť) come from this area. The largely rural residents of Slovácko are known as well for their love of → *slivovice*, which they refer to as their morning toothbrush. Slovácko's favorite son is the country's first president, → Masaryk, who was born to

a Czech-German mother and Slovak father in the town of Hodonín. A popular book and television show entitled *Slovácko sa nesúdi* (Slovácko Doesn't Pass Judgment) played on these stereotypes and created the folk figure *Strýček Pagáč* (Uncle Pagáč).

Slovensko (Slovakia). Though most foreigners assume that Czechs and Slovaks have always been joined at the hip, for centuries there was little contact between the two. Slovakia was ruled with a firm hand by Hungary (and was even known as Upper Hungary, → *Maďarsko*), while the Czechs were governed more benignly from Vienna. In the nineteenth century, when both peoples were working to revive their languages and cultures, it appeared that they might become one. Several Slovaks, like Ján Kollár and Pavel Josef Šafařík, contributed enormously to the Czech National Revival (→ *Národní obrození*), and Anton Bernolák tried to standardize the Slovak language with a dialect very close to Czech. Indeed, numerous patriots, including Josef → Dobrovský, Milan Rastislav Štefánik, and T.G. → Masaryk propagated the idea that Czechs and Slovaks were simply two parts of one nation. The founding of the Czechoslovak state (→ *Československo*) seemed to support this idea, though some believe the Czechs took on the Slovaks to counter their own large German minority. In fact, the differences between the two halves of the country—Slovakia is poorer, less educated, and more religious—proved a problem as Slovak national awareness grew. Despite generous economic subsides, Slovaks felt themselves exploited by their fellow countrymen, as all major decisions were taken in Prague by Czech politicians. The Slovaks, moreover, tend to regard Czechs as immoral atheists. Czechs tended to view Slovaks as their little brothers and tried to help raise them up—sending teachers, administrators, and financial aid. As a result, they feel hard done by Slovak betrayals: whether joining the Nazis after Munich (→ *Mnichov*) or selling out the Prague Spring (→ *Pražské jaro*). It continues to be a mystery to Czechs why Slovaks sometimes pushed for separation and independence when they were so much better off in partnership with the Czechs. Slovaks are often referred to by Czechs as *haluśky* (short strips of boiled dough characteristic of Slovak cuisine) or → *Jánośíci* (the Slovaks' Robin Hood-like national hero). Czechs savor the sound of the Slovak language and praise its softness. Especially beloved is the Slovak word for blueberries—*čučoriedky*.

složenka (payment slip). Rent, telephone, heat, and water bills all arrive in mailboxes on similar strips of paper known as *složenky*. Payment is made after waiting in long lines at the post office. *Složenky* used to be instantly recognizable in the mail slot by their green hue; today they are red.

smažený sýr (fried cheese). A common lunch meal consisting of a thick slice or two of edam cheese dipped in breadcrumbs and deep-fried. It is usually served with a side order of French fries and tartar sauce or alone in a bun. It is typically the cheapest food on the menu and therefore popular with students. For mysterious reasons, foreigners visiting the country develop happy memories of the dish.

Smetana, Bedřich (1824–1884). Classical music composer. Though he could never write mistake-free Czech, there was no more nationalistic composer than Smetana. His opera → *Prodaná nevěsta* (*The Bartered Bride*) is a paean to Czech village life and begins with a traditional → polka. Many of Smetana's operas dealt with Czech history: the rebel Dalibor, the Brandenburgs in Bohemia (→ *Moravské pole*), and the beloved → *Libuše*, which opened the National Theater (→ *Národní divadlo*). In life, Smetana was plagued by hardship, suffering from constant financial difficulties, the early death of most of his family, and ultimately deafness. It was after he had lost his hearing that he wrote what is possibly the most beautiful love song to a country, → *Má vlast* (My Country). A cult of Smetana has reigned in the country since his death, with the communists—especially their first Minister of Culture, Zdeněk Nejedlý—taking a particular shine to his strong melodies and nationalist feeling.

Smolíček pacholíček. Fairy tale (→ *pohádka*) character. Smolíček is a small boy who incongruously lives with a stag in a forest cottage. Though he is warned by the stag never to open the door to strangers, Smolíček twice lets in forest sprites who drag him away and is only rescued at the last minute by the stag. Czechs often cite the entreaties of the sprites, "Smolíček, Smolíček, open up your door so we can warm up."

smysl českých dějin (the meaning of Czech history). For most Czechs, the meaning of Czech history lies in a myth created by scholars like František → Palacký, Alois → Jirásek, and T. G. → Masaryk. They argued that the Czechs were at heart a democratic, humanistic people living according to the religious ideals of the medieval Hussites (→ *husité*) and Union of Brethren (→ *Jednota bratrská*). In this interpretation, only Habsburg rule and the Counter-Reformation prevented them from becoming an independent, democratic nation. It was the national awakeners (→ *Národní obrození*) who then revived (or simply embodied) the earlier traditions and laid the basis for a democratic Czechoslovak state. The historian Josef Pekař opposed this interpretation in his classic article, "On the Meaning of Czech History," where he objected both to the distortion of history to serve current ends, and to the conclusion that Habsburg rule was not beneficial to the Czechs. Rather than viewing the Hussite rebellion as a great moment in Czech history, he saw it as revolutionary anarchy and called the defeat of the radical Hussites at the Battle of → Lipany a "happy day in Czech history." Needless to say, it is the image of a fundamentally democratic and moral people that Czechs hold dear.

Sněžka (Mt. Snowy). The highest mountain in the Czech Republic. The split of Czechoslovakia (→ *Sametový rozvod*) deprived the

Czechs of their highest mountain range, the eight-thousand-foot tall Tatras, which lay in Slovakia. Nevertheless, they continue to take pride in their own Mt. Snowy, which rises 5256 feet (1602 meters) in the Giant Mountains (→ Krkonoše). The peak is popular among hikers and even casual walkers can reach the summit after half a day's walk.

SNP (Slovenské národní povstání/Slovak National Uprising). The Slovak partisan rebellion against the Nazis that became one of the key founding myths of the communist state. On 29 August 1944, Slovak partisans took control of a large area in the center of the country around Banská Bystrica and held onto their gains for almost two months before Nazi units put them down. Though not all the rebels were communists, it was the communists who took credit for the uprising and portrayed themselves as the sole defenders of the nation. To this day, almost every larger city in the Czech Republic and Slovakia has a square or street known by the initials SNP, and Slovaks continue to celebrate August 29 as a national holiday. See also → *Květnové povstání*.

Socialismus s lidskou tváří (Socialism with a human face). Philosophy of the reformist communists during the Prague Spring (→ *Pražské jaro*). The slogan was invented by the First Secretary of the Communist Party, Alexander Dubček, to describe the new course that he and the reformers he brought into government hoped to embark on. "Socialism with a human face" meant that society would be liberalized—people would be free to say and write what they wished—but political power would remain in the hands of the party. It was thus an attempt to walk the narrow line between the democratic West and the socialist East. In the end, the line became too narrow. Liberalizing the system meant that citizens would demand democracy, but moves in the direction of democracy would threaten communism and provoke a Soviet response, which is exactly what happened (→ *srpnová invaze*). Despite this, the idea of socialism with a human face continues to appeal to leftists the world over and even leads some Czechs to ask, "What if the Soviets had not intervened?"

Sokol (Falcon). A patriotic organization founded in 1862 by the philosopher Miroslav Tyrš and the businessman Jindřich Fügner. Inspired by the German gymnastics associations, the *Turnvereine* (and in turn inspiring analogous assocations in other Slavic nations), *Sokol* was designed to promote both national awareness and physical fitness. It proved a hit with the Czech public, growing to over a million members. By the thirties, every town in the country had its own *Sokol* Hall. The organization was best known for its annual public display of gymnastics (called *slet*, a word that means flocking together), which ultimately became so large that it required the building of → Strahov Stadium. In addition to collective exercise, Sokol offered public lectures, artistic exhibitions, concerts, dances, and summer camps. The organization was founded on democratic principles: members used the informal (→ *tykání*) form of address and called each other brother or sister. They also wore distinctive red blouses (following Garibaldi) and sometimes national costumes (→ *kroj*). Members included such members of the country's elite as → Masaryk and → Beneš. *Sokol's* nationalism caused it to be banned not once, but three times (in 1915 by the Austrians, in 1941 by the Nazis, and in 1948 by the communists). Indeed, it was *Sokol* that represented the last mass resistance to the communist dictatorship when during the 1948 *slet*, its members symbolically turned their heads away from President Gottwald as they passed his tribune. Sokol branches can still be found in Czech émigré communities, but efforts to revive the organization since 1989 have been met with public apathy.

sorela. Acronym used to refer to the socialist realist style imported from the Soviet Union. Sorela meant enormous murals and sculptures, which portrayed workers and peasants joyously building a better tomorrow and celebrating their communist leaders. Architecturally, it is associated with massive neoclassical buildings plunked down in the historical centers of cities. The style enjoyed its heyday in the fifties, but was produced until the very end of the regime. Today citizens debate whether outstanding examples of the genre should be preserved as historical relics or consigned to the ash heap of history. See also → *budovatelský*.

soudruh (comrade). Unlike its Russian counterpart *tovarishch*, which can also mean a friend, *soudruh* was used only for fellow travelers. Under communism, it was a required form of address replacing the word → *pan* (mister). Thus, one's doctor was comrade doctor, one's teacher was comrade teacher, and the first secretary was comrade first secretary. Today the word is only used ironically to refer to communists.

španělská vesnice (Spanish village). The Czech equivalent of the English phrase "It's all Greek to me." When something is foreign and unknown, Czechs call it a Spanish village. Germans interestingly use the expression *"Das sind mir böhmische Dörfer"* (It's a Bohemian village to me). Hungarians refer more logically to Chinese.

Sparta/Slavia. The two great teams in the Czech football (→ *fotbal*) league. Both are based in Prague (Sparta on the Letná Plain, Slavia in Eden) and both were founded in 1893. Sparta wears solid maroon (the color of royalty), while Slavia's dress is red on one half and white on the other. The two clubs dominated the Czech league between the wars, featuring stars like Pepi → Bican, František Plánička (Slavia), and Oldřich Nejedlý (Sparta). At the time, Czechs could be divided into those who rooted for Sparta and those who rooted for Slavia, though Karel Poláček (→ *Bylo nás pět*) wrote a popular novel about a fan of Prague's third team, Viktoria → Žižkov. Under communism, Sparta and Slavia were forced to change their names and

even dropped into the second division for a time as the army team → Dukla Praha rose to the top. Only in the eighties did they finally start to regain some of their former glory, Sparta even breeding its own band of football hooligans, immortalized in the pseudo-documentary film *Proč?* (Why?). Since the revolution, Sparta has become the Yankees of the league, buying up every player in sight and winning the league with mind-numbing consistency. Regardless of their relative success, the annual matches between Sparta and Slavia, known as derbies, are among the hardest fought and eagerly anticipated of the season.

Spartakiáda. A mass gymnastics performance held under communism every five years from 1955 to 1985. It featured thousands of performers doing coordinated exercises in the enormous stadium in → Strahov. Its roots are both in the mass exercise programs organized by the patriotic → *Sokol* before the war, and similar festivals held in the Soviet Union—also called *Spartakiáda* and originally intended as a substitute for the Olympics. The participants were selected through year-long training programs and competitions in towns and schools across the country. Television broadcast the routines so people could learn them at home. The highlight of the *Spartakiáda* was the acrobatic feats of soldiers who formed towering human pyramids—frequently breaking bones in the process. The purpose of the event was not only to entertain and promote physical fitness, but also to show the nation's unity.

Spejbl and Hurvínek. The stars of the country's oldest puppet theater (→ *loutkové divadlo*). Both are bald and have prominent noses and large ears sticking up straight out of their heads. Created in 1930 by Josef Skupa, the two puppets play father (Spejbl) and son (Hurvínek), and the theater's humor works on these generational differences. The theater was one of the first to put down permanent stakes—traveling puppet theaters used to be more common—but is now one of many such theaters throughout the country; indeed, Czech children grow up on a heavy dose of puppet theater with frequent school field trips to see performances.

špekáček (spekwurst). A short, thick sausage as essential to Czech campfires as the marshmallow is to American ones. The name *špekáček* comes from the word for fat, and the sausage itself is marbled with pieces of fat. Before roasting it on a stick over the campfire, campers cut crosses in the ends of the sausage so that the four corners on each side turn up as it cooks. It is then eaten with a slice of bread and mustard. While *špekáček* is mainly associated with the outdoors, another sausage known as *utopenec* is served only in pubs. The name means "the drowned man," a reference to the fact that the sausages are stored in a glass jar full of vinegar and onions.

spisovná čeština (standard Czech). Ever since Czech national awakeners revived the language in the nineteenth century by renovating the lexicon and standardizing the grammar, there has been a distinction between *spisovná* (literary or standard) and *obecná* or *hovorová* (spoken) Czech. Much like RP in England, *spisovná čeština* is considered the correct way to speak. It is what you expect to hear from TV announcers, stage actors, or school teachers, and it carries the cachet of intelligence. While people generally use *spisovná čeština* when they write, in everyday interactions they are far more likely to speak *obecná čeština*. The difference between them involves vowel shifts (→ *polévka* becomes *polívka*) and consonant additions or deletions (*vono* instead of *ono*, *eště* in place of *ještě*). The reason for the large gap between the two forms is the Germanization of intellectual culture under the Habsburgs—written Czech maintained its medieval form, while spoken Czech evolved. Intellectuals and moralists have for ages lamented the decline of *spisovná čeština*, yet they, like everyone else, use *obecná čeština* to communicate orally in all but formal situations. See also → *čeština*, → *pravopis*.

srpnová invaze (August invasion). The invasion of Warsaw Pact forces in August 1968. As the Prague Spring (→ *Pražské jaro*) progressed, the Soviet Union gave the government increasingly strident warnings about the dangers of the path it was taking. The ending of censorship and the prospect of multiparty elections finally provoked the Soviet Union and its Warsaw Pact allies (with the exception of Romania) to attack Czechoslovakia in the early hours of August 21. The invasion was justified by the Brezhnev doctrine of the collective responsibility of socialist countries for the fate of the entire socialist community, and was referred to as fraternal aid against a counterrevolution. Indeed, the Soviet leadership received an infamous *zvací dopis* (invitation letter) signed by the hardest of hardliners in the Czechoslovak Communist Party (→ KSČ). The arrival of 750,000 soldiers and 6000 tanks, however, was a complete shock to most Czechs who responded with street demonstrations and such subversive activities as defacing road signs so that the invaders would not know where to go. Though the Soviets did not immediately succeed in creating a "worker-peasant" government of hard-liners as they had hoped, they did kidnap the country's leaders and after three days of constant pressure in Moscow forced them to agree to the "temporary presence" of the Soviet army. The signature of reformists like Dubček on these Moscow Protocols disillusioned the public and legalized the invasion. The hard-line minority then used any pretext they could find to push out supporters of the Prague Spring (→ *prověrková komise*) until they finally took complete control of the country and introduced the repressive regime known as normalization (→ *normalizace*). These events continue to provoke arguments over whether the reformists acted irresponsibly, whether the West should have intervened, and what would have happened if the invasion had not taken place. August 21 was the darkest day in recent Czech history, and it is doubtful whether citizens have yet recovered from it. Its only positive effect was to finally and completely destroy faith in communism, but it did so at the price of twenty years of further rule of the worst sort of opportunists.

SRPŠ (Sdružení rodičů a přátel školy/Association of Parents and Friends of the School). The Czech version of the Parent-Teacher's Association. Parents were invited during each school quarter to talk with their children's teachers and find out, in front of their neighbors, how their children were doing.

SSM (Socialistický Svaz Mládeže/Socialist Union of Youth). Modeled on the Soviet *komsomol*, the SSM was supposed to socialize young people into the communist system. Seen as a continuation of the Pioneers (→ *Pionýr*), membership was more or less mandatory in high school and college, but only those who wanted to rise in the system stayed on after that. Members of the organization were known as *svazáci* (unionists) and were easily identifiable by their blue shirts. SSM existed mainly to organize cultural events, trips, seminars, and demonstrations. The organization also published the daily newspaper *Mladá fronta* (Young Front) and the magazine *Mladý svět* (Young World). After the revolution, *svazák* became a pejorative term for those who had cooperated with the communists. The large property holdings of the SSM—including hotels, campgrounds, and other facilities—have quietly been stolen or privatized by former members. But oddly enough, the newspaper *Mladá fronta*, now known as *Dnes* (Today), has become the country's best selling daily.

Starci na chmelu (The Hops Pickers). Popular filmed musical from 1964. It tells the story of two teenagers who fall in love on a work brigade (→ *brigáda*) for collecting the hops (→ *chmel*) harvest. The hero, played by Vladimír → Pucholt, refuses to participate in the collective activities required of socialist youth and elopes with his young love, thus giving viewers their first whiff of sixties rebellion. The film is most remembered for its catchy songs—played by three guitarists dressed all in black—and a romantic portrayal of summer love in a context with which all Czechs were once familiar.

Staré pověsti české (Old Czech Legends). Written by the nationalist → Alois Jirásek, *Staré pověsti české* laid down the definitive version of Czech myths and legends. Mixing apocryphal stories and real history, Jirásek related the history of the Czechs from their arrival in Bohemia to the victories of Jan → Žižka. The best-known legends tell of forefather → Čech founding the country from the top of the mountain → Říp, Princess → Libuše's marriage to a commoner, and the War of the Maidens (→ *Dívčí válka*). Also to be found here are mythical figures like the White Lady (→ *Bílá paní*), King Barley (→ *Král Ječmínek*), → Jánošík, and the → Blaník knights as well as real ones like Saint Wenceslas (→ Svatý Václav), Emperor → Karel IV, and the creator of the Prague astronomical clock. Jirásek's tales are required reading for all elementary-school students and are as well known to Czechs as stories of Paul Bunyan and Daniel Boone are to Americans.

StB (Státní Bezpečnost/State Security). Like the KGB and CIA, the Czech secret police was known by its initials. The StB were plain-clothed officers who spied both abroad and on the country's own citizens. Any activity that could be remotely considered anti-statist—from passing secrets to the West to complaining about lines in front of stores—fell under the StB's purview. The StB would stoop to any level to do its job, using violence, torture, and threats against friends and family to get suspects to confess or agree to cooperate and become informers (→ *udavač*). Activities like surveillance, opening mail, and wiretaps were the bread and butter of the StB's work. Potential collaborators were often invited for a friendly chat at the organization's Prague headquarters at No. 4 Bartolomějská Street. At these interrogations, the StB usually played good cop/bad cop with one officer offering to help and the other ranting and raving. Czechs got back at this intimidation by telling jokes about *estébáci* (StB officers). For example, "What are the four hardest years in the life of an StB officer?" "First grade." Despite their violent, inhumane behavior, agents were never put on trial after the revolution. One enterprising dissident, Petr Cibulka, however, did manage to publish a widely sought-after list (known as Cibulka's List) of all those who worked with the StB . See also → VB.

S tebou mě baví svět (With You the World Is Wonderful). Eighties film voted by Czechs as their favorite film of all time. It opens with three married men preparing to take their annual men-only ski vacation. Instead, their wives force them to take along their children. The film's folksy humor lies in the ingenious ways the husbands find to care for and entertain their charges. Its closest Western parallel might be *Three Men and a Baby*. The film is typical both of the innocuous comedy preferred by the communist regime and of Czech tastes in popular entertainment which tend towards unsophisticated sentimentality.

Strahov. The Strahov district of Prague is home to what the Guinness Book of World Records still lists as the stadium with the largest playing field. The *Velký* (Large) *stadión* measures 301 by 202 meters and holds approximately 130,000 spectators as well as 33,000 performers. Looking for all the world like a communist monstrosity, it was actually built by the patriotic → *Sokol* organization in 1934 for its mass gymnastics program. The communists, of course, could not let a good thing pass them by and adopted it for their own massive → Spartakiáda displays. They also turned the vast changing rooms into university dormitories that became known as Changing Room City. Despite its resemblance to a sports stadium, Strahov has never hosted sporting events—spectators would be too far from the action. Currently, it is used for large concerts (the Rolling Stones have played there twice) and trade fairs. The quar-

ry on which the stadium was originally built was the site of Josef K's execution in Kafka's *The Trial*.

Strakova akademie (Straka Academy). Building where the governing cabinet meets. As the name reveals, this neo-baroque palace on the left bank of the Vltava just below Letná Plain was not always the seat of government. It was built in 1896 to fulfill the will of Baron Jan Petr Straka, who back in 1720 had left finances for a school for young Czech nobles. The school served various functions during the First Republic (→ *První republika*), when the aristocracy (→ *šlechta*) was deprived of its privileges. In 1945, the Czech government chose the former school as its offices (the occupying Germans had previously used it for this purpose). Though the Academy is the equivalent of Britain's Whitehall, it has not developed as powerful a set of associations, probably because Czechs still have little respect for government officials.

střední Evropa (Central Europe). A term that has referred to various combinations of the countries of Austria, Czechoslovakia, Germany, Hungary, Poland, and occasionally the Baltics and Balkans. It was invented by German scholars who called it *Mitteleuropa* and saw it as Germany's natural sphere of influence. Though the designation disappeared after the debacle of Nazism, it was revived by Czech, Hungarian, and Polish intellectuals in the eighties. They argued that the great cultural achievements of their countries had been conveniently written out of European history as the Cold War divided Europe into East and West. In turn, they hoped that their countries would one day escape from the grip of non-European Russia and return to Europe (→ *Evropa*), their true home. Now that all of Central Europe has entered the European Union, the designation is mainly used to emphasize the singular contributions of the individual countries. Czechs say, for example, that Prague (→ *Praha*) is the most beautiful city in Central Europe and Charles University is the region's oldest university.

stopování (hitchhiking). Even with the latest automobile boom, many young people still rely on hitchhiking to get around. Along just about every highway, one can spot hitchhikers, often with signs for their destinations. Probably the most common were soldiers (→ *vojna*) taking a weekend leave from mandatory service. Drivers of passing cars often use hand signals if they are making a turn or stopping soon (and thus not going in the hitchhiker's direction). *Stopování* is most successful if one of the hitchhikers is a woman, but even men rarely fail to get rides.

Strč prst skrz krk (Stick your finger through your neck). The best-known Czech tongue twister (*jazykolam*). It may look unpronounceable, but in reality it is not that difficult, because the *r* in each of the words is a vowel. Foreign speakers will have more trouble with tongue twisters such as "*Tři sta třiatřicet stříbrných křepelek přeletělo přes tři sta třiatřicet stříbrných střech*" (Three hundred and thirty-three silver quail flew over three hundred and thirty-three silver roofs) that focus on the hard-to-pronounce letter → *ř*. While English tongue twisters are mainly a parlor game, Czechs like to point to them as evidence of the difficulty of their language. Benjamin Kuras notes that Englishmen tell the following joke about difficult to pronounce Eastern European languages. A Czech patient stands in front of an eye chart with the random sequence of letters "XSLKJSDFG." The English doctor asks him if he can read the letters. The Czech replies, "Read it? I know the guy."

sudetští Němci (Sudeten Germans). Name given to ethnic Germans (→ *Němec*) living in historically Czech territories. Many of these Germans were descendants of colonists invited to settle the country in the Middle Ages, while others arrived during Habsburg rule. Ultimately, they formed a majority in the country's border regions as well as in certain towns. With the establishment of an independent state in 1918 and more so with the rise of Nazism, the Sudeten Germans began to agitate against Czech domination of government, and most welcomed the Nazi seizure of the Sudetenland in 1938 (→ *Mnichov*). It was this treason that led to their expulsion (→ *odsun*) from the country after the war. Most Sudetens then settled in Bavaria, where they kept alive their folk traditions and after 1989 began to campaign for the revocation of the Beneš decrees (→ *Benešovy dekrety*), which had confiscated their property.

Šuhaj, Nikola. A Czechoslovak outlaw who like Butch Cassidy became a folk hero. In the 1920s, Šuhaj terrorized traveling merchants—though also reputedly spared the poor—and killed the police sent to track him down before being murdered by former comrades for the reward on his head. Šuhaj's romantic allure came from his surroundings—he lived in the Czech version of the Wild West, the primitive and unspoiled region of Subcarpathian Ruthenia (→ *Podkarpatská rus*)—and his fateful love for the beautiful Eržika. Šuhaj's story was a sensation in newspapers of the day and was given legendary form in Ivan Olbracht's novel, *Nikola Šuhaj, Robber*. In the seventies, the playwright Milan Uhde turned the story into a cult musical entitled *Ballad for the Bandit*, though because of his dissident (→ *disident*) activities he had to write under a pseudonym.

Šumava. A forested natural preserve in southeastern Bohemia on the border with Austria and Germany. Šumava is one of the last areas of unspoiled wilderness in the country. Its name is onomatopoeic as the word *šum* (murmur) evokes the sound of wind rustling through the trees. The region attracts legions of cottagers (→ *chata*), hikers (→ *Klub českých turistů*), and campers (→ *tramping*), especially during the summer months when its numerous lakes and trails are packed with vacationers. Because of its dense forests and hard to navigate swamps, many would-be emigrants tried to leave the country through Šumava. The possibility of flight meant that parts of the region were off-limits and several border villages were evacuated. Potential refugees would pay guides to lead them across the frontier. Some of these guides were provocateurs who turned their clients over to the police (→ *pohraniční stráž*), but the legendary *Král Šumavy* (King of Šumava) delivered dozens to safety in the West and was never caught (except in an eponymous film from the fifties).

sunar. The brand name of the single line of baby food and drink under communism. Fathers were often sent to the store with orders to bring back sunar.

Supraphon. Record label. Foreigners know Supraphon for its recordings of the greats of Czech classical music (→ Smetana, → Dvořák), but for Czechs the label was more associated with middle-of-the-road pop music like Karel → Gott of which it was the monopoly distributor.

svačina (snack). All Czech schools break from 9:45 to 10:00 for snack time. The most common snack is rolls (→ *rohlík*) with butter and spreadable cheese accompanied by an apple or radish. Schools usually provide heavily sweetened tea as a beverage. The term also refers to coffeebreaks for adults either in the midmorning or the midafternoon.

Švanda dudák. The hero of a popular nineteenth-century play by the dramatist Josef Kajetán Tyl. Švanda is a small-town bagpiper (the word *dudák* means "bagpiper") from the → Chodsko region who falls asleep in the forest and breathes into his bagpipe the spirit of a forest sprite which grants him great talents. He sets off to explore foreign lands and wins riches by entrancing a mute princess. His intended Dorotka then arrives to stop him from marrying the princess, and Švanda ends up on the gallows. But it all turns out to be a dream, and in the end Švanda is glad to be alive and well at home. The play is meant as a tribute to Czech musicality (→ *Co Čech, to muzikant*) and a paean to the simple life at home (→ *u nás*).

svařené víno (mulled wine). A popular winter drink sold at outdoor stands or in cafes. Mulled wine is made by heating (but not boiling) wine along with cinnamon, cloves, and sugar.

svatba (wedding). Under communism, women tended to marry young—because of few opportunities for career advancement or self-realization—and were frequently divorced by their mid-twenties. Early weddings were also common under the old regime because they were the only way to secure an apartment (→ *dekrety na byty*). Indeed, divorced couples often had to live in the same apartment. While the age at first marriage has been rising since then, it still remains relatively young. Most weddings take place at the town hall in a secular ceremony; however, picturesque castles (→ *hrady a zámky*) and churches are also popular sites. Weddings are usually followed by a small reception only for close family and friends at a pub or restaurant. Several folk traditions accompany weddings. For example, friends of the groom may kidnap the bride on the way to the reception and the groom must find her and pay a ransom (usually the bar tab of the kidnappers). This is supposed to teach him to keep a close eye on his wife. To show that they are truly ready for married life, the bride must sweep the shards of a broken plate into a dustpan held by the groom. Both then eat from a single bowl with one spoon. A popular danish known as a *svatební* → *koláč* (wedding cake) is often served at the reception.

Svatý Václav (Saint Wenceslas, 905–929/935). The patron saint of the Czechs. Václav was king of the Czechs in the tenth century and was proclaimed a martyr and saint for his lifelong devotion to the church. Indeed, in contrast to other patron saints, Václav was not a fighter. He really was a "good" King Wenceslas. His favorite activity was studying the liturgy and he tried to ensure peace by making continual concessions to the growing Holy Roman Empire. It was frustration with this policy of appeasement that led to his murder at a church door by his brother Boleslav. Boleslav then ascended the throne and led the country into successful battle with the encroaching Germans. Nevertheless, it is Václav who is considered the symbol of the nation's essential goodness. In medieval times, a popular cult grew up around his memory—he was seen as both patron and savior of the Czech lands and language. The cult's undiminished strength can be seen in a recent political poster with the writing, "Vote for → Havel, after all, he is a Václav." His statue on horseback—looking unrealistically militant—at the top of Wenceslas Square (→ *Václavské náměstí*) in Prague is the site of political rallies as well as a common meeting spot for friends. A national holiday honoring Václav, now celebrated on September 28, was instituted in the year 2000, though most Czechs remain unaware of its existence. The popular English Christmas carol, "Good King Wenceslas," was composed by an English deacon and has no equivalent in Czech.

Svazarm (Svaz pro spolupráci s armádou/ Union for Cooperation with the Army). Paramilitary organization founded by the communists. Though intended to keep the population in military readiness, Svazarm ultimately became an organizational home to dog trainers, canoeists, pilots, shortwave radio operators, and any other group whose activities had a tangential relation to national defense.

Švejk. The hero of Jaroslav → Hašek's comic novel *The Good Soldier Švejk*. The novel follows the Czech soldier Švejk as he faithfully serves in the Austrian army during World War I. Through kind-mannered idiocy and over-the-top obsequiousness, he proceeds to subvert army precision and discipline, while managing to survive unscathed. Much of the novel's color comes from its zany cast of supporting characters—like Mrs. Müller, Bretschneider, Lieutenant Dub, Chaplain Katz, and Sergeant Major Vaněk—where

Critics' Choices for Novel of the Century

This list represents the choices of twenty-three leading Czech literary critics for the best Czech novel of the century. They were each asked to choose twenty prose works and to divide them into a top ten (which each received three points) and a second ten (which received one point). The results were published in *Týden* magazine in December 1998. Asterisks (*) indicate books that have been translated into English.

	CZECH TITLE	ENGLISH TITLE	AUTHOR	YEAR	POINTS
1	Osudy dobrého vojáka Švejka*	The Good Soldier → Švejk	Jaroslav → Hašek	1921– 23	60
2	Příliš hlučná samota*	Too Loud a Solitude	Bohumil Hrabal	1976	46
3	Markéta Lazarová	Markéta Lazarová	Vladislav Vančura	1931	35
4	Zbabělci*	The Cowards	Josef Škvorecký	1958	34
5	Žert*	The Joke	Milan Kundera	1967	34
6	Český snář	Czech Dreambook	Ludvík Vaculík	1981	28
7	Obyčejný život*	An Ordinary Life	Karel → Čapek	1933	27
8	Obsluhoval jsem anglického krále*	I Served the King of England	Bohumil Hrabal	1971	22
9	Golet v údolí*	Golet in the Valley	Ivan Olbracht	1937	18

	Czech Title	English Title	Author	Year	Points
10	Kulhavý poutník	Limping Pilgrim	Josef Čapek	1936	16
11	Rozmarné léto	Capricious Summer	Vladislav Vančura	1926	16
12	Bloudění*	Wandering/Descent of the Idol	Jaroslav Durych	1929	15
13	Povětroň*	Meteor	Karel → Čapek	1934	14
14	Naši	Ours	Josef Holeček	1888-1929	14
15	Život s hvězdou*	Life with a Star	Jiří Weil	1949	12
16	→ Bylo nás pět	There Were Five of Us	Karel Poláček	1946	12
17	Stříbrný vítr	The Silver Wind	Fráňa Šrámek	1910	12
18	→ Nikola Šuhaj, loupežník*	Nikola Šuhaj, Robber	Ivan Olbracht	1933	12
19	Hordubal*	Hordubal	Karel → Čapek	1933	11
20	Pan Theodor Mundstock*	Mr. Theodor Mundstock	Ladislav Fuks	1963	11
21	Příběh inženýra lidských duší*	The Engineer of Human Souls	Josef Škvorecký	1977	11
22	Sekyra*	The Axe	Ludvík Vaculík	1966	10
23	Neviditelný	Invisible	Jaroslav Havlíček	1937	10
24	Boží duha	Divine Rainbow	Jaroslav Durych	1955	10
25	Hra doopravdy	A Game for Real	Richard Weiner	1933	10
26	Sestra*	City Sister Silver	Jáchym Topol	1994	9
27	Krysař	The Ratcatcher	Viktor Dyk	1915	9
28	Směšné lásky*	Laughable Loves	Milan Kundera	1963/65/68	9
29	Tovaryšstvo Ježíšovo	Society of Jesus	Jiří Šotola	1969	9
30	Zapomenuté světlo	Forgotten Light	Jakub Deml	1934	9
31	Život a dílo skladatele Foltýna	The Life and Work of the Composer Foltýn	Karel → Čapek	1939	9
32	Povídky z jedné kapsy a Povídky z druhé kapsy*	Tales from Two Pockets	Karel → Čapek	1929	7
33	Válka s mloky*	War with the Newts	Karel → Čapek	1936	7
34	Hranice stínu	Edge of Shadow	Jan Čep	1935	7
35	Rekviem	Requiem	Jaroslav Durych	1930	7
36	Dotazník*	The Questionnaire	Jiří Gruša	1976	7

	Czech Title	English Title	Author	Year	Points
37	→ Temno	Darkness	Alois → Jirásek	1915	7
38	Havířská balada*	Ballad of a Miner	Marie Majerová	1938	7
39	Hrdelní pře aneb Přísloví	Capital Case or Proverb	Vladislav Vančura	1930	7
40	Krakatit	Krakatit	Karel → Čapek	1924	6
41	Děravý plášť	Coat Full of Holes	Jan Čep	1934	6
42	Všeobecné spiknutí*	The Plot	Egon Hostovský	1960	6
43	Okresní město	County Seat	Karel Poláček	1936	6
44	Kámen a bolest	Stone and Pain	Karel Schulz	1942	6
45	Pole orná a válečná	Plowed Fields and Battlefields	Vladislav Vančura	1925	6
46	Pekař Jan Marhoul	The Baker Jan Marhoul	Vladislav Vančura	1924	6
47	Konec starých časů	The End of the Old Times	Vladislav Vančura	1934	6
48	Moskva—hranice	Moscow—Border	Jiří Weil	1937	6
49	Smrt krásných srnců*	Death of Lovely Roebuck	Ota Pavel	1971	5
50	Mistr Kampanus	Master Kampanus	Zikmund Winter	1906–7	5

This list ranks the authors above, rather than the works, according to the total number of points that all of their works received. It is thus the critics' ranking of the best/most productive authors.

Rank	Author
1	Vladislav Vančura
2	Karel → Čapek
3	Bohumil → Hrabal
4	Jaroslav → Hašek
5	Milan Kundera
6	Josef Škvorecký
7	Ludvík Vaculík
8	Ivan Olbracht
9	Jaroslav Durych
10	Jan Čep

Hašek skewered every conceivable human type. The work's subversive, vulgar feel can be seen in the opening scene (here in Cecil Parrott's translation):

"And so they've killed our Ferdinand," said the charwoman to Mr. Švejk, who had left military service years before, after having been finally certified by an army medical board as an imbecile, and now lived by selling dogs—ugly, mongrel monstrosities whose pedigrees he forged...

"Which Ferdinand, Mrs. Müller?" he asked, going on with the massaging. "I know two Ferdinands. One is a messenger at Průša's the chemist's, and once by mistake he drank a bottle of hair oil there. And the other is Ferdinand Kokoška who collects dog manure. Neither of them is any loss."

"Oh no, sir, it's his Imperial Highness, the Archduke Ferdinand, from Konopiště, the fat churchy one."

Švejk became a folk hero almost immediately after the novel was published. Many know by heart whole swatches of the text and Josef → Lada's illustrations to the novel continue to be instantly recognizable. Švejk's peaceful demeanor, humorous storytelling (→ *tlachání*), aversion to authority, and general incompetence came to be seen by both Czechs and foreigners as typical of the country's national character. And in fact, Švejkian passive resistance has been a common tactic in dealing with repressive rulers. Communist ideologues, on the other hand, considered Švejk a friend of the proles. Though the novel is almost universally loved—the country is full of Švejk buffs who can cite chapter and verse—it has also had its share of detractors among Czech nationalists. Besides criticizing Švejk's spinelessness, they also worry about his colloquial, beerhall way of speaking (→ *spisovná čeština*), another characteristic that makes the novel appealing to everybody else. At a recent demonstration against NATO, a protestor showed up dressed as Švejk and chanted, "To Baghdad, Mrs. Müller, to Baghdad." (In the original, he says, "To Belgrade.")

Svěrák, Zdeněk (1932). Originally a high school teacher, Svěrák first gained fame as one of the founders of the Jára → Cimrman Theater. To his resume, he then added credits as screenwriter on several films about contemporary life, which stood out under communism for their intelligence and gentle humor. For example, in *Na samotě u lesa* (Solitude by the Woods), where he played the lead role, he showed the joys of and obstacles to buying and fixing up a summer cottage (→ *chata*). Besides his work as writer and actor, Svěrák also found time to pen many of the most popular children's songs of the last quarter century, which he performs often on television in a show called "Singing Lessons." By the time he won the best foreign film Oscar for *Kolja*, the story of a Czech who ends up taking care of a Russian child, he had become a national icon. His boundless curiosity, heartfelt sincerity, and love for all things Czech have thus led many to view him as the nation's conscience, or at least its favorite teacher.

svíčková (sirloin with cream sauce). A classic Czech dish consisting of thick slices of roast beef accompanied by bread dumplings

Favorite Czech Foods

The daily *Mladá fronta Dnes* recently conducted a poll asking Czechs what their favorite food was. The results are presented here.

Food	English equivalent	Calling it their favorite (percent)
→ svíčková na smetaně	beef tenderloin in cream sauce (usually served with bread dumplings)	12.1
→ vepřo-knedlo-zelo	pork-dumplings-sauerkraut	7.1
smažený → řízek	Wiener schnitzel (usually served with boiled potatoes)	5.7
biftek	beefsteak	2.9
rajská → omáčka	tomato sauce (usually served with bread dumplings or stuffed cabbage)	2.9
čínská masová směs	Chinese beef stir-fry	2.9
párek v → rohlíku	hot dog in roll	2.1

Food	English equivalent	Calling it their favorite (percent)
kachna	baked duck	2.1
chléb se sýrem	bread with cheese	2.1
→ smažený sýr	fried cheese (usually served with french fries and tartar sauce)	1.4
dršťková	tripe soup	1.4
škubánky	potato dumplings (usually served with butter, sugar, and poppy seeds)	1.4
bramborák (→ brambory)	potato pancake	1.4

Source: Poll reported in *Mladá fronta Dnes*, 10 April 2003

(→ *knedlík*) and a cream sauce. The dish takes a long time to prepare because the meat is marinated for several days in a broth made of carrots, celery, and vinegar, which is later added to sour cream to form the sauce (→ *omáčka*). A dollop of sour cream, cranberries, and a lemon slice top off the dish. *Svíčková* appears on every restaurant menu as one of its selections of *hotové jídlo*, or ready food, and is a staple of Sunday afternoon lunches.

Svoboda, Ludvík (1895–1979). Army general and later president. Svoboda's first experience with the military was serving in the Czech legions during World War I (→ *legionáři*). After rising through the army ranks, he managed to escape the Nazi takeover and join up with Czech units in the Soviet Union. After a number of close shaves, he became head of the Czech army in exile and led his troops in the bloody but triumphant journey "From Buzuluk to Prague," a phrase that would later grace his autobiography. As a supposedly nonpartisan minister of defense, he allowed the communists to take power in 1948—he famously told Gottwald that he would "go with the people (→ *lid*)." He later played a controversial role in the Soviet invasion (→ *srpnová invaze*), ultimately siding with the new normalization regime (→ *normalizace*). Despite his association with the communists, he is still looked upon by many as a national hero.

T

tablo (tableau). Graduating high school students prepare posters with pictures of their entire homeroom class that are known as tablo. These posters are displayed in storefront windows around town. While the posters used to be formal pictures of the entire class standing in front of the school with their teacher, recently students have chosen more original approaches. One can see, for example, students photographed as cadavers, as lead stories in magazines, or in their bras (at a girls' school).

televizní pondělky (television Mondays). Communist control of the mass media meant that it was rare for innovative programs to get an airing. One of the few exceptions were Monday evenings when the Bratislava television studios—less regulated than their Czech counterparts—were allowed to put on relatively adventurous productions that were religiously followed by the Czech educated class. In general, the two channels of Czech Television alternated between broadcasts in Czech and Slovak with the daily news featuring both Czech and Slovak anchormen, who took turns reading the news. Today Slovaks continue to watch Czech television, while Slovak shows rarely find their way into Czech living rooms.

temno (darkness). The period of Habsburg rule from 1620 to the start of the nineteenth century is viewed by Czechs as their country's dark ages. After the Battle of White Mountain (→ *Bílá hora*), the Habsburgs undertook a massive campaign to wipe out the autonomy of the Czech lands. The population was forcibly converted to Catholicism, the aristocracy exiled or Germanized, and Czech high culture reduced to insignificance. It is for these reasons that history textbooks play down this era and play up the National Revival (→ *Národní obrození*) at the end of the eighteenth century. The term *temno* comes from Alois → Jirásek's eponymous novel, which tells the story of a fanatical Jesuit priest who tries to re-educate the two children of a Czech religious heretic (→ *jezuité*). While most Czechs prefer to forget the period, the years of "darkness" gave the country both its religious faith, its relatively advanced economy, and its visual appearance (→ *české baroko*).

tepláky (sweatpants). When they arrive home from work or school, Czechs immediately change into "home clothes," usually sweatpants or boxers and a T-shirt. This is done both to keep the house or apartment clean and to lengthen the life of one's good clothes.

tepouš (gay; literally the "warm one"). Slang term frequently used to refer to gays. One must thus be careful about pronouncing the sentence, "I am warm." As in most matters of → sex, Czechs are quite tolerant of homosexuality, and parliament came close to passing a registered partnership act.

tesilky. Name given to communist-era clothing, particularly pants, made from the artificial material *tesil*. They were not only ugly and poorly-made, but came in unappealing colors like green, brown, and gray. They were, however, cheap and available, as opposed to the more expensive and rare blue jeans (→ Rifle). *Tesilky* now stand as a symbol of the lack of consumer choice under communism, or lack of taste for those who continue to wear them.

teta (aunt). Besides one's real aunt, the word is used, mostly by children, to refer to adult family friends of the female sex. The equivalent *strýc* or *strejda* (uncle) is used for male family friends.

tlachání (chattering). A Czech national pastime. There are few things that Czechs are better at or enjoy more than spending the day gabbing with friends or acquaintances in one of the country's many pubs (→ *hospoda*). Conversation topics range from family to sports to politics. The habit of *tlachání* (or more colloquially *kecání*) has been immortalized in the literary works of → Hašek and → Hrabal. Even in the age of mass entertainment, the most popular celebrities are the raconteurs who can spin stories for hours (see → Bohdalová, → Menšík, → Werich). The darker side of *tlachání* is the tendency of politicians and citizens to bicker and discuss endlessly while enemy forces prepare to overwhelm the country.

totalita (totalitarianism). The term totalitarianism was invented in the forties by Western scholars to describe communist and fascist regimes that appeared to have total control over their societies. While an accurate description of the fifties in Czechoslovakia, the word faded from academic discourse when the violence of the Stalinist period passed. Perhaps because of the re-imposition of repressive practice during normalization (→ *normalizace*), the term *totalita* is popular among Czechs in referring to the old regime. It is commonly used in the phrase *za totality* (during the totalitarian regime), which prefaces memories of the period from 1948 to 1989.

totální nasazení (literally "total exertion"). Term used to describe the position of thousands of Czechs who were forced to work in Nazi camps during World War II. While one might have thought that the elimination of the Jews would have been the sharpest memory of the war, it is rather the fate of Czechs assigned to forced labor that has entered the collective memory. This was a consequence of communism's founding myth, which saw the world divided between communism and fascism with no space for victims of the Germans besides heroic workers.

tramping (hiking, camping). Saturday morning trains in the Czech lands are packed with scruffy-looking people of all ages wearing green camouflage uniforms, carrying large backpacks and lugging along guitars. They are not army reservists but "tramps." The words *tramping* and *tramp* were borrowed from the Jack London memoir *The Road*, but in the Czech lexicon they refer to ordinary students or working people who spend every free weekend sleeping under the stars (*pod širákem*—under the wideness in Czech). Tramps are not just individual nature lovers, but highly organized groups with their own leader (known as a sheriff) and name (usually something in English like Dakota, Red River, or Yukon). Each group has its own set of rules—there are attendance requirements and everyone is assigned a nickname—and usually claims a special place in the woods known as a *trampská osada* (tramp settlement). The tradition began as a fad in the twenties, an escape from urban life, but acquired new meaning as a form of protest during the war and under communism. The tramping movement has spawned its own musical genre with songs like *"Bedna od whiskey"* (A Crate of Whiskey), *"Rosa na kolejích"* (Dew on the Rails), the tramp anthem *"Vlajka"* (Flag), and even the Czech translation of John Denver's "Country Roads," all of which celebrate life on the open road, unspoiled wilderness, friendship, and love. While most young people grow out of their tramping phase, there are a select few who remain tramps for life.

tramvaj (streetcar). Since the early twentieth century, most major Czech cities have been crisscrossed by streetcars, and they remain the most common form of city transportation. Riders are on their honor to stamp their tickets when they board (→ *revizor*).

trezor (vault). Artistic work that was seen by the communists as subversive was locked up in a vault where only high-ranking party members could view it. Such was the case with a number of films made in the late sixties that became unpalatable after the Soviet invasion (→ *Nová vlna*). Some of them, including Menzel's *Skřivánci na niti* (Larks on a String), Schorm's *Den sedmý, osmá noc* (Seventh Day, Eighth Night), and Balada's *Archa bláznů* (Ark of Fools) (finished belatedly only after the revolution), remained unseen by the public until the fall of communism. Films, television shows, and records could also enter the *trezor* if one of their creators became a dissident (→ *disident*) or fled the country. A corollary of the *trezor* for writers was the desk drawer. The common expression *psát do šuplíku* (to write for the drawer) means to write knowing that the work would never be published (whether for reasons of politics or talent). See also → *samizdat*.

Tři králové (Three Kings Day). The arrival of the biblical three kings and their presentation of gold, frankincense, and myrrh to the newborn Christ are celebrated on January 6. Traditionally children dress up in white robes with crosses around their necks to represent the kings Caspar, Melichor, and Balthasar (the last of which has his face painted black). They then go from door to door singing a song beginning, "We three kings come to you / We wish you health and good fortune." In return they receive donations for charity. Today, the holiday is mainly celebrated by Roma children (→ *cikán*) who have found it to be an excellent money-making opportunity.

Třicetiletá válka (Thirty Years' War). The religious war that wracked much of Europe between 1618 and 1648 had its origins in the Czech lands. It began with the defenestration (→ *defenestrace*) of two pro-Habsburg officials in Prague by members of the Protestant Czech estates. This touched off reprisals from the Catholic Habsburgs who soon defeated the Czech estates at White Mountain (→ *Bílá hora*) in 1620. While this spelled the end of the Czech-speaking nobility, war raged on as other Protestant nations intervened, with the Swedes in particular holding large portions of the country over the next three decades. The war devastated the Czech lands, but the country was soon rebuilt in baroque (→ *české baroko*) style under Habsburg hegemony. It also gave Czechs their great traitor, the double-dealing Albrecht of Valdštejn (Wallenstein)

tunelování (tunneling). A term used to describe the way post-communist CEOs embezzle the assets of their companies. After the fall of communism, managers were given the freedom to negotiate contracts with other firms. Since the state no longer exercised rigid control over enterprises, it was relatively easy for managers to sell off the assets of the firm to friends and relatives. Even when a firm was privatized, the method of voucher privatization (→ *kupónová privatizace*) produced a set of dispersed owners who rarely exercised control over entrenched managers. Tunneling, perhaps better translated as asset stripping, led to the bankruptcy of many of the country's showcase firms and the enrichment of their formerly communist managers. While Czechs often view the practice as their own invention, a result of their golden hands (→ *zlaté ručičky*) going too far, it is in fact common throughout the world. Such eminent figures as Leland Stanford made their fortunes through tunneling. Nevertheless, tunneling has considerably shaken the faith of Czechs in both the new capitalist order and the honesty of their politicians.

Tuzex. A store where, under communism, citizens could buy Western consumer goods such as designer jeans or sneakers. The name is an abbreviation of *tuzemský export* (domestic export), a misnomer if there ever was one. Tuzex stores did not accept Czechoslovak currency as payment, only special coupons known as → *bony*. These coupons could be obtained either from the state in exchange for foreign currency (citizens were legally required to turn in all foreign exchange to the state and explain where it came from) or from a black-marketeer (→ *vekslák*). The reason for the existence of Tuzex was the regime's permanent shortage of foreign exchange as well as citizens' desires for better-made Western goods. Children with fashions from Tuzex were the envy of their schoolmates.

tvarůžky. A particularly strong cheese popular with Czechs. It is sold in stores in small round stacks and taken home to ripen, usually in a glass jar placed inside a dark cupboard. When it starts to *lézt* (crawl, i.e., when it softens), it is served on bread with onions or fried with breadcrumbs. The cheese is associated with the Moravian town of → Olomouc, which has recently inaugurated an annual *tvarůžky* eating contest. The Czechs, however, are not great cheese connoisseurs. The country's most popular and cheapest lunch is the decidedly ungourmet → *smažený sýr* (fried cheese), which consists of a thick slice of edam cheese dipped in batter and deep fried. Slovaks are associated with their own brand of strong cheese called *bryndza*, which is melted and poured over *halušky*, a pasta similar to gnocchi.

tykání/vykání (informal/formal forms of address). As in many languages, Czech has both an informal (*ty*) and formal (*vy*) form of the second person. *Vykání*, or using the formal *vy*, is the norm with strangers and elders. Adults use the informal *tykání* only when they get to know each other, and it is the older person, or the female in the pair, who proposes that the two address each other informally. Quirks of these forms of address include forgetting how you addressed long-lost acquaintances, and the ease with which you can insult someone by choosing the wrong form. In the past *vykání*—and even *onikání*, referring to someone in the third person as in "Does the gentleman agree with my opinion?"—was far more common, especially when subordinates addressed higher-ups and even occasionally between parents and children. Under communism, however, *tykání* was preferred as a sign of solidarity between workers and managers. Since 1989, there has been a move back to *vykání* to signal the return to the bourgeois traditions of the First Republic (→ *První republika*). The former Prime Minister, Václav Klaus, has supported this trend and purportedly uses the formal address even with his close party associates. Another peculiarity of the second person in Czech is that it is capitalized in personal letters.

U

u nás (literally "at us"). English has no equivalent for this construction which can mean "in our house," "in our country," or "with us" depending on the context. You may be invited to dinner *u nás* which means "at our house," but you may also be asked how you like living *u nás* which means "in the Czech Republic." The first-person plural finds heavy use among Czechs. A sports-page headline may read "*Naši vyhráli*" or "Our guys won" referring to the Czech national team, and a Czech may be referred to as "*náš fotbalista*" or "our soccer player." A famous novel is simply entitled "*Naši*" (Ours) and details the lives of ordinary Czechs in a small village (→ *vesnice*). The *u nás* construction (found in other languages too, *chez nous* in French or *bei uns* in German) allows Czechs to see themselves as part of one big family. As Tony Judt notes, the construction also allows one "to slide effortlessly from cozy domesticity into ethnocentric exclusivism."

účet (bill). Food and drink orders in most pubs (→ *hospoda*) and restaurants (→ *restaurace*) are marked on a thin strip of paper that is left on the customers' table. Beers are denoted with a slash, while other drinks and meals have distinct abbreviations. Waiters calculate the total manually—which keeps their arithmetic skills sharp—and are paid directly. The sum is rounded up as a tip.

udavač (informer). Informers have always been in high demand in the Czech lands. The Habsburg Monarchy used informers to infiltrate Czech nationalist circles and extract information about their plans; the communists turned the screws even tighter, cultivating a dense network of informers in schools and workplaces. The thin walls of state apartments (→ *panelák*) further gave neighbors the opportunity to snoop on each other. Citizens were motivated to turn each other in for "antistate" activities, not only for material rewards (taking their fired boss's place or their evicted neighbor's apartment), but also by the national trait of envy (→ *závist*). The secret police (→ StB) meanwhile often pressured individuals into becoming agents by threatening their livelihood or family. Since the Habsburgs, many a national icon has had their reputation besmirched by later revelations of their having served as informers (e.g., → Smetana's librettist Karel Sabina or the underground poet Egon Bondy). The moral complexities of informing, however, are substantial with many former informers claiming that they never passed on information that would deliberately hurt someone and cooperated only to help their children. Slang synonyms for informers like *fízl* or *práskač*, however, are evidence of the ubiquity of the phenomenon. After the Velvet Revolution, the hunt for informers took the form of lustration (→ *lustrace*), but otherwise proceeded without punishment.

Ukrajinci (Ukrainians). Since the fall of communism, Ukrainians fleeing their own country's desperate economy have found a home in the Czech lands. They serve as a cheap and reliable labor force in the construction industry, and are sought out by individuals to help with home and cottage repairs.

umělec (artist). While English uses the word artist mainly to refer to practitioners of the visual arts, the Czech *umělec* casts a wider net to include writers, musicians, actors, and entertainers. As a small nation with little to distinguish itself from others, the cachet of being an artist is high. Artists, in the broad sense, created the Czech nation, and it is they who purportedly preserve it (→ *Národní obrození*). Judging by the number of theatres (→ *divadlo*), galleries, and publishing houses, there are probably few countries in the world where more people aspire to be an artist. But since the category includes pop singers like Karel → Gott, it is hard to say that the designation is a guarantee of good art. Among Czechs, however, it is still a symbol of prestige and a reason for artists to look down on everybody else.

Univerzita Karlova (Charles University). Founded by → Karel IV in 1348, Charles University in Prague is touted by Czechs as the oldest university in Central Europe. Its history mirrors that of the country. It served as a home base for the Hussites (→ *husité*), was entrusted to the Jesuits (→ *jezuité*) during the Counter-Reformation, was divided into Czech and German parts in the nineteenth century, and was a site of communist indoc-trination as well as protests against communism. University education in general remains out of reach for most Czechs; though tuition at all of the handful of Czech universities is free, spaces are extremely limited—only about ten percent of students go on to higher education. Students thus choose fields where there is less competition for admission—for example, forestry or physical education. University students, however, are considered a distinct occupational class as evidenced by their proclivity to go on strike. See also → *majáles*.

ÚV KSČ (Ústřední výbor Komunistické strany Československa/Central Committee of the Communist Party of Czechoslovakia). The real power under communism was not the parliament or even the cabinet, but the Communist Party (→ KSČ), and the real power in the Communist Party was the Central Committee and its leadership, the Presidium. The head of the Committee and thus of the Communist Party was known as the *generální* or *první tajemník* (general or first secretary) and all other members were secretaries. No major policy change could take place without the approval of the Central Committee. The initials ÚV KSČ thus denoted absolute power and struck fear in the hearts of ordinary citizens.

V, W

Václavské náměstí (Wenceslas Square). Prague's main square. The long square was once the city's horse market, but as the country grew it became its commercial heart. It was renamed for the Czech patron Saint Wenceslas (→ Svatý Václav) by national awakeners in the nineteenth century, and its upper end was closed with the imposing National Museum (→ *Národní muzeum*) and a statue of Wenceslas on horseback. As the symbolic center of Prague, the square has always been the site of political demonstrations, whether to celebrate independence in 1918 (→ *28. říjen*), proclaim the victory of the communists in 1948 (→ *Vítězný únor*), protest the Soviet invasion in 1968 (→ Palach), and again to celebrate in 1989 (→ *Sametová revoluce*). The square is also a popular meeting place—friends often plan to get together under the tail (*u ocasu*) of the statue of Saint Wenceslas.

Valašsko (Wallachia). A mountainous region in northeast Moravia. *Valašsko* received its name from sheepherders who trace their roots to the Romanian region of Wallachia. The isolated and rugged terrain of *Valašsko* meant that its inhabitants enjoyed a certain degree of freedom from the central government. They were often relieved of feudal obligations in return for serving as border guards (→ Chodsko). This independent spirit survives into the modern era: *Valaši* (Vlachs), as inhabitants are called, cherish their distinctive culture, which includes a recognizable accent and numerous folk habits and customs (→ *kroj*). The region continues to be associat-

ed with → *cimbál* music and homemade delicacies like sauerkraut (→ *zelí*) and the large → *koláč* called *fergl*. A popular folk comedian, Bolek → Polívka, has declared himself King of Wallachia. He issues his own passports and holds festivals for his subjects. Ordinary Czechs treasure the region as much for its old-fashioned ways as for its beautiful scenery and hiking trails (→ *Klub českých turistů*, → *čundr*). The region is also home to the legendary mountain → *Radhošť*.

Vánoce (Christmas). The first sign that Christmas is arriving is the thorough housecleaning that precedes it. Another early sign is the baking of mounds of sweets like Linzer cookies (two round wafers with jam in between) or *vánočka* (Christmas bread—a twisted loaf chock full of raisins and nuts). The holiday itself lasts for three days. The first, known as *Štědrý den* (Generosity Day), takes place on December 24 and includes most of the festivities, with the immediate family (and perhaps one or two other relatives) gathering at home. The day traditionally begins with a fast broken only by *zelná* → *polévka* (cabbage soup) served around lunchtime. If kids can hold out with only soup until supper, they will supposedly see a *zlaté prase* (golden pig), a sign of good luck. Many use the afternoon to visit the cemetery. Supper is served in the late afternoon and consists of batter-fried carp (→ *kapr*) and potato salad. Presents, delivered by → *Ježíšek* (Baby Jesus), are usually opened after supper. The entire holiday is accompanied by countless folk traditions, one of which is

175

cutting an apple in half, width-wise. If the core shows a star, it means there will be a birth, while a cross signifies a death—the same symbols that are used on gravestones. December 25, called *Boží hod vánoční* (Divine Christmas Feast), is usually for visiting other family members or friends and eating leftovers. The next day, known as St. Stephen's Day, sees more of the same and also features door-to-door caroling. Television stations traditionally broadcast popular fairy tales (→ *pohádka*) throughout the holiday, with the result that much time is spent in front of the set.

Vařila myšička kašičku (Mousie cooked porridge). The Czech version of "This Little Piggie Went to Market." It continues as follows: This one (the thumb) she gave a lot. This one (the index finger) she gave less. This one (the middle finger) she gave even less. This one (the ring finger) she gave the least. And for this one (the pinkie) there wasn't anything left, and he ran and ran all the way to the pantry (the child's armpit).

VB (Veřejná bezpečnost/Public Security). Under communism, the police were not called police, but rather public security. Originally known as the SNB (*Sbor národní bezpečnosti*/National Security Corps) and thus called *esenbáci*, they later became the VB or *vébáci*. Members of the VB wore military-style uniforms, an indication of the militarization of society, and drove around in white and yellow cars with the initials VB displayed prominently. Though in many ways a typical police force, they took a much larger role in enforcing public morality and had considerable discretion in using their power. They gave way to the → StB, however, if crimes had any whiff of anti-state activity. Many citizens remember the old VB for frequent stops on the street, where they were asked for their citizen identification card (→ *občanský průkaz*). Those who left their card at home might be hauled down to the police department. While the VB disappeared with the fall of communism, what has not

changed is their corruption: a bribe will almost always make a traffic violation go away and a good number of criminal acts feature police cooperation. Cops are also the punchline of many jokes (the Czech equivalent of dumb blondes). For example, a cop goes into a store and asks the salesman if they have color TVs. When the salesman says yes, the cop says he would like a yellow one.

večerníček (evening cartoon). A short bedtime cartoon for children shown every evening at 7:00. The cartoons were first aired in 1964, originally weekly and eventually daily. From then on, all Czech children and parents remember the most popular of them. Although they included cartoons from throughout the Soviet bloc, the perennial favorites were Czech. The best-loved are the outlaw → Rumcajs, the forest sprites Křemílek and Vochomůrka, the mole → Krteček, the dog Maxipes Fík, the rabbits Bob and Bobek (→ Jiránek), and the third-graders with the magic telephone, Mach and Šebestová. *Večerníček* remains synonymous with bedtime for children across the country.

vekslák (money-changer, from the German *wechseln*, "to exchange"). Overvalued exchange rates and a ban on holding foreign currency meant that black-market money-changers were ubiquitous in communist countries. Citizens with the good fortune to be allowed to travel abroad (→ *výjezdní doložka*) inevitably found that the amount of foreign exchange the state permitted them to purchase was inadequate for even basic necessities. They thus turned to *veksláci*, both for extra currency and better rates. Money-changers also conducted a profitable business in → *bony*, coupons obtainable from the state in exchange for foreign currency. *Bony* allowed citizens to purchase foreign goods in special shops called → Tuzex.

Velehrad. Pilgrimage church and monastery. Located near the heart of the former Great Moravian Empire (→ *Velkomorav-*

ská říše) in south Moravia (→ *Morava*), the church was home to Archbishop Methodius (→ Cyril and Methodius), one of the brothers who brought Christianity to the Czechs. Velehrad later became an important pilgrimage site (→ *pouť*), and hosts popular festivities on July 5—the holiday celebrating the missionary brothers. In 1990, John Paul II held mass at Velehrad to welcome Czechs back to the free world.

Velikonoce (Easter). Easter is accompanied by countless folk traditions and is celebrated in a joyful manner. The holiday begins, like Christmas, with a thorough house-cleaning. The house is then decorated with pussy willows. Eggs are dyed and painted with a variety of techniques (the painted eggs are known as *kraslice*). The main religious events take place on Sunday—with mothers preparing pastry lambs (*beránek*) and hot cross buns (*mazanec*)—but children especially look forward to Easter Monday. It is on this national holiday that boys go around with their → *pomlázky* (whips) and gently whip girls, for which they receive either a painted egg or, more commonly now, chocolate and alcohol. See also → *Hody hody doprovody*.

Velká Javořina. The highest mountain peak on the border of the Czech Republic and Slovakia. On New Year's Day, Czechs and Slovaks hike to the top of the mountain as a symbol of their mutual friendship.

"Velká láska postel praská" (A great love cracks the bed). The first line of a children's rhyme that is the Czech equivalent of "John and Jane, sitting in a tree, K-I-S-S-I-N-G." The rest of the rhyme runs: "The delivery room is working overtime. A baby is on the way." It is often abbreviated and written, along with the two sets of initials, inside of a heart.

Velkomoravská říše (Great Moravian Empire). A loose union of tribes that was the first major organized political entity of the Czechs. It was founded by Mojmír I around 830 A.D. in Moravia (→ *Morava*) and expanded to include much of Slovakia (→ *Slovensko*) and parts of Bohemia (→ *Čechy*) and Poland (→ *Polsko*). Mojmír's successor Rostislav welcomed the missionaries → Cyril and Methodius, who are known for translating the liturgy into a Slavic language and Christianizing the Czechs. The Empire fell under pressure from Hungarian invaders at the end of the ninth century and gave way to the first real Czech state under the Premyslids (→ *Přemyslovci*). It is sometimes referred to as the first common state of Czechs and Slovaks (→ *Československo*), but this exaggerates the national consciousness of both groups at the time.

Velorex. A compact three-wheeled car invented in 1943 by the brothers František and Mojmír Stránský. After the putsch in 1948, their factory was taken over by the communist government, which went on to mass-produce the vehicle and change its name from the original Oskar to Velorex. The car ran on a Jawa motorcycle engine, but was completely enclosed in a canvas tarpaulin or metal shell. Production was definitively ended in 1973, though old models can still occasionally be seen on the roads or at car fairs. Zdeněk → Svěrák's film *Vrchní, prchni* (Run, Waiter) accurately captures the humiliation of having to drive a Velorex when all your neighbors had → Škodas or Trabants.

vepřo-knedlo-zelo (pork-dumplings-sauerkraut). The most traditional Czech meal. It consists of slices of pork chop, bread dumplings (→ *knedlík*), and a dollop of sauerkraut (→ *zelí*). Though its culinary charms are limited and its health benefits even more doubtful, for Czechs it is the ultimate comfort food. It is available at every pub and restaurant and forms a staple of family dinners. It is typical of Czech cuisine in its lack of any spice and its heavy portions of grease and starch. Czechs affectionately refer to it in the shortened form listed here, instead of saying its full name, "*Vepřové maso s knedlíky a se zelím.*"

Traditional Czech Foods

A poll in the newspaper *Lidové noviny* asked readers what they considered traditional Czech food. The results are below.

Rank	Czech name	English name
1	→ vepřo-knedlo-zelo	pork-dumplings-sauerkraut
2	→ svíčková	beef tenderloin in cream sauce
3	→ řízek → bramborem	pork chop with potatoes
4	ovocné knedlíky	fruit dumplings
5	→ guláš	goulash
6	buchty	sweet buns with custard or cottage cheese
7	bramborák	potato pancake
8	husa se → zelím	goose with sauerkraut
9	→ zabíjačka	pig roast
10	kachna se zelím	duck with sauerkraut

Source: Poll reported in *Lidové noviny*, 18 August 2003.

vesnice (village). For centuries, villages have been considered the soul of the nation. A typical village consists of small row-houses crowded next to each other along a main street and surrounded by fields and forests. Cultural life in the village once consisted of an amateur theater (→ *ochotnické divadlo*), a brass band (→ *dechovka*), and an annual village fair (→ *pout*), though many of these traditions have disappeared. The village has been lionized in Czech literature (for example, → *Maryša* and → *Naši furianti*), because it is here that Czech culture survived, supposedly pure and unblemished, through the days of Austrian rule. This has not stopped the country from becoming a highly urbanized, modern nation. Nowadays, younger residents of villages generally take whatever chance they can to flee to Prague or any larger town and return to the village only for weekends. Indeed, many villages today are overrun by → *luft' áci*, a term that refers to city residents who own a village home that they visit only on weekends or holidays. An isolated village with no cultural life at all is referred to as a *zapadákov* (from the word for "get lost, disappear"), probably best rendered in English as Podunk.

věstonická Venuše (Věstonice Venus). The name given to a small clay figure of a naked woman—likely a fertility totem—found during an excavation in the village of Dolní Věstonice. It has achieved notoriety both because of its age—over 25,000 years old—and its exaggerated breasts and behind. The figure appears at the beginning of all history textbooks and has been giggled over by generations of students.

Vídeň (Vienna). As long as the Czechs were ruled by the Habsburgs, Vienna played a powerful role in Czech life. Many a Czech favorite son spent his formative years in Vienna getting an education or engaging in politics. From Vienna, Czechs imported the tradition of coffeehouses (→ *kavárna*), sweets (→ *cukrárna*), and Wiener schnitzel (→ *řízek*). Czech cities imitated Vienna's urban design with copies of the Viennese Opera House and Ringstrasse dotting the Czech landscape. For its part, Czechs have always been an integral part of Viennese life, and distinctively Czech names like Jelínek and Kučera can be seen gracing more than one Viennese business.

Vietnamec (Vietnamese). In the name of socialist brotherhood, communist Czechoslovakia hosted and trained thousands of students and workers from allied countries in Asia, Africa, and the Middle East. Of these, it is mainly the Vietnamese who have settled permanently in the country. They are known mainly for selling extremely cheap clothing and other goods at outdoor markets. While tolerated by most, they are not looked upon positively.

Vinnetou. The Indian hero of dozens of adventure novels written by the German writer Karl May at the turn of the century. Vinnetou teamed up with the German immigrant Old Shatterhand to form an invincible duo fighting against evildoers (often Mormons) across the American West. The books enjoy enormous popularity throughout Eastern Europe and have been eagerly read by Czech children for almost a century now. In the sixties, the West Germans turned them into equally popular films that set box-office records across Europe. Though campy by American standards, the books and films inspired generations of Czechs to play at cowboys and indians and become "blood brothers." Unlike in America, however, the Indian was usually the hero. See also → *country*.

vinobraní (grape harvest). The grape harvest is celebrated annually at festivals known as *vinobraní* in the wine-producing region of south Moravia, especially the towns of Znojmo, Valtice, and Mikulov. Along with the latest vintage, → *burčák* (young wine) flows plentifully, and visitors are treated to music and dancing. Wine itself, however, remains a distant second behind beer (→ *pivo*) as Czechs' drink of choice; it is even frequently mixed with soft drinks.

vítání chlebem a solí (welcome with bread and salt). Traditionally visitors to a Czech home were welcomed with the presentation of bread and salt, an ancient Slavic sign of hospitality. Though the custom came to be seen as old-fashioned in the nineteenth century—the grandmother in Božena → Němcová's classic novel (→ *Babička*) is laughed at for holding to the old ways—even today politicians are welcomed to villages with a symbolic presentation of bread and salt, often by a girl dressed in a folk costume (→ *kroj*).

vítání občánků (welcoming the little citizens). A ceremony introduced in the fifties to replace traditional christenings. Like everything else at the time, it was imported from the Soviet Union, where it was known as an October christening. For the ceremony, young couples gather with their newborns at the local town hall where the babies' names are written into the town register. The mayor then presents them with gifts, for example, a book for recording milestones in the baby's life, and makes a short speech welcoming them to the community. Though christenings have become common again (they never completely disappeared under communism), *vítání občánků* maintains its place alongside them to this day, though without its communist baggage.

Vítězný únor (Victorious February). Shorthand phrase for the *coup d'état* by which the communists came to power in February 1948. Though the Communist Party had won a plurality of forty percent in free elections in 1946, they still had to govern in a coalition, and their heavy-handed methods led to a considerable loss of support. Worried about upcoming elections, they tightened their already strong control of the police forces. Ministers from three of their coalition partners in turn tendered their resignations to provoke a government crisis and early elections. A fourth party, the Social Democrats, however, did not follow their lead and allowed the government to stand. At the same time, the communists began holding rallies—most famously in Old Town Square on February 21—and arresting the opposition. On February 25, the president named a new communist-led government, thus marking the beginning of communist rule. With the help of the newly-formed People's Militia (→ *Lidové milice*), the communists soon controlled the entire country. By May, they had passed a new constitution proclaiming the country a People's Democratic Republic and held elections with a single slate of candidates. In communist nomenclature, these events became known as Victorious February, and February 25 was celebrated annually with parades and speeches as the Day of the Victory of the Czechoslovak Working People. Debates continue today over whether the February events were the result of poor judgment on the part of the democratic parties or whether the communist takeover was inevitable once the country ended up in the Soviet sphere of influence.

Communist-era Calendar

This calendar lists the main holidays, significant days, memorable days, and anniversaries from the year 1985. National holidays are indicated in boldface. If there were more holidays during the year than the plan allowed, working Saturdays were added to the calendar. Church holidays were not included in all calendars. The abbreviation ČSSR stands for Czechoslovak Socialist Republic.

Month	Day	Holiday
January	1	New Year's Day
	4	State Holiday of the Cambodian People's Republic
	10	Anniversary of the Birth of President Gustáv → Husák (1913)
	15	Czechoslovak Rocket Army and Artillery Day
	21	Anniversary of the Death of V.I. Lenin (1924)
February	23	Soviet Army and Navy Day
	25	**Significant Day: Victory of the Czechoslovak Working People (1948)** (→ *Vítězný únor*)
March	1	Beginning of Book Month
	2	Anniversary of the First Flight of Czechoslovak Astronaut Vladimír → Remek (1978)
	8	International Women's Day (→ MDŽ)
	23	Anniversary of the Start of the Great Strikes in Most (1932)
	28	Teachers' Day—Anniversary of the Birth of Jan Amos → Komenský (1592)
Moveable Holiday		Easter (Easter Sunday and Monday) (→ *Velikonoce*)
April	1	Beginning of Highway Safety Month
	4	State Holiday of the Hungarian People's Republic
	5	Anniversary of the Declaration of the Košice Government Program (1945)
	11	Day of International Solidarity of Liberated Political Prisoners and Fighters against Fascism
	12	Anniversary of the First Manned Flight to Outer Space (J.A. Gagarin, 1961)
	17	National Security Forces Day
	22	Anniversary of the Birth of V.I. Lenin (1870)

Month	Day	Holiday
May	1	Labor Day (→ *1. máj*)
	5	Anniversary of the May Uprising of the Czech People (1945) and the Birth of Karl Marx (1818) (→ *Květnové povstání*)
	6	Anniversary of the Signing of the New Treaty of Friendship, Cooperation and Mutual Assistance between ČSSR and USSR (1975)
	9	State Holiday—Liberation of Our Homeland by the Soviet Army (1945) (→ *Den osvobození*)
	14–16	Anniversary of the Founding of the Czechoslovak Communist Party (1921) (→ KSČ)
June	1	International Children's Day
	10	Anniversary of the Destruction of the Village of → Lidice (1942)
	24	Anniversary of the Destruction of the Village of Ležáky (1942)
July	5	Memorable Day of ČSSR—Arrival of the Slavic Missionaries → Cyril and Methodius (863)
	6	Memorable Day of ČSSR—Burning of Master Jan → Hus (1415)
	11	State Holiday of the Mongolian People's Republic
	14	Construction Workers' Day
	22	State Holiday of the Polish People's Republic
	26	State Holiday of the Cuban Republic
August	23	State Holiday of the Romanian Socialist Republic
	29	Significant Day of ČSSR—Slovak National Uprising (1944) (→ SNP)
September	2	State Holiday of the Vietnamese Socialist Republic
	9	State Holiday of the Bulgarian People's Republic and the Korean People's Democratic Republic
	17	Czechoslovak Air Force Day
	21	Press, Radio, and Television Day—Anniversary of the Founding of the Red Right Newspaper (1920) (→ *Rudé právo*)
	27	Czechoslovak Railway Workers' Day
October	1	State Holiday of the Chinese People's Republic
	6	Czechoslovak People's Army Day
	7	State Holiday of the German Democratic Republic
	14	Anniversary of the General Strike Led by the Socialist Council (1918)
	28	Significant Day of ČSSR—Nationalization (1945), Anniversary of the Declaration of the Independent State of Czechs and Slovaks (1918), and Passage of the Law on the Czechoslovak Federation (1968) (→ *28. říjen*)
	30	Anniversary of the Announcement of the Martin Declaration (1918)

Month	Day	Holiday
November	2	Remembrance of the Dead (→ *Dušičky*)
	7	Anniversary of the Great October Socialist Revolution (1918) (→ VŘSR)
	10	International Youth Day
	17	International Students' Day (Jan Opletal, 1939)
	23	Anniversary of the Birth of President Klement → Gottwald (1896)
	25	Anniversary of the Birth of President Ludvík → Svoboda (1895)
	28	Anniversary of the Birth of Friedrich Engels (1820)
	29	State Holiday of the Albanian People's Socialist Republic and the Socialist Federative Republic of Yugoslavia
December	2	State Holiday of the Laotian People's Democratic Republic
	19	Anniversary of the Birth of President Antonín Zápotocký (1884)
	24-26	Christmas (Christmas Eve, Christmas Day, St. Stephen's Day) (→ *Vánoce*)

Source: *http://bimbo.fjfi.cvut.cz/~karpisek/kalendar/data_cz/kalendar/kalcsr85.php*

vlašský salát (Italian salad). A salad in name only, *vlašák*, as it is known for short, is a mixture of mayonnaise, salami, and peas that along with rolls (→ *rohlík*) makes for a popular quick lunch. Most grocery stores stock a variety of these mayonnaise-based salads composed of a varying mix of lunchmeats and eggs. Besides *vlašák*, the most popular is called Parisian though it has little in common with French cuisine.

Vltava (Moldau). Originating in the mountains of → Šumava, the Vltava River meanders its way through southern Bohemia (→ *Čechy*) before gathering the heft and strength to split Prague (→ *Praha*) in two and join with the Labe (Elbe) on its way to the North Sea. The river has long inspired Czech artists, most famously in → Smetana's tone poem → *Má vlast*. It is equally enjoyed by Czech vacationers who spend the summer rafting, canoeing, and kayaking its length.

vodník (water sprite). A common figure in Czech fairy tales. A *vodník*, also known by the German term *hastrman*, supposedly inhabits and rules over every stream, pond, river, and lake. He is typically portrayed in a dripping, green frock coat, top hat, and pipe with multicolored bands hanging from his clothes. These sprites usually figure as man's enemy—they destroy mills or send floods, evade capture by turning into fish, and even collect the souls of the people they have drowned, which are stored in small porcelain cups. They can be stopped only if tied up and kept away from water, the source of their strength. A close relative of the *vodník* is the → *rusalka* or water nymph portrayed in → Dvořák's opera of the same name. A popular film comedy from the seventies is set among the *vodníci* of the → Vltava.

vojna (army service). Though the Czechs pioneered fighting techniques in the late Middle Ages—Jan → Žižka invented the tactic of circling the wagons to defend against cavalry attacks—their military fortunes slowly declined ending in the disastrous defeat at → *Bílá hora*. From then on the Czechs' only experience with military life was service in the Austrian army. The standard tour of duty lasted seven years, which led to the kind of romantic complications described in the play → *Maryša*. Their troops were well-trained, however, as demonstrated by the success of

182

the legionnaires (→ *legionáři*) during World War I. Between the wars, the Czechs built a powerful army and an impressive Maginot-like series of fortifications along the border with Germany. They also, however, supplied arms to the rest of the world and decided to lay down their own weapons rather than resist the Germans (→ *Mnichov*). Under communism, Czechoslovakia was considered a country on the frontlines of the war with the imperialists and thus society was heavily militarized (→ *branná výchova*). A two-year term of military service was mandatory, except for those with → *modré knížky* (blue books) that attested to their physical unfitness. *Vojna* at the time came to symbolize absurdity, waste, and boredom and was portrayed as such in best-sellers by Josef Škvorecký and Miroslav Švandrlík (→ *černí baroni*). Some remember it as the only place where the country's main ethnic groups—Czechs, Slovaks, Hungarians, and Roma—mixed freely. The main event in the life of recruits was the *přísaha* (oath) when after several weeks of training they finally became real soldiers at a ceremony attended by their family members. Only recently has mandatory service been eliminated and the Czech army turned into a professional fighting force. See also → *bažant*.

Voskovec & Werich. Jiří Voskovec (1905–1981) and Jan → Werich were the creators and stars of the *Osvobozené divadlo* (Liberated Theater), an enormously influential theater from the thirties. Their plays—with titles like *Kat a blázen* (The Hangman and the Jester), *Pudr a benzín* (Powder and Gas), and *Hej rup!* (Heave-Ho)—combined absurdist comedy, musical numbers, and left-wing commentary on current events. According to the author Josef Škvorecký they "moulded dadaism, circus, jazz, Chaplin, Buster Keaton, and American vaudeville into a new art form…an intellectual-political musical." The most lasting legacy of the theater are the dozens of popular songs with lyrics by V&W and music by the nearly blind composer Jaroslav Ježek. Some of these funny, romantic songs that became popular standards include *"Život je jen náhoda"* (Life is Just an Accident), *"Nebe na zemi"* (Heaven on Earth), and *"Tmavomodrý svět"* (Dark Blue World). At the outbreak of World War II, the two fled to America to escape arrest and certain execution for their anti-fascist views. After the war, they unsuccessfully tried to revive the theater under the new repressive conditions. Voskovec ultimately decided to return to America where he made a career as a stage and film actor—he starred most famously in *Twelve Angry Men*. Werich remained at home and became a folk hero while struggling to get his work produced.

VŘSR (Velká říjnová socialistická revoluce/The Great October Socialist Revolution). Known by its initials, this national holiday was celebrated annually on November 7 in commemoration of the seizure of power by Russian communists in 1917. (Russians actually celebrated it on October 25 because they were still using the Julian calendar at the time of the revolution.) The holiday was marked by mass parades in every town and village. Attendance was required and everyone had to check in with the manager of their enterprise along the parade route. For children there was a *lampionový průvod* (lantern parade), where they carried Chinese lanterns around town in the early evening. Citizens also had to decorate their house and apartment windows with Soviet flags and red banners. As the initial enthusiasm for communism faded, VŘSR became just another excuse for heavy drinking, though the state ultimately banned hard alcohol on official holidays. The Czech equivalent of VŘSR was the anniversary of the communist putsch, celebrated with similar festivities and known as → *Vítězný únor* (Victorious February). This led to the nonsensical phrase: February is our October.

všimné (baksheesh). Derived from the verb *všimnout si* (to take notice of), this word describes bribes given for extra, faster, or better service. Under communism, *všimné* was most frequently offered to doctors to ensure

183

better care and to professors to help in high school or college admissions (→ *gymnázium*). In both cases, these bribes survived communism, though they have disappeared in the consumer goods sector where they were once common (→ *podpultovka*). *Všimné* is usually delivered in a white envelope with the words, "Thank you for your willingness."

Všude dobře, doma nejlépe (Everywhere good, at home the best). Frequently cited proverb that attests to Czechs' attachment to their homes. Most people rarely move away from their hometown—at least partially because it is so difficult to find an apartment—and are happy to eventually take over their parents' home or apartment. This attachment is one of the causes of current high unemployment—citizens are reluctant to move to find work.

vůl (ox). One of the most popular Czech oaths. Young men frequently address each other with "*ty vole*" or "you ox." The American equivalent might be "Hey man" or "Hey dude," though in different contexts the word can be more insulting and even be interpreted as fighting words. This does not stop Czechs from saying "*To je vůl*" (He's an ox), when they want to emphasize a person's stupidity or ignorance. One of Vlasta → Burian's early films is based on the trouble he gets into when he refers to the emperor as a *vůl*. Other animals are also common in Czech insults. *Kráva* (cow) and *slepice* (hen) are both frequently used to describe shrewish or meddling women, while *tele* (calf) refers to a silly one. Common terms of endearment, by contrast, are *brouček* (beetle), *kočička* (cat), *beruška* (lady bug), and *myšáček* (mouse).

VUML (Večerní univerzita marxismu-leninismu/Evening University of Marxism-Leninism). To get ahead in the communist system, one had to be able to talk the talk. This meant justifying hiring decisions in terms of winning the class struggle or rationalizing purchase of a new computer in terms of the battle against imperialism. VUML was the place where upwardly-mobile workers learned this talk. A degree from VUML was required for anyone who wanted a management position in a factory, hospital, or school. The three-year evening course included classes in the basics of Marxist-Leninist philosophy, central planning, and world politics. The lectures in themselves were boring and useless, but attending VUML proved to the regime that a person was loyal and malleable. It also allowed enterprise managers to make useful contacts (→ *protekce*) with other up-and-comers, networks that would allow them to procure hard-to-find goods among the system's general shortages. Even as Marxist jargon and VUML have disappeared, these business contacts remain.

výjezdní doložka (exit visa permit). Under communism, all travel abroad required a special exit visa permit, which could only be obtained after a thorough background check. Any previous anti-state activities, or even similar activities by relatives, were enough to sink one's application for a permit. In any case, permission to travel outside the Soviet bloc was rarely granted without a compelling reason, as the regime feared invidious comparisons, which would reveal the lie to their propaganda about the corrupt West. The communist authorities also made sure that entire families could not travel at the same time so that they would not be tempted to emigrate. Would-be travellers were allowed to exchange only a set amount of money (known as a *devizový příslib*) and were required to turn in all unused foreign currency to the state in exchange for → *bony* coupons (→ Tuzex). One of the greatest changes in personal lives since the fall of communism has been the end of *výjezdní doložky* and the opportunity to travel freely.

vyjmenovaná slova (exception words). Though almost completely phonetic (that is, each letter represents only one sound), Czech represents the sound "ee" in two ways: with the so-called soft *i* and the hard *y*. This causes difficulty for Czech children who learn the language by ear and do not know when to write the one or the other. Though some rules govern their use, much school time is spent memorizing a list of several dozen exceptions known as *vyjmenovaná slova*. Incorrect usage of *i* and *y*, writing *myslet* (to think) as opposed to *mislet*, for example, carries considerable stigma. Fortunately, besides foreign words, this is just about all the spelling (→ *pravopis*) that Czechs have to learn. See also → *diktát*.

Vynášení smrti (Carrying out of death). A folk tradition for biding farewell to winter. Villagers build an effigy of an old woman from wood and hay and dress it up with various ornaments. Known as *Mořena* or *Smrtholka*, the figure is then thrown into a river or off of a cliff to symbolize the end of winter.

Vyšehrad (High Castle). The oldest home of Czech kings. Founded in the tenth century, Vyšehrad, whose name means "high castle," was built in the Romanesque style on a rocky hill in Prague (→ *Praha*) overlooking the → Vltava River. It was here that the first Premyslids (→ *Přemyslovci*) ruled the country, that → Libuše predicted Prague's future glory, and that the nobleman Horymír escaped a death sentence by jumping over the battlements and moat with his legendary horse Šemík. Vyšehrad was the seat of kings until 1146, when Prague Castle (→ *Hrad*) took its place. → Karel IV, however, paid tribute to his forefathers by beginning the coronation parade of Czech kings at Vyšehrad. The Austrians later used the castle as a military garrison, though during the National Revival (→ *Národní obrození*) it again became a symbol of the Czech nation. A foundation stone for the National Theater (→ *Národní divadlo*) was quarried here, and patriots founded the national cemetery → *Slavín* near the ruins of the old castle.

Vysočina (Highlands). Located almost exactly in the middle of the country, on the border between Bohemia (→ *Čechy*) and Moravia (→ *Morava*), *Vysočina* is the country's natural heartland. Rolling hills alternately covered with spruce trees and open meadows attract scores of visitors from all parts of the republic. Many own weekend cottages (→ *chata*) in the region, while others visit in winter for cross-country skiing or in summer for hiking. The gentle but beautiful landscape inspired the national anthem, → *Kde domov můj*, which celebrates its waters murmuring through meadows and forests rustling on rocky hills.

vysvědčení (report card). Czech students are graded on a five-point scale, the highest mark being a 1 (*jednička*) and the lowest a 5 (*pětka*). Each mark is associated with an adjective, thus 1 is "excellent," 2 is "praiseworthy," 3 is "good," 4 is "adequate," and 5 is "inadequate." A single 5 on the final report card means that the student has to take a makeup exam in the summer and, should he fail that, to repeat the entire year. In one joke, parents ask their child to count to ten. He replies: "1, 2, 3, 4, 6, 7, 8, 9, 10." "Where is the five?" they ask. "On my report card," he says. The one distinctive mark is for *chování* (behavior) where a 2 is considered evidence of extremely poor discipline and cause for much consternation at home.

Werich, Jan (1905–1980). Werich first gained fame as a co-star and co-author (with Jiří Voskovec) in the Liberated Theater (→ *Voskovec & Werich*). After the war, he founded the ABC Theater, which specialized in clever repartee and humorous songs, and was one of the few bright spots in the otherwise deadly dull cultural scene of the fifties (→ *sorela*). Werich soon ran into trouble with the communists who severely limited his performances, yet he became known for his Will Rogers-like folk wisdom. There was hardly an office in the country not decorated with his famous dictum "When a person is a certain way, then he has to look out that he is that way. And when he looks out that he is and he is, he has to look out that he is what he is and not what he isn't—as in many cases it is."

Z

zábava (entertainment). General term referring to any sort of village or small-town festivity with music and dancing. It includes such celebrations as → *masopust* (carnival), → *pouť* (fair), → *letní noc* (summer night), and → *dožínky* (harvest festival). All ages show up for these entertainments, which include rides and games for children, and music and dancing for adults.

zabíjačka (pig slaughter). The rural tradition of slaughtering a pig and preparing its meat. Virtually every part of the pig is turned into some kind of roast or sausage. Even the blood becomes a soup. Delicacies made from the pig include such untranslatable (and for some inedible) combinations of meats as *jelito*, *tlačenka*, *ovar*, and *prejt*. Pig roasts usually take place in winter, though they may also be held before weddings or other celebrations to supply victuals for the reception. The family doing the killing usually invites friends and neighbors over for the event and lives off the leftovers for the next several weeks.

zahrádkářská kolonie (gardener's colony). City-dwellers often buy small plots of land in what are called gardener's colonies on the outskirts of town, where they plant every square inch with carrots, tomatoes, turnips, onions, strawberries, or potatoes. Just about every home and cottage owner similarly takes pains to grow fruits, vegetables, or at least flowers in their yard. These gardens are tended as much for their food products (→ *zavařeniny*) as for the pleasure taken in working on them.

žákovská knížka (student's record book). Small notebook used for recording elementary school pupils' marks. All students have their own *žákovská knížka* and bring it with them to the front of the class whenever they are quizzed orally. The teacher uses it to write down the subject of the quiz and the pupil's mark (in addition to announcing it aloud) (→ *vysvědčení*). Every few weeks pupils are required to get their parents' signature on the notebook. The books are also used for disciplinary purposes. If pupils misbehave, the teacher first requests their record book, and, if the disruption continues, she notes the problem and has the pupil return it with a parent's signature. While these notes are usually of the sort "Not paying attention in class," classics in the genre (now published in joke books) reached depths of absurdity as with the teacher who wrote, "Looks at the teacher through his ruler and claims that she is green."

Zátopek, Emil (1922–2000). Olympic champion long-distance runner. Zátopek became the greatest Czech athlete of all time when he won three golds at the Helsinki Olympic Games in 1952. Indeed, by winning the 5 km, 10 km, and marathon, he achieved a triple that will never again be equaled. More amazing is that he was running his first ever marathon. Zátopek's fame came not just from his athletic ability, but from his charisma. During races, he always appeared to be on the verge of dropping dead from exhaustion, but still managed to outlast his competitors. Zátopek married another Olympic hero from 1952, the javelin thrower Dana

Poll for Czech Sportsman of the Century

This poll asked 14 experts and athletes to choose the best sportsman in each category. The results were announced on 30 November 2000 just a week after the death of Zátopek.

Discipline	First Place	Runners Up
Legend of Czech Sport	Emil → Zátopek	–
Hockey	Jaromír → Jágr	Dominik Hašek, Jiří Holeček, Jiří → Holík
Football	Josef → Masopust	Pepi → Bican, Antonín → Panenka, František Plánička, Ivo Viktor
Tennis	Ivan Lendl	Martina Navrátilová, Jan Kodeš, Hana Mandlíková
Water Sports	Štěpánka Hilgertová	Jan Felix-Brzák, Josef Holeček, Martin Doktor
Gymnastics	Věra → Čáslavská	Eva Bosáková, Alois Hudec, Bedřich Šupčík
Track and Field	Jan Železný	Ludvík Daněk, Tomáš Dvořák, Jarmila Kratochvílová
Combat Sports	Vítězslav Mácha	Jaroslav Skobla, Julius Torma, Bohumil Němeček
Skiing	Jiří Raška	Olga Charvátová-Křížová, Květa Jeriová-Pecková, Kateřina Neumannová, Pavel Ploc
Cycling	Jan Veselý	Anton Tkáč, Jan and Jindřich Pospíšil, Jiří Daler

Source: *Mladá fronta Dnes*, 1 December 2000.

Ingrová. The two were lionized by the communist regime as evidence of its superiority over the West, but then became *personae non grata* for their support of the Prague Spring (→ *Pražské jaro*). Zátopek was voted Czech athlete of the century a week after his death.

zavařeniny (preserves). As many Czechs have access to a garden plot (→ *zahrádkářská kolonie*), they have become specialists at preserving apricots, cherries, pickles, or anything else they can get their hands on. Most pantries and basements are lined with mason jars containing these preserves. Having a store of preserved fruits and vegetables was an essential way to get by in the general shortage economy of communism.

závist (envy). If asked to describe their national character, Czechs will usually begin by talking about envy. Though it exists in all human cultures, a number of historical circumstances gave envy particular currency in the Czech lands. As a largely rural nation (→ *maloměšťáctví*) without its own aristocracy, Czechs were not taught respect for wealth and position, but came to view each other as equals (→ *rovnostářství*). Thus, whoever raised himself above others was viewed with suspicion. The communist regime gave these traits wide scope for expression. Because people had so few opportunities to distinguish themselves from others (they wore similar clothes, lived in similar apartments, drew similar paychecks), they became hyper-sensitive to even minute differences. A general lack of privacy (Slavenka Drakulić describes the post-communist innovation of "discretion zones" at post offices and banks so that people would stop peering over one's shoulder) also made private lives into public ones. Finally, the rewards offered for denouncing others to the police (say, for holding foreign currency or badmouthing the regime) made envy pay (→ *udavač*). Envy can be further seen in the mixed reception at home of Czechs who have made good abroad (→ *exil*).

Závod míru (Peace Race). The Warsaw Pact equivalent to the Tour de France, the Peace Race was one of the highlights of the Czech sports calendar under communism. It was founded in 1948 as a way of commemorating the end of the war and it has always been held in May around V-E Day (→ *Den osvobození*). The race itself connected the three capital cities of Warsaw, Prague, and Berlin. Despite its heavy ideological baggage, it was one of the top amateur stage races of its time. It continues to be held, but the loss of state sponsorship and the end of the communist bloc have hurt its fortunes. Czechs still remember the one-time winner Jan Veselý, who was later punished by the communists for dropping out of the race and thus sabotaging the country's athletic reputation.

zazvonil zvonec a pohádky je konec (the bell has rung and the fairy tale is over). Children are trained from the tenderest age to recognize that the ringing of a bell signals the start of a fairy tale or puppet performance (→ *pohádka*, → *loutkové divadlo*). These same performances also end with a bell ringing and the phrase cited here.

zdrobnělina (diminutive). Czech uses a number of suffixes to signal the diminutive. They can be tacked on to the end of just about any noun to indicate small size. Thus a normal house is a *dům*, but a smaller house is a *domek* and an even smaller one a *domeček*. The diminutive of course connotes more than just size, but also cuteness, preciousness, and in certain contexts lack of respect. Just about every given name (→ Jan Novák) carries one or more diminutive versions that are used between friends more frequently than the proper version of the name. Thus, Petr can be called Petřík or Petříček and Lenka becomes Lenča or Lenička.

železná neděle (Iron Sunday). Under communism, Iron Sundays meant that citizens were required to put spare scrap metal in front of their homes or apartment to be picked up by Pioneers (→ *Pionýr*) or members of other community organizations. Such recycling was essential for an economy plagued by shortages of all possible goods. School children were frequently employed to collect any number of items from herbs to iron, receiving prizes for their efforts.

zelí (cabbage or sauerkraut). Common vegetable side dish. It is usually served alongside meat as in → *vepřo-knedlo-zelo*, but it is also part of a creamy soup or baked inside of dough. Despite the perpetual shortages of communism, sauerkraut was always available in stores and was the main vegetable in the Czech diet.

Žid (Jew). The Jewish presence in the Czech lands is long and complicated. Their troubled history is attested to by the myth of the → *golem* who was supposedly created in the sixteenth century to protect Jews from pogroms. In medieval times, Jews were often forbidden to live in large cities or confined to walled ghettoes. As the country modernized, however, Jews were able to assimilate well into the country's culture, with the result that many famous Czechs have been found to have Jewish ancestors. By the nineteenth and twentieth centuries, Czechs were among the more tolerant peoples in Europe. Prejudice of course never disappeared. Jewish jokes—centered on the stock characters of Kohn and Roubíček—were popular among all classes. Often there were political consequences as when Leopold Hilsner was accused of ritual murder in 1899 (→ Masaryk) or Jewish communists were purged in the 1950s (→ Slánský). Most disturbingly, almost all of the country's Jews—an estimated 70,000—were exterminated in the Holocaust with few Czechs raising a finger to defend them (→ *lágr*). Those who survived the camps often returned to find their homes or apartments seized by Czechs, and many emigrated. The communists had little patience for religious practice, and so by the eighties few of the country's remaining Jews identified openly with the faith. Since the revolution (→ *Sametová revoluce*), there has been a revival of interest in Judaism as many people discover their Jewish roots and even non-Jews take an interest in Jewish spiritualism. Most Czechs though are indifferent or mildly suspicious of Judaism. This can be seen in the popular expressions *židovina* (something that is screwed up; literally "a Jewish thing") or *mít vlasy na Žida* (have a bad hairstyle; literally "to have hair like a Jew").

Živnostenská banka (Trade Finance Bank). In 1869, *Živnobanka*, as it is known for short, became the first modern Czech bank and created a virtual monopoly for itself on the Czech market. After World War I, the bank gained control of many of the newly-independent country's most important enterprises including the → Škoda Works and the heavy machinery firm → ČKD. This financial power gave the bank political power, and many citizens saw its hand behind the government's economic policies. The communists in particular criticized the bank as the cause of the great depression and widespread poverty. *Živnostenská banka* was nationalized along with all of its holdings when the communists took power, and its assets merged into *Česká spořitelna* (Czech Savings Bank), the only bank allowed to serve ordinary customers. *Živnostenská banka* has returned to the market since the revolution, but with nowhere near its prewar power.

Žižka, Jan (around 1360–1424). "Great Czech Military Leaders" is not the world's shortest book (as "Great Italian Military Leaders" is said to be) largely due to the medieval warrior Jan Žižka. A follower of the religious reformer Jan → Hus, Žižka led his followers to victories over far better equipped crusaders of the Catholic Church attempting to snuff out their heresy. Žižka's success was based on two military innovations. The first was tactical: knowing his followers were untrained peasants unequipped to take on cavalry, Žižka had his troops form wagon circles from which they repelled charges with their farm implements. The second was motivational: Žižka's charisma and religious conviction helped turn his soldiers into *boží bojovníci* (God's warriors). His effect on his men was such that after his death, they called themselves *sirotci* (orphans). Žižka's greatest victory was on Vítkov Hill in Prague where he defeated the numerically superior forces of King Sigismund (Zikmund) in 1420. Since that time the quarter of Prague including the battle site has been known as → Žižkov and is home to the world's largest equestrian statue. Žižka's invincibility made his armies the most feared in Europe, and reputedly the sound of his warriors chanting religious songs before battles was enough to send the opposition running. Žižka is usually portrayed with a thick beard, a patch over his left eye (he ultimately lost his second eye in battle as well, though even that did not stop him), and a mace in his hand. After the Battle of White Mountain (→ *Bílá hora*) and the Counter-Reformation, memory of Žižka disappeared, but in the nineteenth century, national awakeners resurrected him as a hero who defended Czechs against Germans. While nationalists and later the communists painted Žižka in unequivocally positive tones, contemporary Czechs—perhaps in reaction to this indoctrination—are just as likely to view him as a bloodthirsty radical who ruthlessly destroyed cultural monuments.

Žižkov. Quarter of Prague (→ *Praha*). Named for the medieval warrior Jan → Žižka, Žižkov has developed a reputation as a slightly seedy, working class district. It is home to Vítkov hill where nationalists built a monument to the Czech unknown soldier on the site of one of Žižka's great military victories. The communists later hijacked the memorial as a mausoleum for the remains of the first communist president Klement → Gottwald.

zkratky (abbreviations). One of the deformations of the Czech language introduced under communism was the use of abbreviations for every political, economic, and social institution. To name a few, there were the police—SNB, → StB, → VB—the neighboring communist countries—USSR, PLR—enterprises—and ČSAO, OPBH, → ČSAD. Satirizing this tendency, the humorist Ivan → Mládek composed a popular song consisting almost entirely of abbreviations.

zlaté ručičky (golden hands). A general term that refers to the superior talents and handyman abilities of the Czech nation. Czechs see themselves as an especially technically adept people. On the one hand, there is the vaunted ability of many Czech males—and females—to put together or repair just about any mechanical apparatus. The skill was a necessity under communism, when repairmen and even spare parts were virtually non-existent. The phrase also refers to the part Czechs played in the invention of new technologies. As the most advanced part of the Austro-Hungarian Empire, Czechs like František Křižík, the inventor of the arc lamp, were the driving force behind the Empire's industrialization. Despite the destruction of the work ethic under communism, Czechs still take pride in their technical ability, pointing to scientists like Otto Wichterle, the inventor of the contact lens. At the same time, they worry about how the same golden hands are adept at embezzling money and skirting the law (→ *tunelování*).

Czech Traits

These are the results of two polls on the traits that Czechs most ascribe to themselves. The numbers indicate the percentage of Czechs that believe the given trait characterizes them.

Trait	1990	1992
Negative		
envious	12	28
conformist	9	15
cunning	7	15
egoistical	10	11
lazy	3	8
Positive		
hard-working	4	17
skillful	3	8
having a sense of humor	3	8

Source: Ladislav Holy. *The Little Czech and the Great Czech Nation.* New York: Cambridge University Press, 1996, p. 76.

Zlatý slavík (Golden Songbird). A people's choice contest introduced in 1962 to choose the country's best male and female singers. Citizens could pick up ballots in popular magazines, and vast numbers of them voted

Winners of the Golden Songbird (→ *Zlatý slavík*)

The *Zlatý slavík* is a people's choice award sponsored by *Mladý svět* (Young World) magazine and first held in 1962. It was discontinued between 1992 and 1996, but re-emerged afterward as the Czech Songbird. Originally, readers of the magazine could send in ballots for the best singer and song. Later this was changed to best male and female singers and best group. The contest is followed closely and considered a barometer of popular taste. The list below catalogs the most frequent winners. Amazingly, virtually all of them continue to perform.

Name	Number of Wins	Notes
Karel → Gott	28	The Czech king of pop. Even today no one rivals his popularity.
Hana Zagorová	9	Star in the seventies and eighties. Her saccharine voice and saccharine songs suited the pop scene of normalization (→ normalizace).

Name	Number of Wins	Notes
Lucie → Bílá	7	Post-revolution pop sensation. Her hit "Love Is Love" caused a scandal by referring to homosexuality. Today her personal life dominates the tabloid press more than her music.
→ Olympic	6	The Czech Beatles. Pioneers of the Czech rock scene, their songs are still sung by young people.
Naďa Urbánková	5	Pop diva of the seventies who stood out more for her Elton John-style glasses than her voice.
Elán	4	Slovak supergroup. Their straight ahead rock and catchy melodies continue to attract fans in both halves of the former Czechoslovakia. The lead singer, Jožo Ráž, was a supporter of Slovakia's autocratic prime minister, Vladimír Mečiar.
Lucie	4	The best, most popular, and most prolific rock group since the revolution. One of their videos was banned from television for promoting drug use.
Eva Pilarová	3	She began her career singing jazz in the musical theater → Semafor and ended up singing pop hits.
Petra Janů	3	Gravelly-voiced rock singer. The title of her biggest hit was "Motorest."
Iveta Bartošová	3	Young star of the eighties. She made her career mainly as a pretty face and was helped along by her romantic association with orchestra-leader, songwriter, and impresario Ladislav Štaidl (see below). After early success she faded from view and made a triumphant comeback after a strange kidnapping incident.
Marta Kubišová	3	The best voice of her generation. Her career as a pop diva was cut short by her opposition to the Soviet invasion and subsequent ban on public appearances.
Dalibor Janda	3	Long-haired unshaven rocker whose power ballads imitated the style of eighties pop-rock singers like Bryan Adams.
Team	3	Another Slovak supergroup from the eighties, though more commercial and less talented than Elán.
Waldemar Matuška	2	Gott's only rival as a crooner. He attracted female fans with his more rugged appearance. Later he turned to country music and emigrated to America.
Ladislav Štaidl Orchestra	2	Karel Gott's backing band with one of Gott's best friends at the helm.
Katapult	2	A straight ahead rock band in the style of The Who, with hits like "The Fool Hesitates."
Helena Vondráčková	1	Known as "Gott in a skirt." A member of the → Golden Kids and then a star interpreter of foreign hits, she was always number two on the hit parade. Amazingly, she staged a comeback in the late nineties as a fifty-year-old purveyor of dance music.
Daniel Hůlka	1	Czech imitator of Andrea Boccelli. Now a stalwart of musicals.
Citron	1	Hard rockers who won in 1988 and soon fizzled out.

Name	Number of Wins	Notes
Miro Žbirka	1	Slovak singer-songwriter. It was a surprise win for this glasses-wearing writer of intelligent Beatles-style hits.
Peter Nagy	1	Talented Slovak singer-songwriter who styled himself Profesor Indigo.
Pavol Habera	1	Another Slovak singer-songwriter, mainly known for his good looks.

Source: Jan Krůta, *Klec na Slavíky*. Praha: Epocha, 2003.

and followed the televised awards show. On the male side, Karel → Gott won the contest almost continuously from the time he first broke on the scene. While the female winners were more variable (multiple title-holders were Hana Zagorová, Naďa Urbánková and Lucie → Bílá), fans usually picked singers and genres close to the regime. Whether this was due to vote-rigging or because Czech taste runs toward the middle of the road is debatable. After being discontinued in 1991, the contest was revived as the *Český slavík* (Czech Songbird) in 1996 and continues to be a major media event, the vote-rigging now the domain of record companies. While the *Zlatý slavík* was the top of the heap, other musical competitions—the *Bratislavská lyra* (Bratislava Lyre), *Děčínská kotva* (Děčín Anchor), *Mladá píseň* (Young Song), and *Festival politické písně* (Festival of Political Song)—were common, and a proving ground for future stars. Even today several such contests run on national television.

znárodnění (nationalization). Private property has never enjoyed a sacred place in Czech society. Even the otherwise liberal First Republic (→ *První republika*) thought nothing of confiscating property. The postwar communists, however, made nationalization an art form. Though they originally promised only to nationalize large factories and major landholders, they ultimately seized everything from restaurants to family farms to barbershops, so that no private business was left in the country. The general lack of respect for private holdings may have its roots in Czech egalitarianism (→ *rovnostářství*)—wealth is typically seen as undeserved—and the frequent regime changes which leave all property rights uncertain and insecure.

zubatá (the toothy one). Death is frequently referred to as the toothy one, because she is portrayed as a skeleton dressed in women's clothes—only her white teeth are visible from under her shroud.

List of Tables

Bibliography

It would be impossible to cite all of the works that helped to create this dictionary. Much of the information came from ordinary conversations, daily newspapers, and radio broadcasts. With apologies to many other historians, journalists, writers, and observers whose works inspired and guided me, these are some of the books that proved most helpful.

Augusta, Pavel, ed. *Kdo byl kdo v našich dějinách do roku 1918*. Praha: Libri, 1996.

Bart, István. *Hungary and the Hungarians: The Keywords*. Budapest: Corvina, 1999.

Časlavský, Karel et al. *Hvězdy českého filmu I., II., III., IV.* Praha: Fragment, 1995–1999.

Churaň, Milan a kolektiv. *Kdo byl kdo v našich dějinách ve 20. století.* Praha: Libri, 1998.

Holý, Ladislav. *The Little Czech and the Great Czech Nation*. New York: Cambridge University Press, 1998.

Honzák, František et al. *Fakta do kapsy I*. Praha: Libri, 2001.

Kirchner, Jaroslav and Jan Slepička. *Hvězdy českého sportu I, II*. Praha: Fragment, 2000.

Kuras, Benjamin. *Czechs and Balances: A Nation's Survival Kit*. Praha: Baronet, 1998.

Lidové Noviny, in particular their "Legends of the Twentieth Century" series.

Pynsent, Robert, ed. *Reader's Encyclopedia of Eastern European Literature*. New York: Harper Collins, 1993.

Reflex, in particular articles written under the "Causa" header.

Sayer, Derek. *The Coasts of Bohemia: A Czech History*. Princeton: Princeton University Press, 1998.

Skalička, Janek and Libor Balák. *Hvězdy české populární hudby*. Praha: Fragment, 1999.

Škvorecký, Josef. *All the Bright Young Men and Women: A Personal History of the Czech Cinema*. Toronto: Peter P. Martin Associates, 1971.

Tomeš, Josef. *Slovník k politickým dějinám Československa, 1918-1992*. Praha: Budka, 1994.

Vondrušková, Alena. *České zvyky a obyčeje*. Praha: Albatros, 2004.

Vykoupil, Libor. *Slovník českých dějin*. Brno: Georgetown, 1994.

Index

The main dictionary entries are grouped here under thematic headings. Several entries appear under more than one heading.

Appearances

beauty queen	miss
beret	rádiovka
clothing brands	Jitex
folk costume	kroj
hippie	mánička
jeans	Rifle
long hair	háro
nakedness	nahota
overalls	montérky
pants	tesilky
purple jacket	fialové sako
slippers	pantofle
sweatpants	tepláky

Art

artist	umělec
cartoonist	Jiránek, Vladimír
Czech baroque	české baroko
national/merited artist (award)	národní/zasloužilý umělec
painters	Lada, Josef
	Mánes, Josef
	Mucha, Alfons
People's School of Art	Lidová škola umění
socialist realism	sorela

Celebrities

actors	Baarová, Lída
	Bohdalová, Jiřina
	Brejchová, Jana
	Brzobohatý, Radoslav
	Burian, Vlasta
	Hrušínský, Rudolf
	Landovský, Pavel
	Menšík, Vladimír

actors	Nový, Oldřich
	Polívka, Bolek
	Werich, Jan
singers	Bílá, Lucie
	David, Michal
	Gott, Karel
	Mládek, Ivan
	Nedvěd, Honza
	Pucholt, Vladimír
world travelers	Hanzelka and Zikmund

Children (see also School)

bedtime prayer	Andělíčku, můj strážníčku
bogeyman	hejkal
Boy Scouts	Junák
card game	Černý Petr
cartoons	Ferda Mravenec
	Krteček
	Rumcajs
	večerníček
children's books	Bylo nás pět
	Broučci
	Foglar, Jaroslav
	Honzíkova cesta
	Malý Bobeš
children's songs	Skákal pes
christening	vítání občánků
fairy tales	Dlouhý, Široký a Bystrozraký
	Kdysi dávno
	Kopecký, Matěj
	loutkové divadlo
	Otesánek
	pohádka
	Smolíček pacholíček
	Spejbl and Hurvínek

fairy tales	zazvonil zvonec a po-hádky je konec
games	bobříky
	Člověče, nezlob se
Grandfather Frost	Děda Mráz
rhymes	ententyky
	Vařila myšička kašičku
	Velká láska postel praská
summer camp	bodování úklidu
youth organization	čestné pionýrské
	Pionýr
	SSM

Cities and Towns

Aš	
Brno	
Carlsbad	Karlovy Vary
České Budějovice	
freehold	lhota
Gottwaldov	
Havířov	
Jáchymov	
Kladno	
Lidice	
Olomouc	
Ostrava	
Pardubice	
Pilsen	Plzeň
Prague	Praha

Communism

auxiliary public security patrol	pomocná stráž veřejné bezpečnosti
border guard	pohraniční stráž
bourgeois origin	buržoazní původ
Číhošť miracle	Číhošťský zázrak
Club of Working People	SKP
Colorado beetle	mandelinka bramborová
communism	komunismus
communist leaders	Gottwald, Klement
	Husák, Gustáv
	Slánský, Rudolf
	Svoboda, Ludvík
Communist Party	KSČ
	rudá knížka
	ÚV KSČ
communist language	kůl v plotě
	ptydepe
comrade	soudruh
constructive	budovatelský
cost accounting in a self-supporting unit	chozraščot

defense education	branná výchova
Evening University of Marxism-Leninism	VUML
exit visa permit	výjezdní doložka
five-year plan	pětiletka
Gottwaldov (city)	Gottwaldov
Great October Socialist Revolution	Velká říjnová socialistická revoluce
imported goods	bony
	Tuzex
informer	udavač
lustration	lustrace
mass song	masová píseň
May Day	1. máj
meat will come soon	maso bude vbrzku
miners	Jsem horník a kdo je víc
moneychanger	vekslák
national committee	národní výbor
National Front	Národní fronta
nationalization	znárodnění
normalization	normalizace
Order of Labor	Řád práce
People's Militia	Lidové milice
personnel file	kádrový spis
Public Security	VB
public service work	Akce Z
	Železná neděle
Red Right newspaper	Rudé právo
screening commission	prověrková komise
self-published literature	samizdat
show trials	politické procesy
Socialism with a human face	Socialismus s lidskou tváří
socialist realism	sorela
Socialist Union of Youth	SSM
Solidarity Fund	Fond solidarity
Spartakiáda	Spartakiáda
State Security	StB
television	Major Zeman
totalitarianism	totalita
trade union	ROH
under the counter item	podpultovka
Union for Cooperation with the Army	Svazarm
vault	trezor
Victorious February	Vítězný únor
welcoming the little citizens	vítání občánků
work brigade	brigáda
working Saturday	pracovní sobota

Consumer Products

automobiles	Škoda
	Laurin and Klement
books	knižní čtvrtek

cigarettes	Petra
clothing	Jitex
collectibles	céčka
department store	Prior
dishwashing soap	Jar
explosives	semtex
fourth price category	čtvrtá cenová skupina
garnet	granát
glass/crystal	sklo
grocery store	Jednota
jeans	Rifle
liniment	Alpa
meat will come soon	maso bude vbrzku
medicine	paralen
mineral water	Mattoni
pants	tesilky
plastic bag	igelitka
purple jacket	fialové sako
records	Supraphon
shoes	Baťa
three-wheeled car	Velorex
under-the-counter item	podpultovka
work accessories	fasovat

Czech Places (see also Cities and Towns)

Bohemia	Čechy
castles and chateaux	hrady a zámky
Central Europe	střední Evropa
Chod region	Chodsko
Czech basin	česká kotlina
Czech Paradise	Český ráj
Czech Republic	Česká republika
Czechia	Česko
Czechoslovakia	Československo
Dukla Pass	Dukelský průsmyk
fish pond	rybník
Giant Mountains	Krkonoše
Haná region	Haná
High Castle	Vyšehrad
Highlands	Vysočina
Ještěd Mountain	Ještěd Mountain
Karlštejn Castle	Karlštejn
Kramář's Villa	Kramářova vila
Lány	Lány
Moldau River	Vltava
Moravia	Morava
Mt. Snowy	Sněžka
National Museum	Národní muzeum
Petřín Hill	Petřín
Prague Castle	Hrad
Říp Mountain	Říp
Ruzyně Airport	Ruzyně
Silesia	Slezsko
Slavín burial ground	Slavín
Slovácko region	Slovácko

Subcarpathian Ruthenia	Podkarpatská Rus
Strahov Stadium	Strahov
Straka Academy	Strakova akademie
Šumava region	Šumava
Velehrad Cathedral	Velehrad
Velká Javořina Mountain	Velká Javořina
Wallachia region	Valašsko
Wenceslas Square	Václavské náměstí
Žižkov	Žižkov

Expressions

As on New Year, so for the whole year	Jak na Nový rok, tak po celý rok
at us	u nás
American from Vysočany	Američan z Vysočan
aunt	teta
bourgeois origin	buržoazní původ
breasts (goats)	kozy
Central Europe	střední Evropa
constructive	budovatelský
cucumber season	okurková sezona
death	zubatá
Every Czech a musician	Co Čech, to muzikant
Everywhere good, at home the best	Všude dobře, doma nejlíp
fat cat	papaláš
fateful eights	osudové osmičky
fourth price category	čtvrtá cenová skupina
gay	teplouš
Go, home Ivan!	Běž domů, Ivane
God bless you	Pozdrav pánbůh
golden hands	zlaté ruce
good day	dobrý den
honor to labor	čest práci
Jesus and Mary	Ježíšmarjá
kiss-ass	Hujer
mister	pan
national/merited artist	národní/zasloužilý umělec
nicely Czech	hezky česky
non-Gypsy	gadžo
Our land is not blossoming	Naše země nezkvétá
ox	vůl
people, the	lid
petty theft	malá domů
post-February	poúnorový
purple jacket	fialové sako
respectfully report robot	poslušně hlásím
Shake, Donkey	Oslíčku, otřes se
shit	hovno
Spanish village	španělská vesnice
stake in the fence	kůl v plotě
Stick your finger through your neck	strč prst skrz krk

to success	nazdar
to your health	na zdraví
topsy-turvy place	Kocourkov
Truth triumphs	Pravda vítězí
up yours	do prdele
We were here before Austria...	Byli jsme před Rakouskem...
weather-lore	pranostika
work ennobles	práce šlechtí

Folk Traditions (see also Holidays)

bogeyman	hejkal
Burning of the Witches	pálení čarodějnic
carnival	masopust
carrying out of death	vynášení smrti
chimneysweep	kominík
Easter	Velikonoce
Easter whip	pomlázka
evening bell	klekání
fair	jarmark
folk costume	kroj
folk song	lidovka
grape harvest	vinobraní
harvest festival	dožínky
King Barley	Král Ječmínek
lace	krajka
maypoles	máje
nativity scenes	betlémy
pilgrimmage	pouť
Ride of Kings	Jízda králů
village fair	posvícení
wayside cross	boží muka
weather-lore	pranostika
welcome with bread and salt	vítání chlebem a solí

Food and Drink

baby food	sunar
beer	pivo
bread roll	rohlík
cabbage	zelí
cafeteria	bufet
cake	koláč
carp	kapr
coffeehouse	kavárna
cola	Kofola
crepes	palačinky
deli meat	Gothajský salám
dumpling	knedlík
food	jídlo
fourth price category	čtvrtá cenová skupina
fried cheese	smažený sýr
goulash	guláš
grape harvest	vinobraní

Home Cookbook	Domácí kuchařka
hops	chmel
Italian salad	vlašský salát
lard	sádlo
liquor	Becherovka
meat will come soon	maso bude vbrzku
mineral water	Mattoni
mulled wine	svařené víno
mushrooming	houbaření
odorous cheese	tvarůžky
open-faced sandwiches	chlebíčky
pig slaughter	zabíjačka
pizza	pizza
plum brandy	slivovice
poppy seed	mák
pork filet	řízek
pork-dumplings--sauerkraut	vepřo-knedlo-zelo
potatoes	brambory
preserves	zavařeniny
restaurant	restaurace
rice souffle	rýžový nákyp
rum	rum
sauce	omáčka
sirloin with cream sauce	svíčková na smetaně
snack	svačina
soup	polévka
spekwurst	špekáček
sweetshop	cukrárna
tea	čaj
Unity Store	Jednota
welcome with bread and salt	vítání s chlebem a solí
young wine	burčák

Foreigners and Ethnicities

America	Amerika
Austria	Rakousko
Bulgaria	Bulharsko
Europe	Evropa
exile	exil
expulsion of Germans	odsun
German	Němec
Gypsy/Roma	cikán
Habsburgs	Habsburkové
Hungary	Maďarsko
Jew	Žid
non-Gyspy	gadžo
Poland	Polsko
Russia	Rusko
Russian language	ruština
Slovakia	Slovensko
Solidarity Fund	Fond solidarity
Spanish village	španělská vesnice
Sudeten Germans	sudetští Němci

Ukrainians	Ukrajinci
Vienna	Vídeň
Vietnamese	Vietnamci
Yugoslavia	Jugoslávie

Historical Figures

Beneš, Edvard	
Charles IV	Karel IV
Dobrovský, Josef	
Franz Josef	
Fučík, Julius	
Gottwald, Klement	
Havel, Václav	
Havlíček Borovský, Karel	
Horáková, Milada	
Hus, Jan	
Husák, Gustav	
Jiří z Poděbrad	
Jungmann, Josef	
Kosmas	
Maria Theresa	
Masaryk, Tomáš Garrigue	
Palach, Jan	
Palacký, František	
Remek, Vladimír	
Rudolf II	
Slánský, Rudolf	
Svoboda, Ludvík	
Žižka, Jan	

History

apolitical politics	apolitická politika
August invasion	srpnová invaze
Bach's Absolutism	Bachův absolutismus
Battle of Lipany	Lipany
Battle of Moravian Field	Moravská pole
Battle of White Mountain	Bílá hora
Beneš Decrees	Benešovy dekrety
Charter 77	Charta 77
concentration camp	lágr
defenestration	defenestrace
dissident	disident
Dukla Pass	Dukelský průsmyk
Era of Darkness	temno
expulsion of Germans	odsun
First Republic	První republika
five political parties, the	pětka
Great Moravian Empire	Velkomoravská říše
Habsburgs	Habsburkové
May Uprising	Květnové povstání
meaning of Czech history	smysl českých dějin
Munich	Mnichov
National Revival	Národní obrození
Nazi repression	Heydrichiáda

nobility	šlechta
October 28	28. říjen
peasants at Chlumec	sedláci u Chlumce
post-February	poúnorový
Prague Spring	pražské jaro
Premyslid dynasty	Přemyslovci
Protectorate	Protektorát
regional governor	hejtman
resistance movement	odboj
show trials	politické procesy
Slovak National Uprising	SNP
Straka Academy	Strakova akademie
Thirty Years' War	Třicetiletá válka
Velvet Divorce	sametový rozvod
Velvet Revolution	sametová revoluce
Věstonice Venus	Věstonická Venuše
Victorious February	Vítězný únor
Young Czechs	mladočeši

Holidays

All Souls Day	Dušičky
birthday	narozeniny
Christmas	kapr
	Ježíšek
	Vánoce
Easter	Hody hody doprovody
	pomlázka
	Velikonoce
Grandfather Frost	Děda Mráz
Great October Socialist Revolution	Velká říjnová socialis-tická revoluce
International Women's Day	MDŽ
Liberation Day	Den osvobození
May Day	1. máj
name day	jmeniny
New Year's Eve	Silvestr
Nicholas and the Devil	Mikuláš a čert
October 28	28. říjen
New Year's Day	Jak na Nový rok…
	PF
Three Kings Day	Tři králové
Victorious February	Vítězný únor

Home, Work, and Daily Life

apartment leases	dekrety na byt
asset stripping	tunelování
baksheesh	všimné
banking	Živnostenská Banka
bill	účet
building superintendent	domovní důvěrník
buses	ČSAD
cost-accounting in a self-supporting unit	chozraščot
cottage	chata

country house	chalupa
courtyard	dvůr
fourth price category	čtvrtá cenová skupina
funeral	pohřeb
gardener's colony	zahrádkářská kolonie
highways	D1
identification card	občanský průkaz
Kolben-Danek Machinery Works	ČKD
local PA system	místní rozhlas
meat will come soon	maso bude vbrzku
moneychanger	vekslák
mushrooming	houbaření
payment slip	složenka
petty theft	malá domů
plastic bag	igelitka
polyclinic	poliklinika
prefabricated apartment building	panelák
privatization	kuponová privatizace
public service work	Železná neděle
pull	protekce
purple jacket	fialové sako
restitution	restituce
rubber stamp	razítko
sales clerk	prodavačka
sick note	neschopenka
slippers	pantofle
Standard Farming Cooperative	JZD
streetcar	tramvaj
sweatpants	tepláky
ticket inspector	revizor
tourist agency	Čedok
trade unions	ROH
under-the-counter item	podpultovka
village	vesnice
weekender	lufťák
work accessories	fasovat
work brigade	brigáda
work enobles	práce šlechtí
worker	dělník
working Saturday	pracovní sobota

Language (see also Expressions)

abbreviations	zkratky
communist language	ptydepe
Czech language	čeština
dialects	hantec
	krátký zobák
diminutive	zdrobnělina
exception words	vyjmenovaná slova
female names	ová
first and last names	Jan Novák

informal/formal forms of address	tykání/vykání
letter ř	ř
Russian language	ruština
spelling	pravopis
standard Czech	spisovná čeština

Literature

feuilleton	fejeton
Granny	Babička
Kingscourt Manuscript	Královédvorský rukopis
May	Byl pozdní večer, první Máj
Nikola Šuhaj the Outlaw	Šuhaj, Nikola
Old Czech Legends	Staré pověsti české
Proud Princess	Pyšná princezna
Otto's Encyclopedia	Ottův slovník naučný
self-published literature	samizdat
Švanda the Bagpiper	Švanda dudák
Švejk	Švejk
writers	Bezruč, Petr
	Čapek, Karel
	Erben, Karel Jaromír
	Hašek, Jaroslav
	Havel, Václav
	Havlíček Borovský, Karel
	Hrabal, Bohumil
	Jirásek, Alois
	Mácha, Karel Hynek
	Němcová, Božena

Media (see also Celebrities)

actors	Baarová, Lída
	Bohdalová, Jiřina
	Brejchová, Jana
	Burian, Vlasta
	Hrušínský, Rudolf
	Menšík, Vladimír
	Nový, Oldřich
	Polívka, Bolek
	Pucholt, Vladimír
	Svěrák, Zdeněk
film	Barrandov
	DAMU/FAMU
	Homolka
	Jak svět přichází o básníky
	Limonádový Joe
	Nová vlna
	Pyšná princezna
	S tebou mě baví svět
	Starci na chmelu

film	trezor
	Vinnetou
magazines	Dikobraz
	Květy
	Milá Sally
	Mladý svět
newspapers	Lidové noviny
	Rudé právo
radio	Rádio Svobodná Evropa
	Radio Luxembourg
television	Bohouš
	Dietl, Jaroslav
	Kavčí hory
	Major Zeman
	Nemocnice na kraji města
	televizní pondělky
	večerníček

Military and Police

army life	bažant
	Černí baroni
	modrá knížka
	vojna
auxiliary public security patrol	pomocná stráž
Battle of Dukla Pass	dukelský průsmyk
Battle of Lipany	Lipany
Battle of Moravian Field	Moravské pole
Battle of White Mountain	Bílá hora
concentration camp	lágr
criminals	Babinský, Václav
Czech fighter pilots	čeští letci
defense education	branná výchova
legionnaires	legionáři
May Uprising	květnové povstání
military leaders	Svoboda, Ludvík
	Žižka, Jan
Pankrác Prison	Pankrác
People's Militia	Lidové milice
Public Security	Veřejná bezpečnost
rebels	květnové povstání
	Mašín
	SNP
respectfully report	poslušně hlásím
State Security	StB
Thirty Years' War	Třicetiletá válka
Union for Cooperation with the Army	svazarm
War of the Maidens	Dívčí válka
work camps	totální nasazení
Ye Who Are God's Warriors	Ktož jsú boží bojovníci

Music

brass band music	dechovka
children's songs	Skákal pes
Christmas mass	Hej, Mistře
cimbalom music	cimbál
country music	country
	Porta
classical music	Dvořák, Antonín
	Má vlast
	Prodaná nevěsta
	Rusalka
	Smetana, Bedřich
Every Czech a musician	Co Čech, to muzikant
folk song	Hašler, Karel
	lidovka
Golden Songbird contest	Zlatý slavík
mass song	masová píseň
national anthem	Kde domov můj
People's School of Art	Lidová škola umění
polka	polka
protest songs	Modlitba pro Martu
Radio Luxembourg	Radio Luxembourg
rock and roll	bigbít
Semafor Theater	Semafor
shopkeeper's ballad	kramářská píseň
singers and groups	Bílá, Lucie
	David, Michal
	Destinová, Ema
	Dvorský, R.A.
	Golden Kids
	Gott, Karel
	Kryl, Karel
	Mišík, Vladimír
	Mládek, Ivan
	Nedvěd, Honza
	Olympic
	Plastic People of the Universe
	Reed, Dean
Švanda the Bagpiper	Švanda dudák
Unrequited Love (song)	Škoda lásky
Voskovec & Werich	
Ye Who Are God's Warriors	Ktož jsú boží bojovníci

Myths and Legends

Blaník Knights	Blaník
Forefather Čech	Čech
golem	
Jánošík	
King Barley	Král Ječmínek
Libuše	
Nepomuk, Jan of	Nepomucký, Jan

Old Czech Legends	Staré pověsti české
Radhošť Mountain	Radhošť
War of the Maidens	Dívčí válka
water sprite	vodník
White Lady	Bílá paní
witch	ježibaba

National Traits

artist	umělec
comfort	pohoda
Czech Question, the	Česká otázka
Czechness	češství
dove-like character	holubičí povaha
egalitarianism	rovnostářství
envy	závist
Everywhere good, at home the best	Všude dobře, doma nejlíp
golden hands	zlaté ruce
intelligentsia	inteligence
little Czech	malý český člověk
meaning of Czech history	smysl českých dějin
Mr. Brouček	pan Brouček
provinciality	maloměšťáctví
stupid Jack	hloupý Honza
what we are like	jací jsme
work ennobles	práce šlechtí

Religion

Catholic Church	Katolická církev
Číhošť miracle	Číhošťský zázrak
Comenius, Jan Amos	Komenský, Jan Amos
Cyril and Methodius	Cyril and Metoděj
Czechoslovak Church	Československá církev
Hussites	husité
Jew	Žid
Kralice Bible	Bible kralická
Protestant	evangelík
Saint Wenceslas	Svatý Václav
Union of Brethren	Jednota bratrská
Velehrad Cathedral	Velehrad
Ye Who Are God's Warriors	Ktož jsú boží bojovníci

School

Charles University	Univerzita Karlova
children's primer	Ema má mísu
cultivation work	pěstitelské práce
dictation	diktát
engineer	inženýr
Evening University of Marxism-Leninism	VUML
high school	gymnázium
May student celebration	Majáles

Parent-Teachers' Association	SRPŠ
People's School of Art	Lidová škola umění
recitation	recitace
report card	vysvědčení
required reading	povinná četba
school	škola
student's record book	žákovská kniha

Social Life

card games	mariáš
coffeehouse	kavárna
courtyard	dvůr
Czech Hikers' Club	Klub českých turistů
entertainment	zábava
Falcon Education and Physical Fitness Association	Sokol
form	ples
overnight hike	čundr
polka	polka
pub	hospoda
public square	náměstí
Radio Yerevan	Rádio Jerevan
sex	sex
spa	lázeň
summer beer garden	letní zahrada

Sport

athletes	Bican, Josef
	Čáslavská, Věra
	Holík, Jaroslav
	Jágr, Jaromír
	Masopust, Josef
	Panenka, Tonda
	Zátopek, Emil
bicycle soccer	kolová
Dukla Prague Sports Club	Dukla Praha
Falcon Education and Physical Fitness Association	Sokol
football tennis	nohejbal
hockey	hokej
Peace Race	Závod míru
soccer	fotbal
soccer clubs	Sparta/Slavia
Spartakiáda	Spartakiáda
Strahov Stadium	Strahov

Symbols

chalice	kalich
crown	koruna
linden/lime tree	lípa
lion	lev

206

Theater (see also Actors)

amateur theater	ochotnické divadlo
black light theater	černé divadlo
Kludský Circus	Cirkus Kludský
plays	Lucerna
	Maryša
	Naši furianti
puppet theater	loutkové divadlo
Theater and Film Schools	DAMU/FAMU
theater	divadlo
theaters	Cimrman, Jára
	Divadlo Na zábradlí
	Laterna magika
	Národní divadlo
	Semafor
	Spejbl a Hurvínek
	Voskovec & Werich